Saab 92–96V4
THE ORIGINAL SAAB

The Complete Story

CROWOOD AUTOCLASSICS

Alfa Romeo 105 Series Spider
Alfa Romeo 916 GTV & Spider
Alfa Romeo 2000 and 2600
Alfa Romeo Spider
Aston Martin DB4, 5, 6
Aston Martin DB7
Aston Martin V8
Austin Healey
BMW E30
BMW M3
BMW M5
BMW Classic Coupes 1965–1989 2000C and CS, E9 and E24
BMW Z3 and Z4
Classic Jaguar XK – The Six-Cylinder Cars
Ferrari 308, 328 & 348
Frogeye Sprite
Ginetta: Road & Track Cars
Jaguar E-Type
Jaguar F-Type
Jaguar Mks 1 & 2, S-Type & 420
Jaguar XJ-S The Complete Story
Jaguar XK8
Jensen V8
Land Rover Defender 90 & 110
Land Rover Freelander
Lotus Elan
Lotus Elise & Exige 1995–2020
MGA
MGB
MGF and TF
Mazda MX-5
Mercedes-Benz Fintail Models
Mercedes-Benz S-Class 1972–2013
Mercedes SL Series

Mercedes-Benz SL & Noakes SLC 107 Series 1971–1989
Mercedes-Benz Sport-Light Coupé
Mercedes-Benz W114 and W115
Mercedes-Benz W123
Mercedes-Benz W124
Mercedes-Benz W126 S-Class 1979–1991
Mercedes-Benz W201 (190)
Mercedes W113
Morgan 4/4: The First 75 Years
Peugeot 205
Porsche 924/928/944/968
Porsche Boxster and Cayman
Porsche Carrera – The Air-Cooled Era 1953–1998
Porsche Air-Cooled Turbos 1974–1996
Porsche Carrera - The Water-Cooled Era 1998–2018
Porsche Water-Cooled Turbos 1979–2019
Range Rover First Generation
Range Rover Second Generation
Range Rover Sport 2005–2013
Reliant Three-Wheelers
Riley Legendary RMs
Rover 75 and MG ZT
Rover 800 Series
Rover P5 & P5B
Rover P6: 2000, 2200, 3500
Rover SD1 – The Full Story 1976–1986
Saab 99 and 900
Subaru Impreza WRX & WRX STI
Toyota MR2
Triumph Spitfire and GT6
Triumph TR7
Volkswagen Golf GTI
Volvo 1800
Volvo Amazon

Lance Cole

Saab 92–96V4
THE ORIGINAL SAAB

The Complete Story

THE CROWOOD PRESS

First published in 2022 by
The Crowood Press Ltd
Ramsbury, Marlborough
Wiltshire SN8 2HR

enquiries@crowood.com

www.crowood.com

© Lance Cole 2022

All rights reserved. No part of this publication may be reproduced or transmitted in any form or by any means, electronic or mechanical, including photocopy, recording, or any information storage and retrieval system, without permission in writing from the publishers.

British Library Cataloguing-in-Publication Data
A catalogue record for this book is available from the British Library.

ISBN 978 0 7198 4017 3

Designed and typeset by Guy Croton Publishing Services,
West Malling Kent

Cover design by Sergey Tsvetkov

Printed and bound in India by Parksons Graphics

CONTENTS

Dedication & Acknowledgements		6
Timeline		7
Introduction		8
CHAPTER 1	ORIGINS: WINGS TO WHEELS	18
CHAPTER 2	UrSAAB: DESIGN AND DEVELOPMENT	42
CHAPTER 3	92: SOUL OF SAAB	62
CHAPTER 4	93: ESSENTIAL SAAB	84
CHAPTER 5	95: ESTATE CAR SAAB	104
CHAPTER 6	96: DEFINING SAAB	120
CHAPTER 7	SAAB 96 V4: CONTINUOUS IMPROVEMENT	152
CHAPTER 8	SUPER SPORT: MR SAAB AND MOTOR SPORT MOMENTS	180
CHAPTER 9	BUYING AND RESTORING A CLASSIC SAAB	202
References		205
Bibliography		206
Index		207

DEDICATION & ACKNOWLEDGEMENTS

DEDICATION

To all the men and women of Saab's cars and notably to my personal heroes: Gunnar Ljungström, Sixten Sason, Björn Envall, Rolf Mellde, Josef Eklund, Erik Carlsson, Stig Blomqvist, Robert Sinclair, Ingvar Lindqvist and Squadron Leader Robert Moore DFC.

Gentlemen, thank you for your brilliance and the Saabs that resulted.

ACKNOWLEDGEMENTS

Erik and Pat Carlsson, Chris Partington, Alex Rankin, Robin Morley, Graham Macdonald, Chris Hull, Martin Lyons, Chris Redmond, David Dallimore, Chris Day, David Lowe, Alan Sutcliffe, Mike Philpott, Tony Grestock, David Lowe, Arthur Civill, Jim Valentine, Dave Garnett, Richard Simpson, Iain Hodcroft, Ian Meakin, Ellie and Shaw Wilson, Peter and Janet Turner, William and Bridget Glander, Jean-François Bouvard, Joel Durand, Alain Rosset, Tom Donney, Bruce Turk, Jim Valentine, Drew Bedelph, Steven Wade, Gunilla Svensson, Krzysztof Rozenblat and the Rozenblat Family Foundation, the late Etienne Morsa. A salute to David Hines, Ken Coe, Andrew Mason, Vernon Mortimer, Don Cook, Alan Lawley (and respective wives where appropriate) for all their work at the Saab Owners Club GB and its publications in the early 1960s and the 1970s. Motoring noters to thank include: Steve Cropley, Hilton Holloway, Mark McCourt, Richard Gunn, James Walshe. Specific thanks go to the Saab Club GB, Saab Enthusiasts Club, Saab Club Sweden, Saab Club Australia and, of course, Saab Car Club North America and its *Nines* magazine.

A salute to the wonderful Club Saab Uruguay and Alberto Domingo, and to the family Abeiro. A further salute to the Buenos Aires Saab Club and Charles Walmsley. With thanks to: the Västergötlands Museum, Sweden; the Saab Car Museum (Gunnar Larsson, Roy Beaufoy, Albert Trommer, Per-Olof Rudh, Peter Bäckström, Gunnel Ekburg); the Saab Veterans Association (Saabs Veteranförening); Svenska Saab Klubben/*Bakrutan* magazine and editorial team; Swedish Motor History Association (Motorhistorika Sallskapet i Sverige) and Per-Borje Elg; the Marcus and Amalia Wallenberg Memorial Foundation. Acknowledgements also to: *The Daily Telegraph*; *The Independent*; *Classic Cars*; *Autocar*; *Teknikens Varld*; *Saab Cars* magazine. With thanks to the many others who have taught me about Saabs or published my words on Saab.

I would particularly like to thank Alex Rankin, Robin Morley, Chris Redmond, Martin Lyons, Mike Philpott and Mark McCourt for all their support and kindness and in the research for this book. A salute to my tutors and mentors at KLM Royal Dutch Airlines, and at Qantas, for teaching me to think, to fly the plane and never be seduced by the computer and the complacency it engenders.

Note: The author Lance F. Cole has no connection to 'Lance Cole Photography', its entity, website or any claims or actions made by such. The author has no connection to social media claims of religious or political content made by any other 'Lance Cole' entities as known to be extant.

TIMELINE

1937	The defining amalgamation of the main Swedish industrial engineering companies into a SAAB group on 20 April 1937, locating aircraft production and engineering output at Linköping and using offices of Nohab Company.
1939	SAAB of Linköping establishes its first main engineering works and offices at Trollhättan to include a new airfield, and expands the design office at Linköping. Marcus Wallenberg oversees the final merger to create the greater amalgamated Saab entity, which is completed in 1939.
1940–43	Saab's first three aircraft emerge, notably the Saab-designed twin-boom S21/J21.
1944–5	First discussions about a Saab car from late 1944. The design team includes Saab aircraft designers. Ljungström and Sason produce sketches of the car.
1946–8	Twenty four pre-production cars including three prototypes.
1949	First final specification 2-stroke Saab 92 production-series car leaves factory on 12 December.
1950	The dealer Philipson makes the first official customer deliveries from 16 January.
1953	Saab 92B launched with boot aperture, larger rear window, and relocated fuel tank.
1954	Further revisions as B/2 specification.
1955	Saab 93 announced as heavily re-engineered for 1956 model year with new 3-cylinder engine.
1956	Last 92B cars built late in 1956 for sale into early 1957.
1957	Saab 93B announced.
1958	Saab 93 Granturismo 750 launched: becomes 'GT750'.
1959	Saab 93F and 95 estate car announced: mass volume sales begin in 1960.
1960	Saab 96 developed from 93B: GT750 now with 96 body.
1962	Saab 96 850 Super Sport launched, known in the USA as the GT850/Monte Carlo by 1964.
1966	Restyled Saab 96 launched with major specification revisions: 850 becomes Super Sport Monte Carlo in all markets.
1967	Saab 96 V4 1.5-litre announced alongside new 95V4 option. 2-stroke sales continue for more than 12 months, notably in the USA.
1968	Bodyshell modifications with larger front windscreen aperture.
1969	Saab 96 V4 revised with new styling and specifications.
1970	Saab-Scania and Valmet Oy collaborate to begin production at Uusikaupunki, Finland.
1971	US market 96 V4/95V4 engine offered as 1.7-litre low compression type.
1975	Saab 96 V4 1.7S Rally Special Edition on sale. Further exports and domestic market special editions of the 96 V4 follow as 'Souvenir' and 'Jubilee'.
1976	Saab 96 with major revisions and 5mph 'impact' type cellular self-repairing bumpers.
1978	Saab 95 estate withdrawn from model line-up.
1979	Final 96 V4 cars, all built in Finland.
1980	Last 96 V4 leaves factory driven by Erik Carlsson in January. Final sales ex-showroom continue across Europe into mid-1980.

INTRODUCTION

Original Saab – an engineering excellence and elliptical ethos

Mainly, I think it is due to a common philosophy. It's a little difficult to fully explain, almost as difficult as to why a new melody, just a few notes of music, suddenly catches on to become very popular ... I think however that our design and engineering philosophy was right, from the start. We considered it very important to design a robust and safe car, having a high degree of refinement. The car had to stand out above the rest and be appreciated for its practicality, performance and overall quality level.

Tryggve Holm, engineer and Saab CEO (1950–67), discussing the reasons for the success of the first Saab car (1961)

There are some cars that touch the soul, cars that are so inherently correct and so 'right' that their size or engine

Erik Hilding Carlsson's Saab 96 2-stroke tribute car seen heading the Saab convoy at his memorial service in 2015. Erik was Saab and there is nothing quite like a red rally Saab 'stroker'.

INTRODUCTION

Saab 92 early model (without boot/trunk lid): this is the grail-cup of early Saab and the 'face' of the car says it all. Tony Grestock's amazing 728 XUR has to be one of the rarest and most valuable Saab's in the world. Tony drives it as intended, educating people about the magic of Saab.

capacity seems utterly irrelevant. The brand is not the point: the car and how it was engineered and designed, and consequently how it drove, was (and remains) the point.

Among the small number of cars that fit this description in the last half of the automobile's greatest century were the Saab 92 and its direct offspring, the 93 and 96 (as 2-stroke cars), and then as the 4-stroke cycle 96 V4.

Before everything became computerized, digital and electric, at a time back when man's mechanical interaction with his machines was the point of the mechanism, the original Saab car was, like a few others, a direct, visceral, mechanical driving experience utterly devoid of the effect of consumer 'clinics', 'marcomms', fashion, foible or celebrity opinion through self-proclaimed 'influencers'.

In the early 1960s the little Saab was the most successful rally car in Europe, irrespective of price or size classification. Look at the fuss Ford, followed by Audi, made in later decades when their cars achieved such status: Saab were entirely justified in their self-proclaimed brilliance.

The Saab car or 'Bil' ('bil' is Swedish for car) was, like the original Porsche, the original Citroën or the original Lancia (to mention a few other candidates), an act of adult engineering design and driver delight all wrapped up in a 'pure' car. Grown-ups were in charge when creating the Saab car, not corporate-speak lemmings with an eye on passing trends and quickly dating fashion, expressed in 'new-speak' Orwellian design languages, meaningless clichés and pointless phrases. Saab never touched such things. This is why Saab's cars were so very real and utterly timeless, untouched by the dating of fashion. You cannot really say that about a Ford Cortina, a Honda Civic or a Morris Marina. The compromises of coalesced 'group-think' were not required at Trollhättan.

From its initial '92' iteration, then to becoming the 93, and through to its 96 2-stroke and 96 V4 forms across the thirty-one years it was on sale, here was a car that was so correct, so clever, that it excelled on the world's stage as a family car and as a race and rally car too. A car that was a useful hold-all you could go camping in, yet also a coupé that raced and rallied to the top of the world's motor sport stages. Indeed, in the 1960s Saab Great Britain Ltd ran an advert citing such dual, weekend and workday use of a family

INTRODUCTION

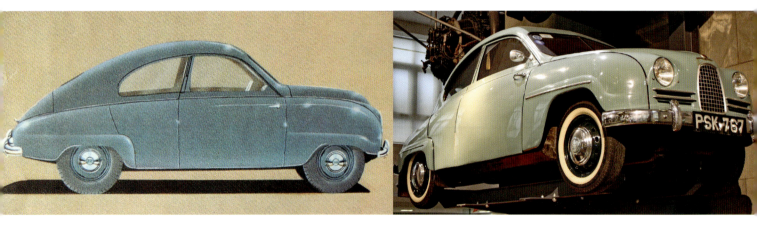

This original watercolour artwork for the 1950 brochure was painted by Sixten Sason's own hand. Green paint ruled.

The Saab 93 on display in the Science Museum, London, is a symbol of its importance.

Saab as both a rally car and family driver as owned by the mysterious 'George'. Apparently George had a sports car of his own, but never used it, instead preferring his wife's 96.

The little Saabs are 'real' cars for real driving and real fun. Rev a 2-stroke to 7,000rpm and let it fly and you will get the message. Yet do not forget the sonorous V4 and its sheer throbbing urge. Today these older Saabs are the subject of huge interest and have a growing following, matched by rising prices. As always with the 92, 93 and the 96s, a dedicated bunch of Saab enthusiasts who are clearly emotionally attached to their steeds remains the core of the movement worldwide.

If you want to know just how famous these Saabs became, consider the fact that it was not just in Sweden where the Saab 92 and 93 appeared on official postage stamps. In the unlikely location of Grenada, the post office issued a $2.00 stamp with three views of a large red 1963 Saab 93. The stamp was part of Grenada's centenary celebrations on 1 June 1988: but why a Saab? Saab really does get to parts that other cars do not.

In the Science Museum, London, there is a display of cars cited as being of importance in the history of the motor car, and among these is a 1956 Saab 93.

The little Saab may have been Swedish, but there were many ingredients in its DNA, with influences from Czechoslovakia, Italy and France. Its design was new yet evoked themes of 1920s 'Aerodyne' engineering from airships, to locomotives, to yachts, to cars. Even Paul Jaray and the Tatra cars he created for Hans Ledwinka get a citation in the annals of Saab 92 design.

Intriguingly, the 92's chief engineer Gunnar Ljungström, although Swedish and essentially an aircraft designer, had some of his initial engineering training in England. He was also a railway enthusiast and a yachting fanatic, and some degree of knowledge transfer is obvious. Of interest, Gunnar's father Fredrik had also influenced railway locomotive design and other aspects of Swedish engineering, including yacht hulls and sails.

Karl Erik Sixten Andersson (later known as Sixten Sason) was Saab's first chief designer/stylist. He had trained in France and toured Europe in a quest for design. He was one of the forerunners and founders of the movement of international renown that today we recognize as 'Swedish design'. Sason's influence at Saab and upon Swedish design is far deeper than many people realize and this book contains a detailed tribute to his life and works.

Rolf Mellde was a young engineering enthusiast, inventor, rally driver and engine tuner who joined Saab in 1946 and hugely influenced the first Saab car and later models. The often forgotten Olof Landbü was an experienced 1930s rally and trials driver. As lead test engineer/development driver, he was the first to test the new Saab in 1946–8 and guided Mellde in the early days: Landbü drowned in a non-car-related accident in 1948 and consequently Mellde's role expanded.

Josef Eklund became Saab's 3-cylinder, 2-stroke engineering genius for the 93 and 96 2-strokes, helping to produce a design that one of his colleagues, Dick Ohlsson, summed up to the 'Save Saab' campaign at the time when

INTRODUCTION

Saab was fighting for its survival in 2011: 'There's something magical about Saab.'

In the first Saab with wheels not wings, there was to be found a small, exquisitely engineered, northern European sporting car that was something genuinely new. It was not a basic 'people's car', but neither was it a conservative or middle-class saloon of upright values and appearance: it was transverse-engined and employed front-wheel drive long before the Mini. The Saab pioneered 2-cylinder and then 3-cylinder power in the mass market decades before today's smaller petrol engines of 'Eco' fame.

The little Saab drove with style and sensation, with true feedback and with superb levels of steering and dynamic intuition. This car could even traverse rutted snow, ice and mud in off-road conditions thanks to its flat under-floor, and go on to toboggan its way across roads and rally stages that would stop rear-wheel-drive cars in their tracks. Or the Saab could be a family hold-all and daily driver.

Sometimes Saab's engineers and designers went against their senior management's conservatism. Secret or special projects were run internally by people like Mellde and Eklund, only for such ideas to prove successful and to effectively save Saab in the early 1960s at a point when the board's pervasive 2-stroke 'obsession' was causing sales to wane. The special rebellious Saab spirit had a Swedish term 'Saabandan', meaning to be daring and go against orders.

There are many reasons why the Saab car company (not the aerospace company) died. More than one hand was to blame and solely citing General Motors (GM), or criticizing Mr Müller, is far too easy and too simplistic, although GM's stewardship raised many questions that not even Bob Lutz and his talented team could manoeuvre around, rebadging Subaru and Chevrolet cars as Saabs in a desperate act of 'badge engineering'. One of the key reasons Saab failed, yet a reason so often overlooked, however, was its *own* utter failure to reinvent its core, key car: the small Saab that as the 92 to the 96 had launched Saab, made Saab, and which for decades *was* Saab.

The point when Saab abandoned its roots in a small, sporty, intelligently designed cheaper car was when the company lost the opportunity to reinvent its brand, its marque equity, its ethos and its values, which were rooted in a defining 'core' car that would create high volume production number profits.

Even the most dedicated Saab enthusiast might have to admit that the company was so wrapped up in doing its own Saab 'thing', with all the engineering quality inherent in that status, that Saab was partly the author of its own downfall. Is this a dreadful thing to say? Maybe, but many Saab veterans believe it to be so. Some rival car makers thought that the Saab car was too high quality, but at Saab you did not think like that: quality and the effort to strive for it could never be too high. How did such a device get to be so 'right' and of such high quality from the word go?

As a tribute to Stig Blomqvist, the hero of Saab's second rally generation, Graham Macdonald took a rally specification V4 with American-type headlamps and recreated pure heroic Saab glory. It is now under new ownership and soon to be seen on the historic events calendar.

INTRODUCTION

Curiously, back in 1949, despite the very advanced design of its first car, some of Saab's upper management displayed an innate conservatism that would later create tensions with those who wanted to expand – perhaps too radically, at the other end of the corporate behavioural spectrum.

Yet other car companies correctly reinvented their 'core' car icon and brand equity: imagine if Saab had reinvented the 96 as a VW Golf crossed with an AlfaSud injected with Saab DNA. What a car that could have been.

But no, long before Fiat, GM or Victor Müller got their respective hands on the levers of power, Saab chose to go up market. There were many correct reasons for this decision, yet it seemed strange indeed to abandon the vital, founding, core model range and brand equity that was the 92, 93 and 96.

I suppose it was all about money and production unit volume (or the lack thereof), and tough choices had to be made with one hand tied behind the corporate back. The Saab 96 sometimes just about touched 100,000 units a year, but Saab struggled to make enough cars to earn the profit to sustain itself. It was left to Volvo to produce two smaller cars (the 340 and 66) to fill the void created by Saab's decision to ignore that market sector.

The truth is that Saab's later cars would not have been born without the Saab 92–96 story, yet it was the eventual move upmarket that led to the death of that early original manifestation of Saab and what many now specify as 'Saabism'. Swedish car buyers, and those in other markets, soon turned to other small- to medium-sector cars.

Today the old Saabs, which some contentiously describe as the 'real' Saabs, have a massive following. Describing them by such tags as weird or quirky simply reflects jealousy or the blinkered vision of conventional minds (a later Saab advertising strapline told you to 'move your mind').

Saab fans, sometimes known as 'Saabists', apparently suffer from 'Saabism' and it is said that they fall into three categories: fans of old original 2-stroke Saabs 92–96, as well as 96 V4 fans; then comes the followers of the developed 99 and 900, which still encapsulated 'Saabism'; and after that are the enthusiasts of the much later Saabs right up to 2012 and the death of Saab as a carmaking brand.

A curious emotional bond infects the Saab fanatic, such as the respected veterinarian Chris Day, who had a yard full of old Saabs. Chris raced a 900 and restored an old 92, transporting his Saabs on a blue Scania-Vabis truck and inspiring many with his Saab enthusiasm.

The early organizers of the Saab Owners Club of Great Britain in the 1960s and 1970s showed huge commitment and much humour in its publications: 'Bengt Krankshaf' was the alter ego of Vernon Mortimer, who developed the club's *Saab Driver* magazine.

Many years back, another big Saab fan was Tony Percy, who headed the Saab Owners Club GB in 1984. He owned two 96s, a 95, a 99EMS and later took care of the 'SaaBSA' motorcycle, a home-built design devised by Ray Pye in 1975 that combined a Saab 841cc triple, a BSA Rocket frame, a Triumph gearbox, a Vincent primary chain and a BMC 1000 radiator. Former Saab Motors USA director Robert Sinclair rode the 'SaaBSA' for a while in the 1980s. It then went through several owners before returning to Great Britain. Such is the free thinking of the Saab fanatic.

Sinclair was so admired by American Saab dealers that when he retired as president of Saab-Scania America/Saab USA, all 130 American Saab dealers clubbed together and bought him a restored Sonett II 'stroker' as a retirement present.

Also in America are the respected names of old Saab expertise led by the likes of Tom Donney, and Bruce Turk, who has been described as America's most obsessed-with-Saab man! Chris Moberg has a Sonett and is fascinated by 2-strokes. Mike Grieco, of Grieco Brothers in New Jersey, seems to have got the old Saab collecting bug quite badly. The famous Saabist and nuclear physicist Walter Kern (of Saab Quantum fame) also built (with David Homer) an electric-powered Saab Sonett in 1975.

Members of the national Saab club in Japan own both the newest and the oldest Saabs in its membership, including a 96 V4 that lives in Tokyo. A representative fan of all things Saab among these was the an aviation technican and classic Saab owner Kazumoto Yabe. The German love of old Saabs thrives across northern Germany and even touches the hallowed turf of Swabia and Bavaria. Not surprisingly Saab still has a strong presence in Denmark.

The same goes in Africa (a dark green 96 exists in fine fettle in Tanzania), America, Australia, New Zealand, Canada, Chile, Argentina, Uruguay, France, Poland, Portugal, the Netherlands and Norway – *everywhere* seems to have a family of Saab fanatics. As a Saab advertisement stated: 'The Saab Spirit: Some people have it.'

The Saab Club of Australia has individual State sections and Aussies all over the nation love old Saabs. A decade ago I flew to Tasmania to meet Steven Wade, who founded the world's first Saab blog and went on to Saab social media

INTRODUCTION

Purists might disagree, but this heavily modified 96 captures the spirit of Saab sport and modification.

fame. Even the Captain of the Qantas 747-400 owned an old Saab. On my visit Wade introduced me to geologist Drew Bedelph, who has a warehouse-sized collection of early Saabs tucked away in this forgotten corner of the world.

On my last foray to Australia, not only were there dozens of Saabs on Tasmania, more were to be seen on the 'big island'. Way out beyond Alice Springs, on the way to Mount Sonder in the Glen Helen Gorge amid the West Macdonnell ranges, I found a property with a sun-bleached and faded old 96 that might once have been pale blue but now was almost white, resting out its dotage in the red dust driveway to a homestead. Apparently it still ran and was used for local runs – 'local' being anywhere within a hundred miles. A shopping trip to Alice Springs in a near sixty-year-old Saab? How normal.

On the twin islands of New Zealand there is a massive Saab subculture and up to a dozen Saab 2-strokes and V4s are currently active there. Head down to the bottom of South Island and you might bump into a 96! Saabs can be found in the islands of the Pacific too.

Of all the Saab outposts, imagine seeing a 96 V4 in Korea in 1970: a regular sight there driving up into the de-militarized zone between South and North Korea was the 96 V4 of the Swedish Ambassador, which was the only Saab in Korea then and for years afterwards.

Princess Beatrix of the Netherlands once owned a 1958 Saab 93, as did the Swedish royal family led by Prince Bertil, starting with a Saab 92; the Danish royals followed their example. The famous British comedian Eric Morecombe ran a 96 V4 and a 99 Turbo, and then a 900 Turbo. Ernie Wise also had a 96. The actor and thinker Stephen Fry once owned a Saab. The wrestler Jackie Pallo drove a 96 V4 and was the first president of the Saab Owners Club of Great Britain.

INTRODUCTION

Reflections on Saab: a 96 captured in a 92's hub cap.

What else would Raymond Baxter, Britain's much missed broadcaster, writer, thinker and ex-Spitfire pilot, drive but a Saab. His friendship with Robert Moore, who headed Saab GB and happened to be a former Hurricane and Tempest fighter pilot, might just have influenced Raymond's choice. Baxter (as well as Erik Carlsson's co-driver Stuart Turner) was a member of the curious Ecurie Cod Fillet (ECF) rally team and it is said that an ECF decal was on Erik's Saab when he (with John Brown) won the 1961 RAC Rally, but Saab peeled it off before the car arrived at the winner's podium.

Visit Buenos Aires or Montevideo and you may spot Saab 92s, 93s, 96s and 99s on the streets, some of which were built locally as officially sanctioned South American Saabs. A plan to manufacture Saab cars in Brazil came to nothing (even though a Brazilian airline named VASP operated Saab-Scandia airliners for decades), but a Uruguayan-built Saab materialized after ten Saab 92s were shipped to Uruguay in 1952 and eighty were shipped to Peru. Several found their way up to Venezuela and down to Chile, where 93s and 96s can still be found rusting away in glorious peace. Havana, Cuba, boasts a bright yellow 92 with some non-standard modifications too. Saabs were sold in Ecuador from 1960 and the local concessionaire Marco Baca and his brother both raced Saabs (including a GT750) in local Ecuadorian events.

In Uruguay, where Saabs were being locally built in the early 1960s by the Automotora Company, its director, José Arijón Rama, raced a 96 Sport both in Uruguay and in Argentina. Héctor Marcial Fojo was the Saab South America 'name' in a 96 Sport with co-driver Nestor Uccellini.

The principal pillars of Montevideo's Club Saab Uruguay, which was founded in 2008 by Alberto Domingo, are currently Carlos and Juan Abeiro. Alberto has run a Saab for fifty years, and he and his wife career around in their little red Saab. If we can agree that Alberto Domingo is our Saab hero in South America, then are the Abeiros the torch bearers for Saab in South America?

Besides Uruguay, there is also the Club Saab Argentina, which I first encountered when hearing about Buenos Aires resident Charly Walmsley, who has owned a lovely black 92B for more than forty years – one of two 92s and several 93s seen running around the wonderful city of Buenos Aires for decades.

In 2008 Walmsley's other Saab, a red 96, and several other early Saab owners and their cars came together as the (now defunct) Grupo Saab Rioplatense ('Saab Group of the River Plate Area') to take part in an historic event in tribute to forty years of the Uruguay 19 Capitales rally, joining forces to create a team of three Saab rally cars, including two 96s, to compete in the 2008 re-enactment.

Erik Carlsson was a passenger in Walmsley's red 96 when he visited Argentina and Uruguay in the 1990s. The great Argentinian driver Juan Manuel Fangio is said to have driven a Saab 96 and 'got' what the car was all about. (For more on Saabs in Argentina and Uruguay, see Chapters 3, 4 and 6).

INTRODUCTION

Bruce Turk, possibly the most obsessed Saab enthusiast in the USA, has a barn full of early Saab beauties ranging from the 92 to the 96, including a 93, 95 and Sonett. It is Saab heaven for collectors.

Classic Saab profile as the Sax-O-Mat equipped 'stroker' gets going.

A last-of-the-line, Finnish-built 96 V4 showed off the updates to an original bodyshell first created in 1949.

■ INTRODUCTION

An early 96 'long-nose' captured low down to show off the lobed styling and revised front grille and lights.

INTRODUCTION

From 92 to 96, the Saab sculpture retained its unique shape, scale and stance.

Perhaps less well known was the involvement of Saab and its designer, Sixten Sason, in the emergence of the globally admired Swedish design movement, providing key support. In the 1950s and 1960s Swedish design topped the world, being innovative and broad in its reach and details, as well as being of the highest quality. From cars to glass, furniture, chairs and architecture, and beyond to areas of interior, exterior and industrial design, fabrics, colours and consumer goods, Swedish design had an effect far beyond its domestic scale. Today we have 'Scandi Design' as an enduring legacy and Saab had a hand in its orgination. Saab's story, therefore, is very much one of design mixed with engineering in a functional yet stimulating manner.

As a young designer I was fortunate enough to contribute something small to Saab design. In this book I have tried to convey my love of Saab's contribution to the sheer brilliance of Swedish design, setting down the story of the original Saab, an icon, a true hero of an age of the automobile that has passed. Today's digital highway has little space for such ingredients from the great epoch of the motor car prior to the 1980s. In Saab lay the difference: here we found the true Saab design language and the Saab philosophy.

Saab is sometimes written as Svenska Aeroplan Aktie Bolaget, but in correct Swedish it is Svenksa Aeroplan Aktiebolaget.

Saab was also part of the social science of Sweden and forged its relationship with its workforce and the towns where they lived. Today the wonderful Saab Museum and the Saab Veterans Club preserve historical documents that outline the relationship of the Saab 'family' and its workers through a form of social contract within Sweden's advanced societal structure that, at that time, was possibly unique in Europe.

This book has taken many years to research and is my attempt at a detailed yet accessible history of Saab's first car and, crucially, all the factors that created both it and Saab as not just a company, but a philosophy. Apart from Porsche or Citroën, I can think of no other carmaker with such a fascinating personality construct.

Here is the story of the speedy little Saab that so many loved as the 'svenska bil med flygplansqvalitet' ('the Swedish car with aircraft quality').

Lance Cole
Villa Saab

CHAPTER ONE

ORIGINS: WINGS TO WHEELS

Although the Saab 92, launched in 1949, was Sweden's first mass production front-wheel drive, safety-built and aerodynamically effective small car, Volvo had actually produced cars from 1927, starting with the 'Jakob' OV4 car, but these were rear-wheel-drive devices influenced by American designs. Dig deeper, however, and you will find that the history of Sweden's first 'car' goes back a further three decades.

The origins of engineering and industrial design in Sweden began with railway locomotives, rolling stock, commercial vehicles and aircraft. Trollhättan was to become 'locomotive city' and later the home of Saab's car production, while nearby Linköping was focused on aircraft; both towns would become manufacturing bases during the second half of the twentieth century.

The earlier attempts at Swedish car production were overshadowed by the manufacture of heavy goods vehicles, buses, and various engines and machines. It was these industries that laid the foundations of knowledge and aircraft design, making possible the rise of production facilities.

The first recorded Swedish-designed motor car and engine can be credited to Gustaf Erikson in 1897 and the design was then refined through to 1901 and beyond. This car and the early Swedish trucks and buses of the era were produced by manufacturers who would, three decades later, amalgamate to become the Saab Company. Erikson's ideas, undertaken in collaboration with Peter Pettersson on behalf of the Vabis Company, would then contribute to the first cars built by Scania-Vabis.

This very rare artwork by Sixten Sason shows off his idea for a more upmarket version of the original 92 equipped with American-style chrome and faired-in headlamps. A case of future-vision unrequited.

The name Vabis is an acronym of Vagnfabriks-Aktiebolaget i Södertelge Company (with a different spelling of the placename Södertälje) and was applied by Philip Wersén from 1891 to a company building railway rolling stock originally derived from David Ekenberg's railway stock coachbuilding concern. Vabis merged with Scania in 1910 to create Scania-Vabis, which was involved with limited Swedish car production up to 1920.

Scania originated in Malmö in 1891 as the Maskinfabriks-Aktiebolaget and took over the Svenska-Aktiebolaget Humber & Co of Malmö – Humber being a British agency. Scania started on an experimental design for a Swedish car in 1901 and by the following year had built two such concept cars and a light truck. In 1903 Scania built Sweden's first 'production' car, although this was limited to just five units.

In 1909 Scania built the world's first truck fitted with proper axles that ran with ball-bearings (Sweden led the world in ball-bearing manufacture). Before 1910 was out Scania would build a series of proper trucks and several more of its cars.

By 1919 Scania-Vabis, based in the town of Södertälje, had produced 830 car chassis units and another 341 car/light commercial chassis types, some of which were sold for export. So the truth is that Scania made 'Swedish' cars, of a type that mirrored other early European cars, long before the first true mass-produced, Swedish-designed Saab with its wing-with-wheels car design. Scania eventually went on to become Saab's partner decades later and Saab cars wore 'Saab-Scania' badges until the 1990s.

Certain industrial brands became prominent in the affairs of Sweden. The names that became integral to the Saab plot included Bofors, Nohab, Thulin, Nydqvist, Koppaberg and Götaverken, all of which contributed to the heady brew of industrial might as they made links and mergers. AB Svenska Järnvägsverkstäderna (ASJ), with its road, rail and air divisions, was to be a key fulcrum in the creation of the corporate structure that was the final SAAB iteration that we now revere as Saab. It is a rather confusing trail.

Few people beyond the circle of Saab enthusiasts know just how strong was the locomotive, heavy road vehicle and aircraft building history of Sweden between 1900 and 1939, or how it all came together to produce a motor car.

As early as 1921 a company called Svenska Automobil Fabriken (SAF) imported American car engines and components of the 'Continental' brand in an early attempt to build a car in Sweden. Twenty-five 'modified' cars with local content were made, but few sold. This was the little-known early attempt at a Swedish-made (but not designed) car, but like the first Swedish aircraft, it was not home-grown. General Motors (GM) had a pre-1939 factory in Sweden where Completely Knocked Down (CKD) 'kits' of Detroit-designed cars were assembled for the local Swedish

Another rarity: Gunnar Ljungström's own sketch illustrates his very first idea for a Saab car before he spoke to Sason. Note the handwritten thoughts on the drawing.

■ ORIGINS: WINGS TO WHEELS

Before Saab there was Volvo, and before Volvo there was Scania-Vabis, who made a small number of early Swedish cars. This is a rare pre-1925 Swedish-designed and built Scania-Vabis car.

market. GM also owned Opel of Germany by this time and half a century later would swallow up Saab.

Also often unseen in the story lies the fact that the Swedish national car dealership company AB Nyköpings Automobilfabrik, later known as ANA and taken over by Saab in 1960, had been established in 1937 to licence-build CKD kits of Chrysler cars for Swedish domestic purchase. This was how large pre-war Chryslers became popular on Swedish roads (but less popular on winter ice and snow).

Prior to its later purchase by Saab, ANA would be the Swedish agents for Ferguson tractors and Standard Ltd's British cars. ANA had its own assembly workshop and under Saab ownership a plan was drawn up for it to build Saab cars.

Of tangential relevance to Saab was Svenska Aero AB, a company with a corporate structure of confused provenance founded in 1921 with links to Heinkel to circumvent some of the restrictions on German aviation imposed by the Treaty of Versailles. Svenska Aero never really succeded and was absorbed by what was now ASJA in 1932, so bringing it into the Saab story. The later Saab (Svenska Aeroplan Aktiebolaget) should not be confused with this earlier Svenska Aero AB and clarity is required when charting such histories.

Layered within this evolution lay the likes of Enoch Thulin and his company Aero Enoch Thulin Aeroplanfabrik (AETA), which was employing more than 1,000 people building aircraft by the 1920s. Further industrial rationalization would take place by State edict in 1936 under the Swedish Prime Minister, Per Albin Hansson. This threw together all the key players mentioned earlier, and so began the Saab story as an entity.

The Wallenberg family of bankers and investors, which owned a shipping line, transport stocks and the Swedish rights to Rudolf Diesel's engine design, was also influential within the emerging body. So pivotal were the banking activities of the Wallenbergs that they are considered to have been an essential part of Saab's first car.

The company was formally registered as Svenska Aeroplan Aktiebolaget on 20 April 1937. Based at Linköping, as a structural subsidiary of the Nohab/Bofors group with a share capital of SKr 4 million, this new body had powerful and well-connected management within its various internal structures. Axel Wenner-Gren was a key investor.

Work soon started on building a factory at Trollhättan and by 1939 Saab was a stand-alone company. Wenner-Gren was the driving force behind it all. There have been allegations about his activities in the 1930s and 1940s, but recent research has clearly confirmed that, although he made errors, he was not aligned to post-1933 German politics as some have claimed.[1]

The Saab Company that was defined in 1937 had originally been structured to exist alongside the aircraft division of Svenska Järnvägsverkstäderna Aeroplanavdelning (ASJA) and this caused certain internal corporate issues, which were resolved by the creation of AB Förenade Flygverkstäder (AFF) as a new joint entity. By this means ASJA, Svenska Aeroplan AB (Saab) and their respective responsibilities

ORIGINS: WINGS TO WHEELS

1930s futurism from Sason's pen as a precursor to the 92's ellipsoid form.

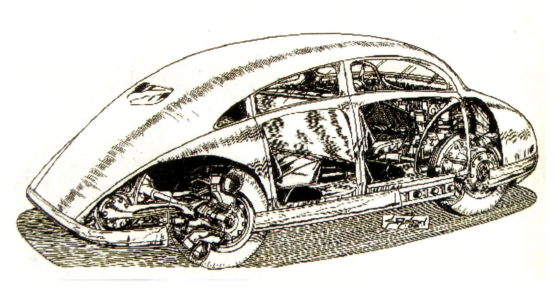

Another Sason 'aerodyne' idea from the mid-1930s with hints of Jaray, Ledwinka and other designers.

within AFF apparently sidestepped any more confusion as they coalesced by apparent State edict, the power of the Royal Swedish Air Force and under the guidance of several well-chosen committees.

That all these companies would end up amalgamated into a greater 'Saab' entity creates an interesting framework for the circumstances and influences that moulded the Saab Company, its aircraft and, notably, its first car – the 92.

By 1939 this confused, expensive and top-heavy construction of ASJA and Saab, under the wings of AFF, was displaying weaknesses in its finances, efficiencies and organization, and it was evident it could not survive the looming events of European tension as Sweden was encircled by geopolitical events. Therefore AFF would effectively be abolished as war clouds loomed and Sweden's political masters and defence chiefs enforced production of Swedish aircraft by a single named structure: Saab.

After producing two licence-built airframe derivatives (one American, one German), Saab created the radical S21 twin-boom design as its first true 'pure' airframe, for which Frid Wänström produced the preliminary design in just ten days.

The fact that Saab should build airframes of both American and German origin under licence before 1939 should not be taken as any sign of allegiance or political preference by Saab, its component divisions or the Swedish state in the 1930s. British aircraft engineering was also linked to both Linköping and Trollhättan and British engineers were working at Saab before 1939.

In the mid-1930s Sweden was essentially 'arming for peace' to defend its difficult position of facing an increasing threat after Hitler took power in the new Germany from 1933. Such needs created the requirement for a new Swedish aircraft industry, which would be met by the new Saab company as it emerged from a complicated corporate and political mess. From here it would be just five short years until corporate confusion was overcome and there would be a clear path to a Saab car built by Saab the aircraft manufacturer.

SAAB'S CAR

The original Saab cars, all derived from one model as the founding 92, were in production for thirty years. This was down to the engineering and design integrity of the underlying design, which itself reflected the integrity of the men who created the car and the company they worked for. What happened at Saab in the years after 1937 at Linköping and Trollhättan, and later at Nyköping, was not just special but very unusual indeed. In fact we might reluctantly have to argue that Saab was so self-absorbed in its own excellence and design brilliance, that it took its eye off the ball of profit and loss in the early 1970s. The same charges might also be directed at Citroën at the time.

The Saab was so charismatic, so brilliant, that it touched the hearts of many men and women the world over across decades. If ever there was a superbly driving motor car with 'designer' character, then it was the original Saab car. It was called Ur ('original') Saab and was affectionately known at the company as 'the UrSaab' (UrSaaben).

From the UrSaab came the 92, which was not quite perfect first time out, and its few flaws were addressed by the 93 and then the 96. The Saab 92 was essentially a Swedish act of supreme 'design' stemming from a small group of dedicated engineers, headed by one of the greatest industrial designers most people have never heard of.

The Saab 92, 93 and 96 2-stroke cars display the essence of this purity of both line and engineering; the later 96 V4 is best described as the same-but-different. That this Saab should also carve a niche in the United States of America only adds to the mix of the wonderful story of how Saab's first car became a global star in the world of rallying, with Erik Hilding Carlsson as its very own hero.

Saab's products really were the essence of the design philosophy of Swedish engineering. It is worth emphasizing that the people who designed Saab aircraft also designed Saab's car. At the same time as Saab was designing its car, work also progressed on the innovative Saab airframes, such as the amazing Saab 35 Draken, which first flew in 1955. This crank-winged, delta configuration jet fighter was perhaps even more advanced than the Saab 92 and 93 cars: Drakens often appeared alongside the cars in advertisements for Saab 93s and 96s.

The aeronautical link was therefore not hyperbole – it was engineering reality linked to a philosophy that no other carmaker took to such extremes, arguably not even the Bristol Car Company.

The Saab car was never a consumer device that happened to have wheels, which was the fate of so many cars past and present. What of built-in obsolescence? Not at Saab.

Saab cars had soul and still do. Beyond engineering and design integrity, there is the psychology and the very driving of the Saab. From the 92 to the 96 V4 (and beyond) Saabs drove and behaved in a specific manner. These cars had character and a spirit that stemmed from the men who created them. A welcome touch of Swedish intelligence and arrogance was apparent, for this is a car built by people who knew what they were doing and stuck to their decisions.

In the absence of a home-grown Swedish car, the economical and capable German DKW car would dominate Swedish motoring before 1939. For those who could afford them there were also large American cars and, of course, there was always the Volvo. But the large rear-wheel-drive cars of American design were useless in tough Swedish conditions beyond the suburbs of a major city. A rear-driven V8 on a rutted Swedish road covered in frozen snow was a pointless exercise.

The DKWs were sold by Gunnar Philipson and his dealerships, which is where he made his money. But Philipson would soon invest in Saab with cash up front before a Saab car had even been drawn.

1945: A SAAB WITHOUT WINGS

After the interruption of World War II, by 1946 Saab had concocted a recipe for a special type of new car. Informal discussions are believed to have begun in late 1944, with further more detailed work progressing across 1945.

The earlier automotive 'Aerodyne' or 'Streamliner' styles, which mimicked aircraft and airship forms, was influential in France, Germany, England and, to some degree, in the USA during the 1920s and 1930s. Examples of the 1930s Chrysler Airflow had made it to Stockholm. American cars, however, despite such exceptions as the Chrysler Airflow, the Briggs Streamliner and Ford's Lincoln Zephyr prototype, would in the mainstream soon concentrate on cubic capacity and 'fins and bling', stressing fashion over function. It is the aerodyne type, however, that inspired Sason's Saab car design, along with the new trends in aircraft design.

Saab's aircraft and its first car straddled this pre- and post-war world from the 1930s to the 1950s. The prototype from which the Saab 92–96 range derived was known as the 92.001/92.001. The Saab story panned out in a world of wings that became wheels, and the origins of its design DNA meant that its original cars were not just 'aircraft inspired' but were *truly* aircraft derived and designed by aircraft men.

Trollhättan also had a relationship with the British early on, for the Göta Canal, which crosses southern Sweden, was constructed using British expertise from Thomas Telford and British steam-driven dredgers. British aircraft engineers and test pilots worked for Saab and a link with the British de Havilland Company was established early on.

Like Saab, its rival Volvo would focus on integrity of engineering and safety, yet Volvo's early cars were influenced by British and American practices and fashions, notably rear-wheel drive, even though this configuration was almost useless for traction in the ice and snow of a Swedish winter. Here lay the first difference between Volvo and the front-wheel-drive ethos of Saab.

By 1946 Volvo was selling the first of a series of cars that were more relevant for the Swedish market. Good though they were, the PV444, which was developed into the PV544 of legend, retained rear-wheel drive, scant attention was paid to aerodynamics or sports handling, and they still aped American-inspired styling. Saab still had its opportunity: we must be thankful Volvo did not embrace front-wheel drive for another six decades.

Saab took a different route, capitalizing on the growing pride displayed by its workforce and a very distinct engineering ethos and design language.

The very first Saab 92 concept sketch of early 1945: it is not that far off the real thing, despite being a bit more extrovert.

■ ORIGINS: WINGS TO WHEELS

A re-colouring of an early watercolour sketch for the 92.001 UrSaab. Note the faired-in front.

Closer to production form, another evocative sketch of UrSaab development.

Why a car? Why did Saab not revert to its pre-war expertise? Surely it would have sufficed if its in-house experts had returned to their former building of railway locomotives and stock, aircraft, trucks, buses or industrial plant machinery. What of washing machines, boats or fishing rods, all of which were considered. Why cars?

The truth was that, temporarily at least, the aircraft market was saturated with cheap war-surplus aircraft and it would take Saab the aircraft maker years to plan and create its advanced new jet aircraft and prop-powered family of machines. The new Saab J29 Tunnan jet fighter and the S90 Scandia propeller airliner were top class designs, as was the S32 Lansen fighter. All were superb aircraft of world class, but they were long-term projects exposed to the whims of the marketplace and government policies and orders. Converting the S17 from prop- to jet-propulsion was but an interim measure for Saab, no matter how good was the resulting J17R jet. The double-delta-winged S35 Draken was a decade away.

War-surplus Douglas DC-3 (or C47) airliners were for sale very cheaply all over the world and the slow process involved in selling the high-quality S90 Scandia airliner did not in any way reflect upon the aircraft, which was brilliant

ORIGINS: WINGS TO WHEELS

in every respect. The Swedish Air Force would, of course, order the new Saab fighters, but designing and making aircraft is a very expensive business: Saab needed a new project and a cash-rich, cash-quick project at that.

A secure, long-term investment in a strategic plan was necessary to make things, employ people and survive the post-war years of austerity. Saab was also still being advised by the official Swedish Matériel Administration and the thoughts of its Board sometimes conflicted with the suggestions of some of the leading Saab engineers. Even Wallenberg was cautious about building a proposed car. Financial support from the Swedish state investment fund would be welcome, but it would be too limited to create a world famous company or brand in 1945 or 1946.

Saab's management was clever and chased even the smallest contract or opportunity. The designer Kurt Sjögren dreamed up a small hydrofoil powerboat that performed very well. Saab also created a lightweight aluminium rowing boat for tough arctic or tropical conditions and 250 were ordered. How about prefabricated steel buildings? Could Saab supply them? Only if the company could first secure the steel on the world market, and steel supply was to become a major issue in the immediate post-war years.

As Saab embarked on its first car, the aviation division and aero-engine Flygmotor section were about to introduce three new aircraft designs and begin building the de Havilland jet engine under licence. Given all this, money and manpower were in short supply and external recruits were hired to work on the new car project. Only a handful had worked for a carmaker (Volvo) or its suppliers, or with engines and chassis. Less than twenty-five men formed the core team that built the Saab 92 prototype.

Free thinking was about to come to the fore. After discussions with the Wallenbergs, Wenner-Gren and various other parties, notably Gunnar Philipson, the main Swedish car dealer, Saab's President Ragnar Wahrgren suggested examining the idea of making a car, either under licence or of actual Saab design.

Occasionally Sixten Sason went a bit over the top. This is 1947 proposal for a developed 92 is more UFO than 'people's car'. We can see clear hints of later 1950s American styling.

Saab made a crude clay model of Ljungström's first idea. Clearly it was too pre-war in style.

ABOVE AND LEFT: **Sixten Sason** quickly presented his idea and this is the early small-scale model of the design. Notice the aerofoil nose, glazed lamps and sheer style. The model has much larger twin-rear windows than the UrSaab.

In a move not unlike that of Howard Hughes's technique of ordering a new airliner to be designed and built for him and his airlines with payment up front, Philipson told Saab he would order 8,000 cars over three years and pay a large cash sum as a down payment (reputed to be a total of SKr1.8 million). Philipson, however, both expected and received input into the car's specification and pricing. Effectively, the Saab Board (and the Matériel Administration people) had their minds made up for them.

'The Company has examined the feasibility of making cars', Wahrgren told the key decision-makers. Wahrgren would, however, be gone from his role within five years – job done just as the new Saab 92 took to the roads.[2]

In late 1945 the Saab Board approved the design and prototype manufacture of a new car, a Swedish version of the pre-war DKW small 'economy' car that Philipson had sold so many of, but with added refinements and quality. Saab was authorized to spend SKr200,000 in hard cash on developing the car. The new car would sell for between SKr3,200 and up to SKr3,900 on the Swedish market at launch. Selling 10,000 of them within the first three years of production would put the Saab 'car' project in profit and repay Philipson.

The massive sum of SKr800,000 would be needed to take the development prototype to production status tooling-up readiness. This could only come as a grant and as investment. Designed at Linköping and built at Trollhättan would soon become the Saab car legend. The heavy tooling presses, which would cost more than SKr500,000, were to be the most expensive item. American steel was to be ordered but was hard to get, even though Saab's total initial order for the car was less than a day's output for the giant American steel-producing cities.

The 'Aeroplan' men had been used to aeronautical tolerances and the money to achieve them. Weights, thicknesses, resistances, load paths and performance were to be thought about and designed in just the same way as they would for an aircraft or a racing car, that is, with ultimate possible strength and the least possible excess. This new approach, this uniquely Saab ethos, would cost time and money. Decades later, in different economic circumstances, such issues would come home to roost.

The starting point of the new car was not to produce something comparable to the large Volvos or the pre-war American behemoths. Instead it would be new, but retaining a memory of the small, front-wheel drive, 2-stroke DKW that Philipson had sold in Sweden before the war and which had proved very popular. DKW was a German company founded in 1916 by the Danish engineer Jørgen Skafte Rasmussen, and the first DKW cars had been produced in 1928.

FRONT-WHEEL DRIVE

Front-wheel drive had been briefly tried before in big cars by Cord in America and by Citroën in France, as well as by the smaller DKW.

Alvis of England had built a very sporty two-seater front-wheel-drive car in the late 1920s and caused much head-scratching in the emerging British motor industry as a result, but the Alvis was a wood-constructed, metal-panelled, open sportster. Alvis even took out a patent in 1928–9 for its front-wheel drive, front axle lubricator mechanism. Alvis also patented in May 1929 an idea for linking two engines together and providing a single-shaft output that was specifically relevant to front-wheel-drive traction. A variant of such a linked twin-engine configuration would, of course, appear in Rolf Mellde's Saab 93 twin triple-cylinder engined 'Monster' in 1959.

The benefits of front-wheel traction were obvious. Alvis had built 4-cylinder and 8-cylinder front-driven cars about 1928 to 1931 and had raced a front-wheel-drive racing car as early as 1925. Production figures vary for the road-going versions, but approximately 150 such Alvis cars are cited as having been built in total. Alvis were the forgotten path-finders, and Citroën and then Saab would beat the Austin-Morris Mini Minor (the 'Mini') to mass-market volume production of a front-driven car by years.

Saab concentrated on a transverse-engined front-wheel-drive design for the small family car market, yet one with sporting handling and qualities all wrapped up in the safest body shell yet constructed, boasting advanced aerodynamics on a scale never seen before. Did Saab actually know what they were about to dream up?

The Saab Board might not have known what was coming, but the engineers on the ground had realized that they had to do something different to succeed. Just copying everyone else and creating a reheated pre-war car design with leaf spring or lever arm suspension, separate bulbous wing or fender panels and upright styling angles, enclosing a wheezing cast-iron lump of an engine sitting on a hefty chassis clothed in tin, or even a part-wood or a canvas-clad body,

ORIGINS: WINGS TO WHEELS

Two titans of Saab, chief design engineer **Gunnar Ljungström** (left) and chief project manager **Svante Holm** (right), seen with a styling model.

was not going to tempt car buyers or last long in the marketplace once post-war austerity gave way to an economic boom that would, in time, surely arrive.

DKW's 2-stroke thinking and legacy may have been the key influence on Saab's engine choice, but there were factors such as post-war shortages, a scarcity of machine tools and a lack of raw materials to be considered: the 2-stroke had fewer moving parts and was cheap and easy to build and maintain. If Saab could refine the 2-stroke concept and fit such an engine in a car built to aircraft design standards, it might make its mark, or so the 'Aeroplan' men of Saab believed.

Meanwhile, given the employment situation, Saab entered into talks with the Swedish government about seeking support for car production in the 'national interest'. By this time Saab had also discovered that the metal presses to build the car would need another SKr600,000 of investment: the costs were mounting.

When Saab's men sat down to create a car that would meet the needs of the people of their own land, the thought of global sales domination was far from their minds, for the Swedes were not made that way. Yet Sweden already had a carmaker that was well established by 1947: Volvo. In even its popular post-war PV444 model, the Volvo was a large, rear-wheel-drive car of American styling and layout. It was also an oversteering, tail-wagging device with reduced winter traction, but as front-wheel drive was so rare at the time, few people knew what they were missing.

Saab was not in the mindset of building cars to ancient design parameters. Critically, Saab was not hindered or blinkered by established principles: Saab the carmaker could start with a blank sheet of paper and a whole load of new ideas. The Swedish climate and conditions may have been relevant to Saab's first car design, but they cannot have been the sole key arbiter, otherwise Volvo would have been building something far more appropriate (with front-wheel drive) for the very same conditions.

As 1945 closed Saab moved towards its new project, and wing design section leader Gunnar Ljungström would soon draw the first ideas for the design.

1946: THE BIG STEP

What route should Saab follow? Should the car mimic not just the old DKW, but also the rear-engined, rear-driven Volkswagens, Fiats, Renaults and Tatras? What about the Austin, Peugeot or Ford models with front engines driving the rear wheels, all clad in a dinosaur school of car design with running boards and upright windscreens? Remember this was 1945. Even Citroën's advanced Traction Avant was an old-school design no matter how clever it was, and it would remain in production for a decade after World War II.

Saab the Innovator – Before the Issigonis 'Revolution'

In 1945 Alec Issigonis had not yet dreamed up his curvaceous and low-fronted Morris 1000 'Mosquito' prototype, nor then seen it de-radicalized by 1950 into a more conventional 'upright' machine for middle-class British tastes; neither had Issigonis invented the transverse-engined, small-capacity, front-wheel-drive 'Mini'. Saab was ahead of even Issigonis, yet he would be hailed a decade and more later as a 'pioneer'.

Perhaps only the VW Beetle had taken steps to depart from styling convention and few people had ever seen what German aerodynamics experts had been thinking about for cars and aircraft in the 1930s and 1940s. What of Ledwinka, Jaray and their Tatra? Was this where so many designers would glean some ideas – with a bit of help from others? Even a polymath like Ferdinand Porsche was not immune to 1930s streamliner and aerodyne design ideas that had begun with Paul Jaray and a few others.

Saab's approach was not dissimilar to Ferdinand Porsche's aerodynamic focus with his pre-war body designer Erwin Komenda and aerodynamicist Josef Mickl. Did Saab take a cue from it and from VW to become the better teardrop shape that Sixten Sason would focus upon? Ljungström certainly expressed interest in what Porsche was doing and is believed to have considered using the new Porsche design bureau, originally known as Dr.Ing. h.c. Ferdinand Porsche GmbH (Konstrucktionsbüro für Motoren-Fahrzeug, Luftfahrzeug und Wasserfahrzeugbau), as consultants before Porsche came to produce its own Porsche-branded car. Whatever the effects of Porsche's designs, notably his late 1930s streamliners, Ljungström sidestepped the opportunity to use Porsche's rear-engined configuration and instead Saab did its own thing. Ferdinand Porsche's pre-war design theories may have influenced the Saab 92, but Porsche's own mass-market 'teardrop' 356 coupé, with styling co-penned by Erwin Komenda, was several years away when Sason shaped the 92.

What of Josef Ganz who, like Sason, drew up designs for advanced aerodynamic cars in the 1930s and had his ideas published in motoring magazines. Such themes were all in the mix of the era. Add in the design works of Jacques Gerin, Gabriel Voisin, Norman Bel Geddes, Frederick Lanchester and Georges Paulin, and the design curve was moving fast. The Tatra of Ledwinka and Jaray was not to be overlooked at Saab either.

A tension existed in the Saab car design proposal: it had to be new, clever, advanced even, and of the company's typical high-quality engineering, yet also basic, reliable and affordable. Sven Otterbeck, the Saab deputy director under whose wing the car 'Projekt' fell, framed this tension with the view that 'Europe is impoverished by war, the car has to be undemanding and cheap'.[3]

Given such a statement, the reader may wonder how something as radical and revolutionary as the UrSaab 92.001 could result and get approved. Otterbeck's statement suggested that we might have expected a basic, sit-up-and-beg, boxy little reinvention of a DKW, or a copy of an Austin Seven, or a Swedish VW. BMW, for example, had built an 'economy' car of this type under licence to meet an economic need. After 1945 the Germans turned to micro cars: three- or four-wheelers with tiny motorcycle engines and two-seat bodies. Even the British tried three-wheel cars with two-stoke engines and flimsy bodyshells.

The first wooden buck for the 92.002 prototype followed the 92.001 UrSaab in 1948. The more conventional front and headlamp treatment was deemed more acceptable.

■ ORIGINS: WINGS TO WHEELS

Sason's sketch proposal for a halfway-house design between the 92.001 and the more upright 92.002 production shape.

UrSaab caught at rest: what a simply stunning piece of aerodyne sculpture by Sason.

ORIGINS: WINGS TO WHEELS

Incredibly, against all the odds, as its first car design Saab produced a spaceship of a car blessed with aviation engineering. The test of the requirements framed by Otterbeck was to be more than solved.

The first basic design remit from a management decision was that the Saab car should be both faster and more economical than the pre-war DKW that had been so popular. This could only be achieved through an efficient structure and aerodynamic design. Less drag meant more speed and less fuel used. It was a simple equation. Thus was set the foundation of the Saab car ethos.

In Saab's new thinking lay the key that unlocked the gateway to a design specification. Perhaps the subconscious knowledge of just how popular the pre-war 2-stroke German DKW had been in Sweden had played a role. The idea of a home-grown, updated version would have certainly appealed to Saab's most important backer, Gunnar Philipson.

Under the guidance of Otterbeck as vice-president of the Saab aircraft company, who oversaw the URSaab project's initial approval, the engineer chosen to become the engineering 'father' of Saab's first car was Gunnar Ljungström. Ljungström was working as a wing stress engineer at Saab before he became the chief engineer for the new car. He was just about to turn forty and was steeped in engineering tradition and learning that went far beyond airframes.

Project X9248

In 1944 Ljungström was designing a torpedo-launching variant of an existing Saab aircraft. He had risen to the wing-design group leader role through his work on Saab airframe projects, which brought him into close contact with the needs of airflow and aerodynamic behaviour. This was to prove valuable for his next assignment in 1945, the Saab car that was to be known inside the Linköping and Trollhättan sites as 'Project X9248' before gaining its 'UrSaab' tag.

Ljungström brought into the team Sixten Sason, the celebrated 1930s stylist and designer who had been a mechanic/pilot in the Royal Swedish Air Force more than a decade beforehand. By late 1945 Ljungström had sketched out his own potential car body design and style, but he was aware that it lacked innovation and that secret magical ingredient that would make it special. As the project took formal shape in 1946, he turned to Sixten Sason, who had been working on X-ray drawings and design sketches for the Saab aircraft drawing office.

This proposal for 92.002 featured a Viking-type winged emblem that was not far off being a Voisin-inspired logo.

TRYGGVE HOLM

Tryggve Holm may have been born to lead Saab (and not just the car division). His father was the managing director of Bofors, one of the key companies that created the 1930s industrial movement in Sweden from which Saab arose. Tryggve became a qualified mining engineer and then worked for Bofors and ASJA. After moving to Saab in 1950 he was appointed overall Saab CEO, while also serving as a director of Bofors and chairman of the Swedish Employers Association. Holm pushed for an increasing use of electronics at Saab and also worked closely on Saab airframe development.

Tryggve Holm was the big-voiced, 'big beast' of Saab and its 'Captain', yet he could be sensitive and considerate. In essence he pursued the 'classless' Swedish social model in his relations with employees. His international outlook was fostered by a childhood that featured his father's expansion of Bofors and his own time on a Carnegie Scholarship in the USA. ASJA, which was an essential part of Saab's founding structure between 1937 and 1939, was how Holm gained a foothold at Trollhättan (ASJA's director Ragnar Wahrgren was to become Saab's first CEO).

Holm was a key figure in the decisions that resulted in Saab's early aircraft and guided the development of its original car. It was Holm who stressed the importance of the Saab 'quality' ethos. Some witnesses claim that he was reluctant to embrace the move from a 2-stroke engine to a 4-stroke unit, but was persuaded to accept the change.

Tryggve Holm was one of the 92's founding fathers and went on to lead Saab during its greatest years in the 1950s and 1960s.

He certainly embraced the idea and the funding for the 95 estate car and continued to focus on quality.

Without Tryggve Holm Saab would not have created its cars. We owe a great debt to both his vision and his innate caution.

It would be more than a year, however, before the third 'original Saab' car design team member Rolf Mellde would join the project. Mellde was a young engineer with rally driving experience, and also a tuner and inventor, whose skills would become hugely important to Saab, not least in the creation of the rally department.

The small, original team at Saab for what became Project X9248, from the CEO down to the youngest worker, was a family. The hand-picked 'Aeroplan' men included designers, engineers, senior and junior apprentices and experienced artisan craftsmen. In addition to Ljungström and Sason they included Bertil Baerendz, 'Bror' Bjurströmer, Erik L. Ekkers (or Storerkers), Sven Fredriksson, Hans Osquar Gustavsson, Tage Fladån, Hugo Möller, Nils Lidro, Olle Lindgren, Sigvard Lenngren, Ellis Olsson and Tore Svenson. Other names who were to become key elements of the Saab car project's early days included Berth Olofsson, Bo Olsson, Arne Frick, Erik Johansson, Olle Lindkqvist, Lars-Olav Olsson, Gunnar Svanström and Gosta Svenson. Erik Nilestam would also soon play a role in the body engineering department. Rolf Mellde joined Saab in time to influence the production-series 92 of 1949.

Svante Holm, followed by Tryggve Holm, would become managerial leaders of renown. Tryggve Holm indeed was

ORIGINS: WINGS TO WHEELS

The first use of the name 'Sonett' by Saab appears in 1948 when Sason drew this photo-modified image of the 92 with a clear 'Sonett' name badge.

to be CEO of the company throughout its greatest 'original Saab' years from 1950 to 1967.

Hugo Möller, who was in charge of tool design on the project, would go on to become Saab's chief tooling engineer and a patent holder. Svante Holm, the project leader, would become a senior Saab managerial figure. (He should not be confused with Saab CEO Tryggve Holm.) Olof Landbü was the lead test engineer/development driver for the new car up to his death in 1948.

The core of the Saab team dedicated to creating car 'number one', as it was known by the team, consisted of about fifteen to twenty men. More then seventy years have passed since the beginning of the Saab car project. The names given here have been compiled as accurately as memory and research, have allowed (any omissions or errors are entirely accidental).

The mid-1940s Saab family was headed by the CEO, Gunnar Dellner. An early senior Saab engineer was Claes Sparre. Bertil Sjörgen and Svante Simonsson were senior planning managers. Erik Rydberg was to become car production-press and tooling manager and Nils-Gustaf Nilsson became the head of car production. Head foreman of the airfield and at the aircraft factory was Gunnar Westlund. Through these names and others, various randomly obtained spare parts (from DKW, Auto-Union and others) were combined with special one-off panels and handmade prototype toolings to create the prototype that would become a world famous car.

The rock upon which the project relied, and whose role in the process was vital, was Gunnar Ljungström.

GUNNAR LJUNGSTRÖM: A YACHT, A SAIL, A WING AND A CAR – *FRAN FLYGLAN TILL BILAR*

Of principal relevance to the Saab story was the young stress engineer Gunnar Ljungström, who had trained in Sweden and in Great Britain. In later life he was showered with awards and honours for his massive achievements and contributions to both Saab and to Sweden. One of Ljungström's former employees, Gunnar Larsson, who worked on the Saab 99 and 900, and who had a principal role in the development of the 9000, has recently co-written *Saab, We did it! Gunnar Ljungström and his Pioneers*, which can be

Gunnar Ljungström – wing and aircraft designer and the 'father' of the first Saab car.

purchased from the Saab Museum. A follow-up book is also now available.

Born in 1905 to a family headed by Fredrik Ljungström, who was a well-known figure in Swedish engineering, the young Ljungström was to become an engineer of vision, dedicated to pursuing the highest standards in Swedish engineering. His father had been an engineer, inventor and industrial figure who had held patents for inventions related to hydro-power, railway engineering and agricultural engineering machinery. He had also designed a new type of gearbox, which his son Gunnar had tried to promote commercially.

In the 1930s, after graduating from the Swedish Royal Institute of Technology, and working for his father at a company named AB Spontan, Gunnar had gone to England in 1932 to work at the A.J. Wickham Company. This meant that Ljungström had some experience of his father's engineering projects and of automotive- and transport-related engineering in England (however brief). He was to become the only Saab employee to have such experience as the Saab car protoype was initially created.

After his return to Sweden Ljungström joined the nascent Saab via the Nohab Flygmotor Company in 1938. He had a mind full of ideas, not least for the advanced gearbox design his father had dreamed up. Ljungström even conceived an idea for a people carrier or minibus-type vehicle, but production plans came to nothing.

He would work with famed Saab aircraft designer A.J. Andersson on finding a solution to aircraft engine cooling problems by designing a hydraulically actuated cooling system and on solving airflow problems (Jaguar's later designer Malcom Sayer would be doing the same at the

Bristol Aircraft Company shortly afterwards). Ljungström then concentrated on wing design, focusing not just on aerofoils but wing structure, rigidity, weight, strength and performance. It was this work that resulted in the hull of the Saab car prototype from 1947 after he had been asked to join the car project at its initial development stage. But wings were Ljungström's thing at Saab as he attempted to resolve the conflicting requirements of strength, weight, shape and surface smoothness.

Gunnar Ljungström was also highly interested in sailing (his father designed wing-profile yachts in the 1930s), yacht design and marine engines, all of which were to further his interest in hydrodynamics, aerodynamics, wings, structures, engines and then in a car design that stemmed from aircraft design. He would become leader of the Saab Automobile Division's engineering function. In fact Ljungström was not a 'petrol-head' car enthusiast of the type represented by Rolf Mellde: yachts were Gunnar's thing, but he came to a dedication to the Saab car through his applied thinking.

The fact that the Saab car would be equipped with a freewheeling transmission device should come as little surprise when we consider that Gunnar's uncle, Birger Ljungström, had patented a free-wheel device for bicycle gearing hubs long before 1939.

Gunnar Ljungström's father had created a new type of steam engine with a non-condensing turbine powerplant and had founded AB Ljungströms Ångturbin to promote the idea. Fredrik was a high-profile engineer, inventor (he also conceived an early form of extracting shale oil in a fracking-type process during World War II) and leader. A pre-heater designed by Fredrik Ljungström, for example, saves the use of many tons of fossil fuels in the generation of electricity at power stations. Fredrik also worked with the richest man in Sweden at the time, Axel Wenner-Gren, who owned many Swedish industrial companies and was a major investor in the formation of Saab in 1936–7.

An obvious link from Gunnar (and the Saab 92) to his father was that Gunnar created rigid, innovative reinforced wing structures and fuselage hulls at Saab, before designing the first Saab car's unique wing or hull-type ultra-rigid monocoque body using frames and reinforcing posts of similar technical design process.

Where did this idea stem from? The Citroën Traction Avant's 1930s monocoque was all very well, but it was still a pressed steel tub with an all-welded, one-piece body built in thin steel sheet. The Saab car's body was less of a tub and more a boat hull crossed with an aircraft wing and fuselage design, with a thick skin and added reinforcement and special frames.

Many Saab old-timers say that the Gunnar's inspiration was his father's then unique 'Circular Arc' construction method for yacht and boat hulls, which Fredrik had created in the 1930s. This new design of hull structure conferred not just great benefits in hull strength, but also hydrodynamic flow advantages. Specially shaped frames and hoops made for a more rigid hull that was shaped like a wing or aerofoil.

Fredrik's yacht designs (in which Gunnar was involved) also had a new type of rig where the sail was a double-aspect, aerodynamically efficient design that required minimal rigging. There was no boom, no foresail, no forestay and no shroud. The single mainsail was a giant curved wing section mounted on a rotating mast to provide very efficient propulsive effect even in low winds: the mast was unsupported by stays or wires and used Swedish ball bearings to offer the mast a unique rotating mount.

This 'Ljungström Yacht', as it became known, was with its unique structural hull design of unusual ellipsoid wing aerofoil-section profile, and with both a futuristic raked prow and tapered stern and very low hydrodynamic drag, very futuristic. Known in the 1930s as the wing or 'ving' series of yachts, this yacht design was very radical for its time and the blinkered minds of the establishment seemed offended by its challenge to their certainties or the obvious contradictions of so-called perceived wisdom.

In more recent years Fredrik Ljungström's 'cirkelbågsskrov' (circular arc) and 'ving profil' design ideas have been re-purposed by other designers. That they provide a clear visual design link to the shape and, vitally, the structure of the Saab 92 is obvious. Surely even to the most dispassionate observer it becomes very obvious that the design of the Ljungström yacht hull was entirely relevant to the later Gunnar Ljungström-engineered Saab 92 body in structural and hydro- and aerodynamic terms.

Many old Saab veterans have said that, while the 92 was credited to Ljungström and Sason, to them it is obvious that the Ljungström yacht hull designs had played an inspirational role in the car's structural and aerodynamic design. They are convinced that, at the least, there exists a design-language link to the 92 from the yacht design process.

Perhaps we can only regret that the yacht was not a Saab product. After all, in 1945, Saab did consider producing boats when it was searching for new projects and new

■ ORIGINS: WINGS TO WHEELS

The UrSaab captured the light and had a unique down-the-road graphic in designer's terms.

employment and income ideas. Saab's Kurt Sjögren had designed a stunning hydrofoil powerboat, which would appear in early photograph's of the Saab 92.

There can be no doubt that we should look to Gunnar Ljungström to explain the radical engineering in Saab's revolutionary new car that emerged from a corner of northern Europe. Add in Sixten Sason as Ljungström's accomplice and the plot is clear.

When World War II ended and Saab was desperate for something to build, produce and sell, wing designer Ljungström would become the pivotal engineering figure for the new idea: the Saab car.

As with an aircraft wing or fuselage, Ljungström designed the Saab car body to be very stiff in its key sections and to have reinforcements around openings and windows. This was why the Saab 92 had steel reinforcing rails in its windscreen pillars and very strong box sections around the door apertures, just like a reinforced fuselage and wing. The windscreen pillars were like reinforced struts with inner steel rods enclosed in a single pressing that was mounted from the bulkhead running upwards and then over-wrapped with the leading (downwards) portion of the one-piece roof pressing to form a steel-sandwich of a strut. The wing-hull of a body, however, lacked a rear boot aperture to retain stiffness and avoid a weakness-inducing 'hole' in the structure.

Thick sills, closed-off bulkheads and special reinforcing frames and pressings meant that the cabin cell was many times stiffer than any car made at the time or for decades afterwards. Ljungström also fitted the 92 with its flat-bottomed, boat-like under-tray and sculpted wheel shrouds and roof design.

Instead of an opening rear body access panel, Ljungström designed an exquisite spare-wheel carrier in which the spare wheel was tucked up inside the body. When needed, you turned a handle, a body flap opened and the spare wheel was lowered to you, clean and dry.

To prove the point about wing design in car design, witness the 92's monocoque torsional rigidity rating: this was over 11,000lb/ft/degree. Even other monocoque-bodied cars at that time struggled to achieve 3,000lb/ft/degree of torsional rigidity. Over a decade later, Ford's 1960s (super-computer-designed) Cortina Mk1 managed 2,500lb/ft/degree, which, put plainly, was less than a quarter as stiff in the body as the late-1940s designed Saab. Some modern cars exceed 6,000 lb/ft/degree of torsional rigidity – just over half of what Saab achieved. In places the metal used in Saabs was more than 20 per cent thicker than the standard gauge. Thick side-sills and doors and reinforcing fillets all added to the car's supreme strength. Remember, this car remained 'safe' in legislative and crash terms into the 1980s.

The model 92 to 96 Saabs were crush-proof and had anti-intrusion and rollover strength that kept the cab safe and the roof upright when impacted. A roll-cage was added for legislative reasons for rally-car Saabs, but so stiff was the standard car's cabin that you could roll one several times and drive away with the roof uncrushed, as Erik 'on-the-roof' Carlsson proved several times. When a Ford Cortina was dropped on its roof to prove how strong the Cortina rally car was, the results were embarrassing.

Ljungström's key teammates in developing the prototype car's body were Olle Lindgren and Erik Ekkers (also cited as Storerkers). Josef Eklund would join Saab in 1953 and work with Ljungström to develop gearboxes and engines as the 92, soon to become the 93 3-cylinder, evolved.

Intriguingly, the Saab 92 was not too stiff at the front of the car, so with a softer, crushable nose it offered some early degree of crash energy crumple zone, reducing the energy forced into the cabin and its occupants. Neither was the 92 a heavy lump despite its reinforced hull (wing design techniques solving that paradox). It came in at under 900kg in road-use specification, vital given its tiny engine.

So it was that the 92 was shaped like a wing and the Swedes called it the 'Vingprofil' car. It was not just shaped like a wing, it was *built* like a wing (or a yacht hull) and therefore strong in twist, tension and compression qualities. The 92 was a curved, ellipsoid, smooth, forensically scaled piece of genius that was truly a new design statement in a world of austerity. Under the skin it was clever too. This was hardly a basic car for a post-war mindset of poverty.

Ljungström worked on developing the range from the 92 to the 96 across the decades and influenced the Saab 99, itself even stronger in the cabin and windscreen pillars than the 92 to 96 series. He also worked on drivetrain components and suspension.[4]

Gearboxes? Cylinder head design? Both were further areas of Ljungström's expertise for Saab (he would collaborate with engineer Josef Eklund on these items). So too was the choice to go with a front engine and a front-wheel-drive configuration, years before the so-called 'revolutionary' Mini with its front-wheel drive of the late 1950s. Remember the 92 was trendsetting years before the Mini or the Citroën DS.

However clever he was, Ljungström was no designer of car bodywork. His own sketches to shape the first Saab car were good, but he was self-aware enough to know that they were not good enough (see the sketch displayed). Enter Sixten Sason.

SIXTEN SASON: THINKING IN THREE DIMENSIONS – *FFÖREGÄNGARE INOM SVENSKA INDIUSTRIDESIGN*

Alongside Ljungström, there would be another defining character, the industrial designer, pilot, philosopher and all-

The UrSaab's tapered tail is clearly evident in this view.

round polymath who became known as Sixten Sason.

Born in 1912 at Billingehus near Skovde, Karl Erik Sixten Andersson grew up on a smallholding with his mother and a father who was a stonemason and sculptor. The young Sixten learned his sculpting and three-dimensional skills from his father and then developed a passion for motorcycles, cars and all things aeronautical. His first illustrations were published in the Swedish press before he was eighteen years old. He had speculatively sent the Husqvarna Company a proposed design sketch when he was fifteen and the company invited him to visit its design studio.

During his period of National Service conscription in the mid-1930s he served as a mechanic/airman in the Swedish Air Force and trained as a pilot. His artistic mind also developed a functional, engineering process that was focused on ethos and application.

Sason became interested in everything related to design. Some of his early designs for futuristic cars, motorcycles and aircraft were published as sketches submitted to Swedish magazines before 1930.

By 1931 Sason was living on a barge in Stockholm and attended the respected Sköld Painting School to learn illustration techniques. One of his fellow barge mates was Åke V. Pernby, who became a well-known Swedish painter and graphic artist. Pernby also worked at the Sköld school in the 1930s and later ran it. Sason and Pernby had also met up in Paris when studying fine art.

Another Sköld school member and friend of Sason was the famous French-born, Swedish artist Pierre Sager Olofsson, who would contribute to Saab as an industrial designer and colourist under Sason's lead from the 1950s. It was Olofsson who was behind the abstract, eye-searingly bright colours of Saab's 96 and 99 paint schemes of the late 1960s and early 1970s. Bright green, bright beige, bright blue, bright anything – it was all down to Olofsson.[5]

Olofsson would go on to design the Husqvarna Våpenfabriks AB badge and logo and corporate identity, and later worked with the designer Sune Envall, whose career had begun in the Sigvard Bernadotte design studio. Sune Envall was the brother of Saab's later design chief (and Sason's protégé) Björn Envall.

During his National Service Sason was injured in 1934 in a flying accident when a wing strut penetrated his chest. He lost one lung and was struck down by infection for several years. He recovered by re-purposing himself as an illustrator, draughtsman, designer and inventor, turning his hospital room into a studio complete with easel, and had paint supplies brought in for him. He also studied the art of the silversmith. He took a correspondence course on engineering that was to prove very beneficial. Here was a true Renaissance man.

By 1938 Sason had established some profile in Sweden and seen his ideas further published in magazines. He also spent time in Paris studying sculpture and fine art, just as Citroën's famed sculptor-designer Flaminio Bertoni was creating the Traction Avant and the early sketches for a streamlined replacement, the car that after the interruption of World War II would become the revolutionary Citroën DS.

For commercial and profile reasons Sixten had adopted the Spanish name 'Sazon' or 'Sason' (meaning 'spice) in order to distinguish himself from the ubiquitous 'Andersson' surname so common in Sweden.

Sason lived and breathed airflow and styling. His 1930s ideas for a micro-car predated the German Fritz Fend's post-war designs by nearly a decade (being seeimgly mirrored post-war by the Messerschmitt Kabinenrollers and the Fahrzeug-und Maschinenbau FMR TG500 of Flitzer-type lineage). His further 1930s designs included a people carrier and an aerodynamic, low-slung, steam-powered limousine.

Sixten Sason graduated from the engineering course and started work providing illustrations for AB Svenska Järnvägsverkstäderna (ASJ), the Swedish rail engineers, and then he worked for the Husqvarna concern (AB Husqvarna Våpenfabriks). After moving to Saab he drew attention for his futuristic ideas and sketches. He provided early X-ray see-through structural drawings of Saab products and then also sketched out his 'styling' ideas. He would soon design flight deck/cockpits and cabins for Saab aircraft, including the superb Scandia S90 airliner and the S91 Safir light aircraft (an example of which was later owned and flown by Erik Carlsson).[6]

In the 1930s Sason also designed a new type of car suspension that took its inspiration from an aircraft undercarriage leg and strut. He invented a space-saving yet highly effective shock-absorbing telescopic vertical damper and coil-spring combined 'strut' suspension for use in cars, notably in the front engine compartment. The 'Macpherson'-type suspension strut, designed by Earle S. MacPherson and granted a US patent in 1947, was not dissimilar and would soon become ubiquitous. Other telescopic suspension designs were known in the late 1930s but Sason (and then MacPherson) defined the idea with integral springs and fluid-absorbers in a self-supporting 'strut'. MacPherson got his name on the patent and the rest is suspension strut history.

In 1938 Sason drew up a four-wheel-drive car with four-wheel steering, and he also created a chassis-spine design for a sleek, steam-powered car. Another Sason interest was architecture, working on urban planning, circular garages (in 1936) and Le Corbusier-type town planning system designs: it seems his mind rarely rested.

In 1939 he presented an idea for a new bridge across the Öresund to link Sweden and Denmark, as he felt sure that this would become reality. The grand sweeping arch of the bridge's biased-axis ellipse design seemed to pre-date the sweep of the later Saab 92's rear roof and pillar. He would further refine his idea for the bridge in the 1950s.

In a 1941 design drawing he shaped 'Project LX', a delta-configuration, blended-wing type fighter jet with many futuristic motifs; it is still contentious whether that design had any influence upon Saab's later S35 Draken jet fighter, so wonderfully designed by Erik Bratt. We might say that both men had seen advanced research on their subject and seem to have reached similar conclusions, but Bratt was the qualified, top aeronautical engineer, so we give him his due credit. Yet Sason's amazing, intuitive draught-design of a double-delta 'Rocket' jet fighter as his LX design concept predated the actual Draken design by more than a decade, and Saab would also make a part-scale test airframe that more closely mimicked Sason's speculative design sketch.

The level of thought that went into the aerodynamics of Saab's first car was unprecedented. There was more to Sason and his knowledge than many knew, however, for he had also made a close study of Wernher von Braun's uniquely advanced rocket-missiles. During World War II he sketched the details of a crashed V-1 rocket and it is said that he bravely travelled to Britain in the bomb-bay of a clandestine BOAC Stockholm–London de Havilland Mosquito, which operated a neutrality-busting, ball-bearing and spying service, to present his findings to British Intelligence and the Ministry of Aviation boffins in London.

After the war he would shape the first 1950s Saab Sonett roadster and the design of the 'Catherina' concept car. He also designed the Hasselblad 1600F camera (a heavily modified Sason-styled Hasselblad camera went to the moon with the Apollo 11 mission).

During his time at Saab, Sason knew Victor Hasselblad, who from late 1940 manufactured reconnaissance cameras for the air force to use in airframes. Sason dreamed up a commercial model with Hasselblad that was designed to be more compact, lighter and easier to use, yet with detailed features and lenses of high quality: effectively this became the world's best single-lens reflex camera of its era despite being of medium-large format at 6 x 6cm. The camera had interchangeable lenses and film canisters. Hasselblad launched the camera in New York in 1948 and ended up with more orders than he could immediately deliver.

Sason designed the Husqvarna 'Silver Arrow' motorcycle, a 'Monarscoot' moped for Monark of Sweden, and the first Electrolux vacuum cleaner amid a range of Swedish consumer product items including an iron, a cooker and a wonderful waffle-maker that looked like a spaceship from a 1950s American movie.

Husqvarna did not just make chainsaws: they also produced Sason-designed motorcycles, irons, sewing machines, kitchenware and cookers or stoves, one of which was branded 'Regina' at Sason's request in honour of his mother. Husqvarna also manufactured enamelled dishes and saucepans that were almost indestructible and so long lasting that the only way to update them into a revised range was by applying the bright colours of the early 1960s.

In 1947 Sason pitched a radical redesign of the PV444 to Volvo. His concept looked like a cross between a Bugatti 'Tank' type 57G car design and an American 'low-rider': it had a lobed, low, roofless body with an integrated nose and headlamp treatment that had definite shades of the earlier Tatra, yet was also highly original.

Of particular note were the advanced styling elements that Sason incorporated into his early 1945 design pencil sketch for the Saab 92, notably that glitzy, chromed-up front and the one-piece body with wheel shrouds and spats. It looked like something you might see at the 1958 Detroit Motor Show, but it was Sason's Saab sketch of early 1945. Indeed, the Saab Board deemed it too flashy, too advanced, too big, and Sason toned down the design to create what became the 92 – still stylish but with a touch of Swedish puritanism!

Sason's own Saab 92 had a very rare full-length folding sunroof, special paint and numerous cabin and engine upgrades. He also owned one of the very first 93s at its launch.

■ ORIGINS: WINGS TO WHEELS

SASON DESIGN AB: MADDOCK, MONÖ, OLOFSSON

As a freelance consultant (no longer a Saab direct employee as he had been pre-war) Sixten Sason founded Sason Design AB in the Stockholm suburb of Solna as the base from which he consulted for the major Swedish companies including Saab, Husqvarna and Axel Wenner-Gren's Electrolux. Much of this was done in collaboration with the British industrial designer/architect Peter Maddock, who had arrived in Sweden on the Gothenburg ferry in 1955 and married a Swede.

Sason became so famous through his Saab 92 design that General Motors, which had a factory and office in Sweden even before World War II and had also owned Opel in Germany for many years, are known to have offered him employment in America. Sason turned this down for three reasons: he had limited command of English, he had health issues, and he loved Saab and Sweden. Little did he know that, decades later, General Motors would own Saab.

In 1957 Sason collaborated with Pierre Sager Olofsson, who had also worked for both Saab and Husqvarna, on the design of the Electrolux Model 70 vacuum cleaner and the brand never looked back. Design and colour were the key alongside the cleaner's engineering. Sason designed the Husqvarna Coronette moped in 1959, as well as a range of consumer items for the company.

1957: SWEDISH ASSOCIATION OF DESIGNERS

Sixten Sason was also a founding member of the Swedish Association of Designers, which was established on 1 March 1957. Rune G. Monö was elected the association's president and it was through Monö that Peter Maddock had found employment on his arrival in Sweden, which led to time working at Sason Design AB.

Rune Monö had designed trains for Axel Wenner-Gren's engineering company (Wenner-Gren had been a leader of Saab, owned Electrolux, and was a backer of many projects and aspiring inventors, and later created a foundation to benefit global science), and Monö had started at Saab as engineering design draughtsman in Sason's office at Saab before the war.

Maddock would go on to work for the Bernadotte design consultancy and spend his design life in Sweden, as told in his book *Swedish Memories 1955–2007: a Life in Product*

Sixten Sason was not only the father of the Saab style, he was the founder of Swedish industrial design.

Design. He later founded his own design bureau, Utvecklings Design AB, and taught at the University of Umeå's Institute of Design.

Sason was pivotal to these men's careers and to the emergence of both Saab and Swedish design.

A regular visitor to Sweden in the 1950s and 1960s was the hugely influential British industrial designer Robin Day (and his designer wife Lucienne), who is said to have held Sason's work in high regard.

At Saab a series of concept cars (including an idea for the later Sonett) were of Sason design. But above all he had created the domed, wing-hull style of the highly aerodynamic first Saab car. Sason thought in three dimensions and his Saab car design for the 92 was to prove timeless.

Sason's design sketchbook (last exhibited in the Sason exhibition at the Västergötlands Museum in 2008) included numerous elliptically influenced shapes, his vee-tailed, elliptically formed twin-engined airliner being particularly redolent of the advantages of the parabolic form. Lowering body drag, induced drag and interference drag were the key elliptical issues.

Sason and Saab had access to extensive research results, notably from intercepted findings of both pre-war and

ORIGINS: WINGS TO WHEELS

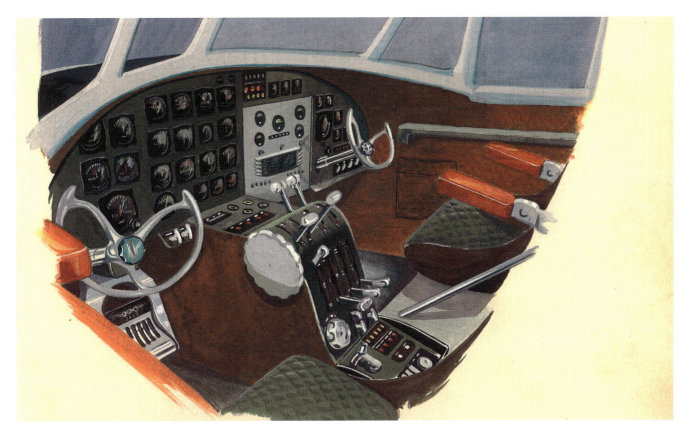

Sason designed Saab's aircraft cockpits, flight decks and interiors. He applied that knowledge to the 92 family series and onwards to the 99.

wartime technical and scientific reports from German sources. To apply such a range of techniques to aircraft was one thing: to use them for a four-seat, small family car – Saab's first car – was noteworthy, but it went unnoticed by a wider audience.

Sason would go on to shape Saabs up to the first 99 before his death in 1967, when his brilliant protégé Björn Envall would take over the task of maintaining Saab's design language.

Hugo Möller, who was the tooling manager in the 1940s UrSaab project, wrote his memoirs in the early 1970s and these can be obtained from the Saab Veterans Archive. In Möller's opinion, 'Sixten Sason was not only a skilled and far-sighted designer, he also had a good understanding of the manufacturing process'.

Ljungström, Sason and Saab were ahead of mainstream practice. Sason's sculptor-trained hand was one of intuitive genius. Ljungström said of Sason that he was 'a genius, an engineer with the talents of an artist, or an artist with the temperament of an engineer ... the ideal partner to work with'.

A practical artist, the tall, debonair Sason possessed what Björn Envall called (in interview with the author), 'a very English sense of humour'.[7] Sason was famed for his practical jokes and amusing sketches and portraits of people he knew. He even drew a design for the Saab 92 with a rear hatch panel that opened in the roof to allow the feathered hats of women sitting in the back seat to protrude.

Sixten Sason died tragically young in 1967 aged just fifty-five. His nephew Leif Hjorden held much of Sason's archive and portfolios. Another curator of Sason's works was of course Björn Envall, whom Sason had originally employed. The pair, in collaboration with Anna-Maria Claesson, ensured that a Sason retrospective exhibition was held at the Västergötlands Museum to great critical acclaim.

In the design world, Sixten Sason surely deserves global recognition in the annals of not just design, but of Swedish, and global, social design history.

CHAPTER TWO

UrSAAB: DESIGN AND DEVELOPMENT

The roots of the first Saab car's style and shape were interesting and international. The influences of French 'Aerodyne' design practice and the 'streamliner' movement on both sides of the Atlantic, allied to knowledge of airframes at Saab, greatly influenced the original 92's design.

Sason's radical shape for the 92, which he created at the end of 1945 and in early January 1946, was utterly coherent and organic, yet swept and sculpted like no other car. It was a delightful, happy little coupé of a car and a defining moment. The windscreen pillars were raked at an incredibly 'fast' angle for the era: 47 degrees of sweep.

It is often stated that Sason walked into Ljungström's office and put down a sketch of a raked, stylish, fast-backed teardrop that had shades of French and pre-war Czech styling trends, yet was styled with a wing or aerofoil chord shape. It was clearly influenced by nature and the wind.

Of particular note, the 'Exper-Vagen' (experimental wagon), prototype car 92.001 or X9248 as it was coded in factory paperwork, had those unique, very highly swept windscreen pillars, which were somewhat American in design architecture. The side panels were curved and flowed into an aircraft-style rear fuselage that allowed the airflow to remain attached as it streamed down the back of the car. At the front, the first prototype had its headlamps faired-in under the unusual perspex fairing as part of a low and wide style that looked like the leading edge of a wing aerofoil.

The front wheels were also faired-in under a somewhat bulbous wing or fender shroud line. The car looked like a wing with wheels and it was revolutionary. The sleek and sculpted prototype, the 92.001, was the 1940s equivalent of a concept car design, a one-off special, the sort of thing designers cook up for the Geneva or Turin motor shows to advertise what they can do. Rarely do such concept cars ever make their way through to the production line. With a few minor changes Sason's flying-wing fantasy become a real car.

The truth was that, above all contemporary designs, Sason's sleek, faired-in shape was new and non-derivative – it was a design hallmark from the word go. Ljungström had recognized immediately that it was the only choice and he told the Board so, advising that the shape would use much less fuel, be more stable and permit higher speeds, even if, as some felt, there was a touch of the 'frog' to its visual demeanour.

RUNES IN THE WIND: THE DETAILS OF DESIGN

Among the many influences that had shaped Sixten Sason's ideas had been the time he spent in Paris at the heart of the 'design' revolution: surely he could not have failed to be awed by the huge, almost architectural cars of the 'streamliner' era, or its locomotives and aircraft.

Sason was known to be greatly interested in such shapes or 'aero' curves. Some of his later aircraft designs were elliptical and were plainly influenced by the Supermarine Spitfire, which Sason is known to have adored, and the likes of Arthur E. Hagg's exquisitely ellipsoidal and sculptural design for the de Havilland Albatross. It is of interest that Hagg was also a yacht enthusiast and designer. Of deeper relevance, Saab would have a close relationship with de Havilland and built the de Havilland jet engine under licence.

The Saab 92 was an amalgamation of 1930s and 1940s ideas and themes that came together, not as a pastiche, but as something genuinely new from the mind of a great designer working in the advanced guard of industrial design.

The rapidly advancing American stylistic trends that later

UrSaab: Design and Development

The sole prototype UrSaab, with its faired-in front, drove thousands of miles in testing. This rare view was captured at Linköping or Trollhättan before the end of 1947.

influenced Sason were reinforced when, after the launch of the 92, a five-strong team of design lecturers from the University of Chicago design faculty lectured in Sweden in 1952 and framed the latest techniques in colours and forms, which Sason quickly embraced. In particular, the 1950s Chevrolet Nomad is often cited as an influence upon Sason's design for the Saab 95 estate car derivative of the 92/93.

Early scale models for wind-tunnel testing at the Swedish Aeronautical Research Institute revealed a coefficient of drag of C_d 0.32, and the full-size production car C_d was a stunning C_d 0.35, far lower than the average drag figure for cars of the era, which was commonly about C_d 0.45–0.60.

The Saab, although initially styled by hand by a pilot and engineer, rather than in a wind tunnel, had an aerodynamic advantage that was real. This was then honed in the Saab wind tunnel: the car's shape had at least 30 per cent less drag than the most aerodynamic car of the day and 50 per cent less drag than a conventional car of the era. This reaped advantages in speed and economy. The prototype's drag coefficient was that world-beating C_d 0.32. This was truly an incredible figure and one that increased only slightly for the production car variant to C_d 0.35.

The 92's aerodynamic credibility, however, was not just about reducing drag. As with all subsequent Saabs, the 92 was tuned to have good crosswind stability, and the point at which the airflow separated, known as the critical separation point (CSP), was also finely tuned to reduce wake vortex 'base' drag behind the car, and to give lower levels of lift, over the tail and under the car.

Sason and Ljungström also made the most of the benefits of the front-wheel-drive configuration that came from a flat floor by controlling vortices and pressure under the car, which, according to later textbook theory, could reduce unwanted lift by 20 per cent. This early advanced thinking by Saab included adding underfloor shaping to tune the airflow's behaviour. Everything that would normally protrude was tucked up to avoid it adversely affecting under-car airflow and pressure.

Saab had grasped the problem early on and Saab had its own advance-flow wind tunnel in use for aircraft and car design in 1947. A scale model of the 92 tested in the wind tunnel of the Swedish Aeronautical Research Institute gave results that were not perfect, but the airflow stayed attached across the body or hull and the boundary layer was not greatly upset by panel junctions, gutters, or trims, all of which had been reduced to smooth the flow of air. Unlike many contemporary designs and some modern cars, the 92 was a 'clean' car, meaning that it did not suffer from extreme airflow upset or a turbulent rear end that sucked up road spray onto the car.

The 92 had to use flat glass in its side windows, so was short of inwards curvature towards its top and roof, known as tumblehome, yet Sason was able to smooth

■ UrSAAB: DESIGN AND DEVELOPMENT

'Styling' model for presentation to the Saab Board. The simple elegance of the design is obvious, yet it is so radical for its time.

and curve in the vital roof dome and rear end shapes to control the airflow.

Sason's intuitive scaling and sculpting, which also reflected his knowledge of boundary layer and laminar airflow characteristics, and the need to preserve localized airflow velocity, delaying airflow breakdown and decay over an aerofoil by creating ultra-smooth surface skinning, was vitally important to the design: Saab as aircraft designers knew that there are key rules to cheating the air and lowering drag in aircraft or cars.

The 92 followed the rules of the science of the time, notably that airflow over the front of the body should be free to flow sideways and not be adversely forced apart. A rounded frontal planform was much better in this respect than a square-edge frontal design.

Crucially, the rear of any fuselage or car body should decrease its cross-sectional area as its depth and width, towards its rear or trailing edge, and should do so, particularly for a car, at an angle that preserves airflow to a chosen point where it can be deliberately severed or separated cleanly, rather than separating inconsistently. Premature separation of airflow must be avoided, according to the theory, but not at the expense of an overly long tail with variable separation points that might cause increased base drag and lift.

Bumps, lumps, ridges and trigger points on the skin surfaces needed to be avoided in order to avoid localized flow separation or airflow velocity slowdown and 'bubbling'. This was Saab's application of aviation-style 'smoothness criteria' and 'boundary layer' thinking to a car.

These rules were crucial arbiters of the Saab 92 shape, as was the consequent control of the respective form, induced and interference drag coefficients. The Saab 92 reflected these rules to a degree greater than any production car at the time and for years afterwards.

The Droplet

The *gouette d'eau* or teardrop school was evident in car design at this time, notably in the Saab 92. Once again, the links between aviation, automobiles, the men that designed them, and the advanced guard of Northern European aero-

UrSaab: Design and Development

dynamic design knowledge came together in a series of coincidences and events. One thing was for sure: if wings, fins and flying saucer styling was a post-war fashion, its roots lay in work by a handful of men from Paris, Stockholm, Stuttgart and London.

Above them all in terms of modernity, cohesion and style stood Saab's flying wing of a car. At the rear of the 92 the car's curvy tail and rear deck angle preserved the airflow down to the rear base of the car. Some designers have argued that the tail is too long and that a more 'chopped' tail would have reduced drag further, but close analysis of woollen tuft and smoke flow results on the 1:5 scale test model (and the full-scale car) confirm that the 92 somehow kept its flow attached down to its rear end. Sason had, in fact, gently bobbed the tail according to the Kamm theories: it was not an overly long, torpedoesque stern, even if it lacked a sharp Kamm 'razor' ridge.

Only the danger of premature airflow separation triggered by a crudely moulded rear window trim strip could ruin the achievement and that did not occur on the 92 or 93. In fact Sason used elliptical shapes to deliberately trigger a degree of airflow separation with minimal drag over the split rear windscreens and provide controlled aerodynamic behaviour. The production car, with its smoother one-piece rear windscreen was even more finely tuned in terms of airflow down the rear rump of the car. The way in which the side panels curved inwards and joined under the rear windscreen was a design highlight, as was the brilliantly simple chromed rear bumper bar. A look at the first in-house body design of the Bristol Car Company in its 401 model will reveal very similar shaping and scaling to the Saab 92 at and behind the rear roof, rear window and rear wing lines, led by the requirements and rules of airflow.

The 92 had low drag and stability and tuning these factors reduced yaw effects in side slip and crosswind sensitivity. Only the roof gutter on the production 92 caused problems, Sason wanted it smoothed down as per prototype 92.001, but there was no other way of realistically securing the roof to the sides: a spot-welded flange and roof gutter was the manufacturing compromise. It did cause local flow disturbance, but to the smallest possible degree.

Why did the 92 have faired-in front wheels? Covered rear wheels were a 1930s streamlining norm, but hidden *front* wheels? The answer was that turbulence from the rotating front wheels and buffeting from the wheel arches could upset the airflow pattern down the side of the car and underneath it. Fairing-in the front wheels reduced bubbles of flow separation and turbulence. This is why 92.001 had completely faired-in front wheels to lessen turbulence and drag. But a compromise had to be reached for a mass-market car as the 92 had to run on real roads, often rural dirt roads.

By curving the sides of the car and the join between them and the roof, Sason tuned the airflow to retain its speed or even accelerate it, and stay 'attached' longer. This not only lowered profile or form drag, it also created a cleaner, smoother aerodynamic behaviour around the back of the car, as Bristol noted in the 401.

'GAS' drew the UrSaab years later and captured its soul.

UrSAAB: DESIGN AND DEVELOPMENT

The early 1:25-scale wind-tunnel model as tested. Note how, remarkably, the tufts show the airflow is still attached down the tail despite its angle.

Crucially, Sason knew that wind-tunnel testing of small models of full-size items was fraught with risk due to the scale-effect of the wind tunnel itself, which might not produce proportional-to-scale results. Even the design of the wind tunnel itself could alter the results. Over-reliance on wind-tunnel results was to become a significant issue in the developing art of aerodynamic design and tuning.

The effects on drag of trims and items such as gutters, panel gaps, mirrors, door handles and window frames were impossible to assess cumulatively and it was even more difficult to assess them as their true behaviours and values changed when scaled down. The cross-sectional area of such items and the smoothness of the overall skin were vital elements in reducing both their actual, shape-engendered and interference-effect drags.

92.001 was a prototype aimed at the best possible low-drag shape. Although it was slightly altered for production, the key attributes of 'aero' styling were retained. It is significant that in the 1970s, when the study of car aerodynamics really came to the fore, scientists tried to create the ideal minimum-drag body shape for a car. The shape chosen was a mixing of parabolas and blended asymmetric half-ellipses with a differing lower lobe shape that was curved and tapered in a different shape than the upper body. The shape was built as a test model and subjected to fluid, smoke and computational analysis. Shades of the forms of the 92.001 and the 92 were clearly obvious.

Despite 92.001's touch of overly bulbous frontal width, the actual blend of part-ellipsoid shapes in front, profile and plan view was very obviously similar to the later scientifically proposed, theoretically minimum drag shape. Top airflow researcher A.J. Scibor-Rylski actually used a profile example of the Saab when discussing aerodynamic form and wake pattern turbulence for a car in his defining book *Road Vehicle Aerodynamics*.[8]

In fact, 92.001's fat, asymmetrically curved frontal lobe turned out not to be as bad as some had thought in the late 1940s, because the 1970s experiment revealed that, despite the cross-sectional area issues, the somewhat bulbous lower body shape aided in reducing the road or ground surface interference drag problem, despite its fullness of shape. The transformations of body panels and shapes further down the 92's body also predates similar, later findings.

There were mixed reactions to the Saab's shape, but whatever the correct metaphor, it was clear that the trends of the late 1920s and Art Deco motifs of the 1930s were obvious: a touch of American feeling was also present in the hints of coupé to the design.

A Tatra-Jaray Rear Fin for 92?

At one stage in 1947 Saab experimented with a Tatra- or Jaray-type tail fin empennage on the rear of the 92. Although it conferred aerodynamic advantages in terms of stability,

UrSaab: Design and Development

Unveiling the original UrSaab to the Saab Board. Note the square, faired-in headlamps, which were soon replaced by podded ovoid lamps.

it was too extreme for production, but the consideration and research into such a fin-device for the 92 showed just how deeply Saab went into aerodynamics for the 92: even some dedicated Saab enthusiasts do not know of this rear fin empennage being considered for the 92 design. Saab's knowledge of aerodynamics for aircraft, and then as it was applied to cars, had been hard won and expensively researched, not least in its own wind tunnel.

At the same time, and in the spheres of auto-aero design, Sason was also coming up with advanced styling ideas for cars and aircraft that were widely published in the Swedish and European motoring press. It should be noted that Sason designed the whole package, not just a detailed tweak. He was developing theories aligned with leading German researchers, and also being multi-lingual he was able to discuss and digest these new developments on a wide platform.

Ford would get involved in advanced aerodyne design through the ideas of Johan Tjaarda van Starkenborgh (or Sterkenburg), which were incorporated in its 1930s rear-engined 'Aerodyne' concept car, which was developed under Edsel Ford's personal charge as the V12 Zephyr. Tjaarda influenced several 1930s cars and his son Tom Tjaarda became a much-admired and well-respected car designer in the 1960s and 1970s. Johan Tjaarda was much taken with the works of Paul Jaray in early automotive aerodynamic design: as to how much Sason was influenced by Tjaarda Senior, or Jaray, we cannot know, but Sason went on to define a unique style of his own for the Saab 92. We should recall that the defined problem of airflow and its management will result in solutions that are of similar type and resulting design. So a designer does not so much 'copy' another, but reach similar solutions through their own design thoughts, which will inherently contain the same science and resultant techniques.

So revolutionary was the Saab that even *Autocar* magazine remarked upon its radicalism, its different appearance and design formula. Surely, if this car had come from Detroit, or Paris or Turin much more fuss would have been made of it, but Trollhättan is a long way north and easily ignored.

With funding for a prototype and a development car to follow, Saab needed a shape, a form and a function. Several ideas were sketched up for the car's shape, and three of these were made into wooden and clay styling 'bucks' as small scale models to help management decide which look to go for.

November 1945: 1:25 Scale Model

The first scale model of the proposed new car design was at 1:25 scale and presented in November 1945, which proved how fast the Saab Board had moved things along. This design was based in part on Ljungström's own original sketch and it was realized, in an act of self-awareness, that it was too tame, too conventional and not the 'new' car that was required.

■ UrSAAB: DESIGN AND DEVELOPMENT

The car with its next frontal treatment and lights. Note the overhangs across the wheels – an area that needed work.

Sason presented his radical design shape in sketches and another 1:25 scale model was created by the end of the year: this design won over the Saab Board and came with Gunnar Ljungström's recommendation. Ljungström is reputed to have commented to those who were shocked by the shape: 'It does not matter if it has the look of a frog if it saves 100 litres of fuel a year.'

Ljungström had said that as soon as he saw the strange, curved, aerodynamic wing-with-wheels that he knew it was correct; he was proven right. It looked like a wing, but it had shades of French, Czech and American design ideas in its wonderfully scaled form and stance. An upturned tortoise or an insect or a frog, or maybe some form of biomorphic device with wheels, or indeed just a UFO born from 1940s aviation developments? Maybe the 92 incorporated all these themes. It looked like something from science fiction, or a future vision of a car that would have been published as an X-ray drawing feature in the *Eagle* comic a decade later.

The Saab Board knew it was radical and nothing like any other car anywhere. With a smoothed-in one-piece 'pontoon' body of monocoque type, this body shape was a huge gamble and one that went against the tide: the new car was a radical departure indeed, especially as a first offering from a company that had never made a car.

Low drag meant less fuel used, and the car was designed to be stable in terms of aerodynamic lift and crosswind stability. The only real issue to solve was the covered wheel openings or shrouds; these had to be productionalized via a more rational approach.

So was born the shape of the Saab 92: a wing with wheels, a UFO of a car in a new age of post-war technology and design. This was no accident nor was it a fashionable feint. It was science and Saab style in its first iteration.

'Bror' Bjurströmer, who was a deputy manager in the car construction project, has been cited as contributing to the initial schedule of design themes under Gunnar Ljungström's lead. Bjurströmer led the men in the scale model design group, creating a 1:25 scale model of the proposed car body, and should not be ignored in the story of UrSaab development.

UrSaab: Design and Development

The UrSaab was a flying saucer of a car that touched on perfection.

With two aircraft in concurrent production, the factory was busy and it was difficult to find space for a new project. It was in the workshop of the Saab tooling department that the sketches of the new car began to be transformed into the wooden models of 1946.

Wooden Full-Scale Prototype

Work started on building a full-scale model on 7 January 1946. Just two carpenters from the aircraft model and prototype shop were available to create the platform and base form, over which the 'styling' shape would be built in hand-carved, filed and sanded, wood.

In order to achieve the full-scale model, the drawings were enlarged using a photographic projector to expand the images onto metal painted with light-reflective material. Templates were then cut and, using these as a guide, the full-scale styling wooden model was built. This itself was modified several times as design changes were made.

A space in the corner of the workshop was allocated for building the first design prototype, created from a wooden base unit, a sort of table top in Swedish pine. At first a team of two woodworkers, later expanded to six, worked on the mock-up. As the wooden 'buck' took shape, Wahrgren, the company chief, his deputy Sven Otterbeck and Sixten Sason, the body designer, would come in and suggest further changes to the shape – asking for more planing and sanding here and there to create the sleek, swept shape that would later become so famous. In this way Otterbeck, the aviation man, had a little-publicized role in helping shape the final form of the car, a fact often disguised by the focus on Sason.

That first styling 'buck' or development shape was built from alder. Men from Saab's own aviation workshops were assisted by woodworking craftsmen from the small local firm called Dahlström and Löfgren of Motala.

After four months' work the shape was finally formed and approved on 15 April 1946. It was painted and then waxed and hand-polished using shoe polish and rag cloths.

After that came the approval to construct the first car in metal as a hand-beaten metal shell. This was created in May 1946 by a team of fewer than six artisan panel-beaters who had been recruited from Nymans Plåtslageri of Linköping. They were led by a seventy-year-old veteran craftsman who had worked for the nearby Thorell Company. He was well versed in the ancient skills of forming the first panels over

UrSAAB: DESIGN AND DEVELOPMENT

the reshaped wooden buck and using dried horse manure to achieve smooth compound curvatures and the correct resilience when being beaten over to smooth the buck's curves for panel beating. The various elements of this 'proof' of the concept full-scale metal body were gas-welded together, helped along by quite a bit of hammer-beating by the veteran team leader.

The railway engineers and carriage builders ASJ also helped with hand-painting and lacquering the first 92.001 prototype 'buck' body. Among the younger men involved at this stage were Hugo Möller and Hans Gustavsson, who had key roles in the early tooling and fashioning the prototype panels, respectively. An engine mechanic came to Saab from the engine repairers Linköpings Motorverkstad to work on the installation of the prototype's DKW engine. An Auto-Union fuel tank that had been purchased secondhand is reputed to have been used in the prototype.

The new car's lead production engineer was Nils-Gustav Nilsson, who oversaw much of the early plans at Linköping and the factory floor production site at Trollhättan.

Hugo Möller and Hans Ingemar 'Osquar' Gustavsson

Hugo Möller was the Saab car project tooling manager. He recalled in his 1973 memoir that the first metal test-body was built from locally sourced steel, but that the following three test-bodies were made of American-sourced steel and that Svante Holm went to America to source steel, presses and tooling assistance. Möller detailed the build process and confirmed that the drawings for the mechanical parts – engine, gearbox and 'chassis' components – were begun in the summer of 1946. He recalled that the machine shop and workshop construction began in late 1946.

Möller's notes reveal that the final costings for the 92's entire four-year development from design to production were of SKr4,577,062.[9] This exceeded the Board's original estimates and can in part be put down to the costs and difficulties inherent in securing the steel, presses and toolings, and their purchase and delivery from overseas into the newly expanded facilities at Trollhättan. Developing the actual prototype design, the body, engine and drivetrain was done remarkably cheaply, often using used components and old-fashioned, hand-worked model-making practices.

Hans ('Osquar' – a deliberate spelling) Gustavsson

Sason created a more upmarket badge/logo for the car, but it was rejected as being too 'flashy'.

was one of the team who created and built the 92.001. Gustavsson worked on creating the hand-formed body panels and frontal design. This required the help of several small engineering companies that were sworn to secrecy. As such Gustavsson must be cited as having contributed to the translation of the design into three dimensions and of influencing it as that happened.

Machined parts, panel beaters and casting skills were provided by ASJ, Thorell and Northern Light, respectively. Much trial and error was involved in creating the world's first mass-produced, ultra-low drag, monocoque body hull of such curvatures, which is what the Saab 92 represented.

Nobody else knew how to make a small, tight, rigid coupé monocoque except other aircraft makers experienced in building airframes. Saab's men visited Nyköpings Automobilfabrik to see what they could learn from the company, which had been building cars from imported knocked-down or kit components. All these cars, however, had been chassis-based examples of the ancient art of coachbuilding. Nobody seemed to know how to build a small, stressed-skin car body.

It was clear that Saab would have to think about wings and fuselages when considering the design of hatches and doors

UrSAAB: DESIGN AND DEVELOPMENT

The interior of the UrSaab had elements of earlier Bugatti and Citroën design in its motifs and shapes.

Under the prototype's bonnet could be found an Auto-Union fuel tank, a DKW-derived engine and spare parts.

in self-supporting hulls, and from there create a wheeled hull or fuselage with suitably reinforced apertures and correct load paths through the structure: Saab essentially built an aeroplane with wheels.

Stunning though the shape was, further development work was needed at the front of the design, since the 92.002 prototype was perhaps almost too futuristic.

Bearing the registration plates of E14783/E1866, it had a broad low aerofoil-profiled front that looked smooth but created a degree of excess cross-sectional drag (C_d) due to its surface area, while the shrouded wheels had a limited steering angle and soon fouled up their wheel arch housings.

Sason came up with a revised, more stylish podded headlamp and grille treatment, seen on car registration E14789 with its 'vee' pointed bonnet and two circular lamps, podded and inclined, either side of the bonnet's 'vee' point. At one stage the 'vee'-shaped bonnet was fitted, but the revised circular headlamps had not been thought of and the car retained its original faired-in square headlamps. Sason also at this stage experimented with a wing motif grille and bumper bar design, which sadly was not deemed acceptable for production. A few rare photos and some archive film

footage exist as evidence for these interim styling experiments that Sason undertook to modify the shape. Production prototype 001 was completed on 1 May 1947 and the revised number 002 less than one month later. There has been some confusion as to whether car 003 was a third car or a revised version of car 002, but records in the Saab Veterans Archive and the Saab are clear that there were three prototype cars (*see* below).

E15892 Becomes F14803

Some prototype chassis confusion exists in the records: Saab 92 test car chassis No.3 (a car with shrouded front wheel arches, prior to their modification for production) originally had the registration number plate of E15892, which was seen when testing on 27 August 1947. It also bore the same registration when Saab deputy director Sven Otterbeck appropriated it for his personal use – under test, of course – and took the car home to show it to his wife, Kerstin Strandman. This has recently been confirmed by photographic evidence of Otterbeck in the car at the family home near Finspång in 1948, prior to the car's launch in 1949.

51

■ UrSAAB: DESIGN AND DEVELOPMENT

ABOVE: **Defining Saab form.**

BELOW: **Pure style – note the spilt-screen.**

SAAB 92 PROTOTYPE DEVELOPMENT TIMELINE AND CHASSIS NUMBERS

Late 1944–1945	Private internal and then subsequent official Board-level discussions about a Saab car leading to approval of project and go-ahead with limited funding tranches for each phase.
1945	Gunnar Ljungström makes his early pencil sketches and then a small scale clay model is built, but he rejects it and approaches Sason.
October 1945	Sason presents his final concept design sketches.
7 January 1946	Construction begins of the first scale-model in wood of the Sason design. Three major revisions of design to follow, notably one with more upright frontal design.
March–April 1946	Further design and model works leading to the first full-scale wooden design 'buck' with continuing on-going design/styling revisions.
15 April 1946	First full-scale wooden 'buck' is completed with its applied black shoe-polish finish.
May–June 1946	First metal body prototype started, leading to first test car ready for painting in June.
4 June 1946	Finished prototype shown internally to Saab.
July 1946	Engine, drivetrain and chassis components finalized and tooling drawings begun. Workshops and new factory floor space/facilities planned.
Late 1946 into 1947	Early prototype testing and test cars.
1 September 1946	Final design changes to prototype made and signed off as Saab 92 model.
27 February 1947	Final Board go-ahead for production car build.
10 March 1947	G.V. Philipson signs order for the Saab car.
April 1947	First castings for production toolings created.
1 May 1947	First test car ready. Name of car yet to be settled.
1 June 1947	Second test car ready.
10 June 1947	The first recognizable Saab 92 car is shown to the Swedish motoring press. The first three prototype cars were 92.002, 92.003 and 92.004. They received early Linköping registrations, at least one of which was later altered to a Trollhättan registration. The original 1947 registration numbers were E1820, E15892 and E15752, respectively. E15892, the car driven by Sven Otterbeck, was changed to the Trollhättan registration F14803 on 5 August 1948.
November 1947	Car project production preparations moved to Trollhättan from Linköping. The early batch of test cars were built in the 'knot Barn' at Linköping site prior to the move.
December 1947	First castings as production toolings delivered.
12 February 1948	First pressings using production presses enacted.
28 April 1948	14,000 people turn up at the Grand Hotel in Stockholm to see the public showing of the new Saab '92'.
September 1948	Olof Landbü, the 92's development test engineer, and his colleagues Karl Nyberg and Börje Garbing drown in a non-car-related accident. Rolf Mellde takes up lead role.
June 1948–1949	20 'pilot' build bodies fitted with drivetrain components to provide the first cars as test examples, starting with chassis number five (92.005) in early June. Cars with differing 'Standard' and 'De Luxe' specifications built. Dark blue paint (not green) applied to the base-specification car. These cars had chassis numbers 92.004 to 92.024.
June 1949	The 92 went on public show in Trollhättan at the 'River County' exhibition.
12 December 1949	First final specification production chassis leaves factory.
16 January 1950	First official customer deliveries made. Philipson, the car's appointed dealer, takes about a dozen new 92s and shows the car in its Stockholm showroom. Full sales begin.

However, this car categorically had its registration number (and therefore its plates) changed to F14803 on 5 August 1948 as a Trollhättan registration, and not as its prior Linköping registration dated 8 August 1947.

At one stage Sason even fitted three headlamps in 'cyclops' style to a 92 body, which was thankfully discarded. One 1947 proposal by Sason saw twin rectangular headlamps mounted high on a squared-off nose with a large chrome grille across the car. It looked very glitzy, very 1950s Americana, and it was ahead of its time – but not right for the little workhorse Saab. It took another restyling attempt to thin down the bulbous wing section nose and create the higher, more upright frontal design that became the Saab 92 production-tooled design after the 92.001/02 prototypes were constructed. Chassis No 92.003, built in April–May 1947, was fitted with the new production front end.

The changes took place before June 1947, when the final production shape was revealed to the Swedish press. The production frontal design was less dramatic than Sason's earlier prototypes, but it was more practical and had a lower cross-sectional drag figure. One of the reasons the front wing line was more vertical and not so elegantly curved like a float or a hull was that the panel beaters struggled to construct such a shape that would pass through the metal press stamping machine. A bumper and a somewhat conventional grille aperture were also added. Sason's pre-space-age shape was being toned down a bit, but the revolutionary teardrop shell retained its purity of line and close relationship with the prototype.

Between 1944 and 1947 Saab's men were very busy with not just the designs and production tooling for the Scandia and the Safir, but also the new 92 car, all of which began at the same time. Gunnar Ljungström and Sixten Sason focused on the car. Led on site by Frid Wänström, Saab's aviation research design chief, who had directed the Saab 17 design project, the team produced a series of brilliant airframes and a car!

Tord Lidmalm directed the Scandia project, and A.J. Andersson designed the Safir. In the background from 1945, Lars Brising developed the initial S.29 Tunnan jet fighter-bomber designs; in 1948 Saab received the go-ahead to design and build the Arthur Bråsjö-designed S.32 Lansen jet fighter. There was very little cash to spare, and even less manpower and factory floor space available. Perhaps this explains why such a small team of men created the car on a tight budget. No wonder the 92 went from concept model to metal prototype in six months. Building the car would take a bit longer.

PRODUCTION BUILD-UP

Behind the scenes, Saab was spending millions of kronor on building the car plant at the new Trollhättan factory and in purchasing the body pressing equipment. The bill for the presses to form the body parts in Swedish kronor was Skr2.24m and the total cost to get the Saab 92 into production was Skr4,577,062. It was a massive amount of money at the time for a project that had begun with just Skr200,000 of development funding. The price of the car had risen, but here Saab had also been influenced by tax banding levels and government regulations. The initial price per car was set to be Skr3,200, but this rose to Skr3,900 and then to more than Skr5,000.

Saab wanted British steel for the car, so it approached the British company Pressed Steel Ltd to supply the body-pressing equipment and to help with securing the steel, but Pressed Steel turned them down. Svante Holm, the 92's lead project manager, rushed off to America and after a visit to the Budd steel fabrication works secured the services of Heinz Manufacturing of Philadelphia, who then shipped over the giant body pressing tools, which weighed between 70 and 300 tons. Parts went initially to the Linköping factory, where the early work on the 92 was done, and then the main presses were sent directly to Trollhättan via the port of Gothenburg. The expensive new presses, Saab's biggest investment, were transferred to canal barges for the journey to Trollhättan. One of the massive pressing machines, vital to the project, nearly capsized its barge and Saab's first car

Car P553 leaves the factory for testing.

production came close to sinking before it was built. The three Heinz employees who travelled to Sweden to oversee the setting up of the giant presses were William Meyers, Joe Slobojan and later Edward Tipper.

Saab built three body presses and their operation was overseen by lead production engineer Nils-Gustav Nilsson. All went well after the initial near-disaster on the canal barge.

Alloys or Just Steel?

One of the earliest questions was what should the advanced new car be constructed from? Surely Saab, maker of aluminium alloy aircraft, could build its car from this strong but light metal and gain a massive advantage in terms of weight, performance and miles per gallon, not to mention rust resistance.

The reality was that Saab had made riveted aluminium aviation structures, but welding aluminium would have been as complicated and expensive as it remains today as a car body material. Saab did not have the money or the experience. Glass fibre and plastics may have been an ideal aeronautical spin-off product from the war, but this was a technology in its infancy. Glass fibre reinforced plastic body panels were time consuming to make and performed very poorly in a crash impact. Cash-strapped post-war Sweden was no place for a 1940s plastic testbed.

Despite the lure of alloy, one of the first decisions was to build the car in high-quality steel as a stressed skin monocoque, yet using thicker steel and more reinforcement than any car had used up to that time (and well beyond it). American steel was used for the early cars. The car would have a fuselage: a one-piece monocoque structure with localized reinforcements where needed. It would have a soft nose and a hard cabin to protect its occupants.

The metal thickness used for the new Saab was more than 20 per cent thicker than on any other contemporary car, the metal of the roof skinning was 1.11mm thick, the body side walls 0.87mm and the crucial, box-section steel sills were 1.59mm in thickness. Most panels were in 18/20 gauge steel, with 16-gauge used in some places.

The 92's main A-pillars or windscreen pillars featured a triple-section, multiply-flanged, 2.5mm-thick steel sandwich triangulated design that made them the strongest A-pillars of any car made then and for many years afterwards. An extra steel insert to these pillars added to the roll-over

The 92 unveiled to the press, and still with the shrouded front wheel arches.

This 92 has the more cut-away front wheel arches, so is closer to the production standard.

Saab's first car seen with the S.21 fully Saab-designed airframe (preceded by two licence-built earlier derivative types).

protection and intrusion resistance, and the main side B-pillars were box-section steel pillars of great strength. The sills were boxes of thick steel unlike any other sills seen on a monocoque until the Saab 99/900 design. Here was the proof of the unique strength of the Saab.

The main, front roof supports, the windscreen pillars, featured extra steel inserts that ran down into the bulkhead and tied into the sills and the B-pillar frame.

Most cars have thin gauge, pressed steel sills that are welded-up from several panels to create the sill. These are easily deformed and can split open in an impact, and they also have seams that can rust. The Saab sills were thick, box-section steel beams of immense strength with high levels of resistance to deformation and intrusion. In the middle of the car the B-pillars formed a roll-over hoop with unheard-of strength. The smoothed-in front wings or fenders featured large steel wheel arches to help absorb offset driver or passenger side-only impacts. The bulkhead/firewall was reinforced at each side and the roof was so stiff that it could later accept a larger sunroof aperture. By having a single piece of pressed steel for the entire roof, the 92's torsional rigidity was greatly increased.

Such thinking was unique. Only in recent years has the Euro NCAP crash test criteria for offset impacts focused attention on the structural design of the front corners and the sill members and footwell/toeboard strength in car design. There were no safety standards extant when Saab made its first car, but amazingly when they became law in later decades the little Saab's ancient underpinnings sailed through new legislation.

Thanks to Ljungström and the work of Olle Lindgren, as stressman, and Erik Ekkers the little Saab had a tough hull that resisted intrusion and could be dropped on its roof from a great height with minimal damage.

The Saab's overall rigidity was very high and load paths through the structure were carefully calculated, a rare move in late 1940s car design. In fact the original 92 in its URSaab guise exceeded 11,000lb/ft/degree of torsional rigidity, one of the highest figures ever achieved. Closely welded and properly undersealed, the body would stay stiff and strong through many Swedish winters. Just as in an aircraft, there were reinforcements around the cabin apertures. Only the rearwards-mounted fuel tank (although it was up under the rear floor and not at the rear bumper) and front-hinged doors betrayed the thinking of its age and these safety-related items were soon dealt with as knowledge advanced: the doors were changed to forward-hinged.

Dynamics

Safety was to be built in, but how would its engine drivetrain work, and what sort of character would it possess? These were the vital questions that hung in the cold winter air as 1945 turned into 1946 and a team about a dozen strong got down to creating the first Saab car, an idea that had been in informal discussion since 1944 but which was now Board-room approved reality.

Ljungström's mind was open, but he later stated that the idea for front-wheel drive came less from him and more from Sixten Sason, who pushed for the efficiencies of the front-drive theory. Driving the front wheels meant better traction, notably in snow and ice, with the engine's weight (70 per cent) over the driven wheels. It also meant that weight was saved by not having a driveshaft running the length of the car back to a rear differential. The floor could be flatter, the suspension easier to locate, and more front cabin room could be found with the transverse engine alignment.

Alec Issigonis at BMC and teams at Renault, Citroën and Fiat would all take years to produce cars with similar claims that were then lauded by the motoring press.

The 92 had torsion-bar suspension, the mountings of which were unusually strong metal plates that were welded into the hull. The new car was to be a two-door, four-seater family vehicle with a large boot, with the ability to fold down the rear seats to create a small luggage deck yet retain two front seats.

Saab also came up with the idea of giving the 92 removable seat cushions and a fold-down rear bench that created a small overnight or camping bed. It was immensely practical, despite not getting a boot opening until 1953! The camping-bed ability of the 92 was a very Swedish thought that reflected the Swedes' need to make the most of summer and go camping in the country or by the sea. The Saab 95 estate would later provide a more comfortable bed.

Two Pots of Torque

The decision to use an aluminium-headed, 2-stroke (2-cylinder) engine was both genius and in the long term a handicap, which would appear to be confirmed by the later decision to re-engine it with a 3-cylinder 2-stroke, and then, with the leap in Saab 96 sales, the adoption of a V4 engine. But that was two decades away and first there came the 2-cylinder,

UrSAAB: DESIGN AND DEVELOPMENT

transverse-aligned, oiled-up, 2-stroke, 25bhp Saab-designed engine with 764cc in the production version.

Again the influence of the little DKW and its 2-stroke engine was to be felt. And what of the early Opel Kadett type that was imported from Germany? That was another car influential in the Swedish market.

Gunnar Ljungström stated that the other main reason to choose the 2-stroke 'twin' was that when Saab started making cars, there was a scarcity of machine tools, metals and materials, so the small engine with less than a dozen moving parts involved less financial cost and ease of manufacture and maintenance in a period of post-war austerity and hoped-for expansion.

Originally patented in 1858 by Pierre Hugon, the 2-stroke cycle engine was valve-less, had fewer moving parts, used piston-controlled ports and had a higher efficiency ratio than a 4-stroke combustion cycle. Of high torque, virtually unburstable and small and light, it could run on low quality fuel and oil, and was simple to maintain. This type of engine was ideal for Saab in post-war Sweden ... at first.

Such engines had done well in Europe before 1939, including in Sweden, because their oil mix did not freeze or wax up in the deep-frozen winter conditions. Swedish mechanics knew how to fettle the engines, even if a de-coke was needed every few thousand miles. Light, with only seven main moving parts, the 2-stroke was simple, cheap and it also revved beautifully. Compared to a low compression 4-cylinder cast iron lump, a Ford V8 or another antique side-valve, there was something alternative about the 2-stroke, even if it did scream, smoke and rasp away like a bee with a loud sting in its tail.

Gunnar Ljungström designed his own improved version of the DKW 2-stroke engine and the prototype engine, with its 'thermo-isophonic' thermal cooling system, was built with help from Albinmotor AB.

Water-cooled, with a three-speed gearbox and with responsive rack-and-pinion steering, as opposed to the conventional choice of the vaguer feeling worm-and-roller type then in mainstream use, the mechanics of the 92 were as honed as the bodyshell.

The engine was mounted well forwards in the under-bonnet void. This brought two major advantages: more weight was over the front-driven wheels and there was plenty of rearwards crush room in an impact, leaving space for the engine to move before it impacted the main bulkhead. The only disadvantage was inherent understeer.

The oil-to-petrol mix was set at 4 per cent. Original 92s used a fuel pump of diaphragm-type, which was activated by crankcase pressure variations rather than the usual mechanism. With piston-controlled ports, no valves and few major castings to move about, this was an engine of 'pure' ethos, yet like all 2-strokes it did emit rather high emissions, especially when cold.

Unusually, the engine had its own mounting cradle featuring a small leaf spring front component with rubber buffers that

All the first cars were green, or so the legend says. But that's not true, as a handful were finished in a smarter blue, reputedly suggested by Gunnar Philipson.

57

UrSAAB: DESIGN AND DEVELOPMENT

SAAB 92 PRE-PRODUCTION BUILD FIGURES

1946	Car 1 as UrSaab 92.001
1947	Cars 2 and 3 as 92.002 and 92.003
1948	Car 4 as 92.004
1949	20 test/production line pilot-build cars. These cars had their own chassis numbers up to 92.024
12 Dec 1949	First full status production car chassis built

ABOVE: **This early 92 has a single front driving lamp. Note the thinner-gauge bumpers, while retaining the shrouded wheel arch.**

LEFT: **Early production was slow and careful. Quality was required and it took effort to shape and weld the heavy-gauge steel into a hull.**

resisted torque shunt. This drastically cut vibration.

Sweden's wartime expertise with roller and ball bearings meant that creating a 3-bearing crankshaft was easy for Saab. The production 92 weighed in 1,775lb (885kg). It was no ultra-lightweight, but neither was it a cast-iron lump and it had low drag and that spiteful, perky engine to row it along. Going over 900kg would have put the 92 into another tax band in Sweden, so weight was crucial, but not at the expense of safety or rust resistance. Despite the weight, top speed was cited as 65mph (115km/h). Fuel consumption, however, was not as good as a small 4-stroke engine.

Even with is low drag shape, the Saab struggled to get to 40mpg (7.06ltr/100km), and oil also had to be added to the 2-stroke mix. Ljungström's design, allied to Mellde's tuning skills, did however produce a car that was fast through the gears, with overtaking speed performance from the 2-stroke being particularly strong and well above class average, provided you kept the engine nicely revved up.

UrSAAB: DESIGN AND DEVELOPMENT

Possibly one of the first advertisements for the 92 in late 1949 or early 1950.

On 10 June 1947, having previously been shown prototype 92.001 on 4 June 1946, the Swedish motoring press were shown the first recognizable Saab 92 car: 92.002. This was the car with the revised chromed grille and with two round headlamps set each side of a raised prow. It was a development of changes made to the original 92.001, registered as E1866 and E14783, after which the aerofoil-shaped and faired-in front was altered to provide a vee-angled bonnet with two podded headlamps set each side of the nose. Larger section bumpers were fitted to 92.003 and 92.004.

Road Testing

The 92 prototypes also racked up thousands of kilometres of testing to ensure that the Saab-designed engine and components were fit for purpose. Test drivers from Philipsons, the dealership that was co-funding the 92, had to deal with a test schedule as the prototypes were driven night and day around the rough rural roads and tracks of Östergötland county and the road to Norrköping. Bumpy roads and exhaust fumes were tiring for the drivers, but many worthwhile changes to the production car specification resulted from this long development period, which was overseen by former rally driver and engine expert Olof Landbü, the Saab 92 chief test driver/engineer. Landbü was sadly drowned in September 1948 with two of his Saab test department colleagues, Karl Nyberg and Börje Garbing, when they went swimming and fishing on the Southern Canal at Trollhättan in stormy conditions. Only Saab draughtsman Kurt Liljevall survived the tragic accident.[10]

Just a single crankshaft failure marred the development of the engine; the car was tested day and night throughout 1946 and 1947, covering more than 170,000 miles (280,000km). With the engine and gearbox as a single integral unit, unlike the DKW design, and with the clutch and input shaft aligned

59

The 92 looked far less utilitarian in the right paint hue and with enough polished chrome. Note the whitewall tyres. Behind can be seen the one-off prototype for a Saab hydrofoil powerboat design.

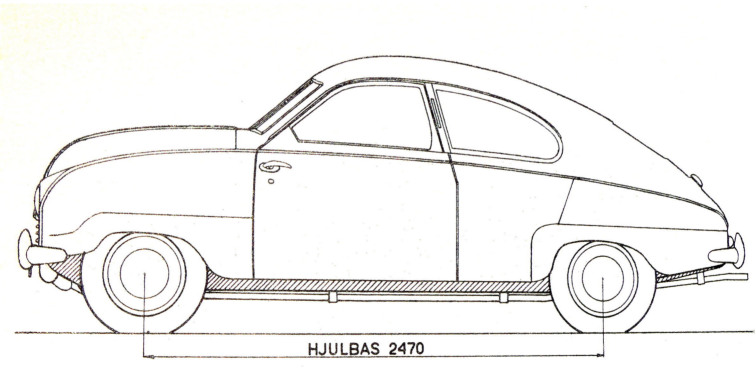

Side profile of the 92 also reveals the bulbous shape and stance with the tapering tail.

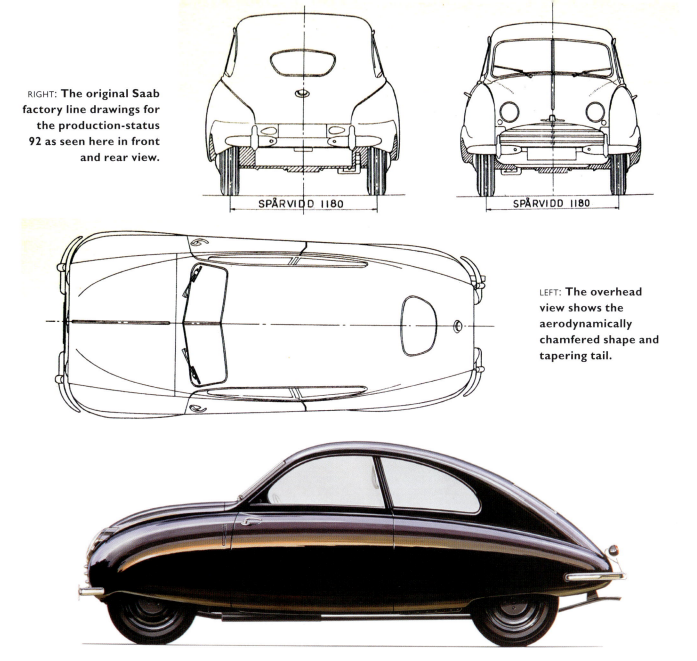

RIGHT: **The original Saab factory line drawings for the production-status 92 as seen here in front and rear view.**

LEFT: **The overhead view shows the aerodynamically chamfered shape and tapering tail.**

Profile of perfection.

with the crankshaft, every rotating shaft was in parallel, thus reducing internal stress and vibration. The car's radiator was mounted behind the engine near the bulkhead, away from cold air coming though the grille. This was fine in winter but gave rise to overheating in the summer, due to a lack of engine bay airflow.

For aircraft men used to no-expense-spared practices in securing the ultimate in efficient design, creating a car on a minimal budget was a new experience. Yet this was a good thing as Saab did indeed use secondhand parts to create the 92.00. Saab also purchased a secondhand Opel Kadett and a Hanomag as reference points.

From UrSaab 92.001 came the Saab 92 production status car of 1949. From sketch to car in just four years was truly something for a novice carmaker even if it had previously built aircraft. From 1947 through to 1949 Saab finished off its car, tested it extensively, and finally settled on a production status specification for late 1949.

Considering that the 92's basic underlying shape and structure remained in production from 1949 to January 1980, the integrity and the essential correctness of its timeless Sason-influenced design can only be confirmed.

CHAPTER THREE

92: SOUL OF SAAB

The 92's debut took place not in Trollhättan, but at Saab's Linköping base in the canteen on an expensive antique rug. The car's debut was attended by everyone from Marcus Wallenberg down. Reaction to the 92 was both favourable and curious, and soon the first stages of production build-up were begun at Trollhättan. The car was to have a name (Sason had wanted to call it 'Sonett' as early as 1948, as shown by the accompanying photograph), but as it was a follow-on from Saab's last product, the Saab 91 Safir aircraft, it seems that the car got stuck with just a number, 92.

After further extensive testing involving the first five cars as the pre-production models in 1948, the first public view of Sweden's new 'other' car had been in April 1948 when 14,000 people turned up at the Grand Hotel in Stockholm to see the 92. Then in mid-June 1949 the 92 went on public show in its home town of Trollhättan. But the early car was a basic specification variant, right down to having only one windscreen wiper and a very sparsely equipped dashboard. Little did the Swedish public know that it would be January 1950 before they could actually purchase and receive the first deliveries of their Saabs.

In the first British-published (but 'Continental' located) road test of the production Saab 92 in 1950, *Motor* magazine reckoned that the new Saab was 'unorthodox' and of 'striking appearance'. *Motor* also stated that the car was so unusual that it was difficult to compare with others as no comparable benchmark existed: 'The whole layout is so ingenious both in conception and in detail

The Saab 92 soon featured an opening boot and some trim improvements: this is the 92B.

A Sason X-ray view of Ljungström's hull for the ultra-stiff 92. It was designed like a wing and fuselage, with a touch of yacht design thrown in.

that it was with extreme curiosity that we collected the latest car from the factory'.[11]

Decades later, in 2010, *Classic and Sports Car* magazine said of the 92: 'When launched, the 92 made almost every other European rival appear positively antediluvian ... In addition the 92's coachwork is some of the most elegant to be found on any post-war car.'

Here was independent opinion agreeing with the Saab ethos yet decades apart. This is not a question of 'confirmation bias', selecting views that support the beliefs of the author and other Saab enthusiasts, but there are multiple examples of independent published opinion concurring. Those believing the opposite will continue to cite their own evidence as unimpeachable and maintain that they are in no way biased. It was ever thus.

The truth was that Saab had got it right.

The British loved the little Saab and sales eventually justified the decision in 1962 to create a direct export service from Trollhättan to Great Britain to support the new outlet. Instead of driving (or transporting new Saabs by truck) to the docks at Uddevalla or Gothenburg for loading onto a ship for the North Sea crossing, Saab reduced the mileage put on the new cars for the British market (and the risk of damage to them from driving and loading on-board) by starting a direct boat service for new Saabs from the factory using the Trollhättan waterway direct to Felixstowe docks. Erik Granlund, who was Saab's shipping manager, initiated this new service in early 1962, but during the very severe winter of 1963, when even Great Britain froze up for three months, the waterway from Trollhättan froze over and the cars had to be driven to Uddevalla port on the main coast instead.

As early as 1952 Saab began considering production of the 92 outside Trollhättan, and even outside Sweden. Enquiries were flooding in for the car from all over the world, notably from North and South America. In 1951 Philipsons, the garage chain that had backed the 92's development, considered setting up their own production plant at the Philipson works near Stockholm, but the plan did not come to fruition. Within a few years, however, Saab would be building cars in South America.

Legend has it that all Saab's early cars were painted green – a particular shade of leftover wartime green paint, but in fact several of the early cars were painted in a very smart navy blue. In December 1949 the Trollhättan factory was ready for proper, series production. It is known that at least one car was produced to public sale specification prior to the Christmas break on 12 December, but rolling production started in the first week of January 1950. On 16 January 1950 Saab delivered the first three of the series production cars for customers.

Only one month after production started, the cars of chassis numbers 7 and 8 were entered in the Monte Carlo Rally, driven by Rolf Mellde/K.G. Svedberg and Greta Molander/Margareta von Essen. They finished in 55th and 69th places, respectively. Better results were to come, but few recall that as early as December 1949 a very early pre-production Saab 92 won its first rally at the Circuit of Östergötland, driven by Svedberg.

92: SOUL OF SAAB

Saab went funky with its early brochures in a modernistic 1950s idiom. This colourful cut-away is a delight of the era.

The 92's very sporting suspension was by torsion bars. It proved to be a hard ride but one ideal for Sweden's country roads where ground clearance was important.

The front suspension loads were transferred into the bulkhead and stiff central tub area, in a manner that aped wing-to-fuselage loading and stress path design. The mounting of the rear suspension arms was well inboard of the wheelbase, reducing weight and pendulum loads and effects on the car. Telescopic shock absorbers and good roll and rebound rates produced a car with deft handling and the responses of something far more exotic, but with that hard ride. It steered like a sports car, a small fighter aircraft or a sports glider, so it was direct with minimal 'play' and little input needed: the Saab told you what it was about to do. In effect the 92 drove, steered and rode with the finesse of a real driver's car. Keeping the engine revs up and learning how to make quick gear changes soon became the key to fast progress in the little car.

ROLF MELLDE: DRIVING FORCE

Erik Carlsson is rightly credited as the man behind the driving characteristics, the dynamics, of what made a Saab a Saab. Carlsson influenced both early and more recent Saabs.

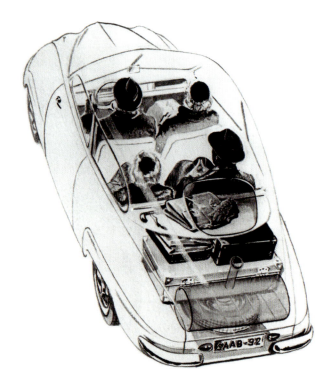

An early Sason vision of the 92. That fuel tank would soon be placed more safely under the boot/seat area.

92: SOUL OF SAAB

Rolf Mellde, who started Saab's rallying in 1949 and engineered some of the company's greatest hits, was a true hero of Saab.

He undertook extensive prototype testing of its cars and ordered changes to make the Saab 'feel' more apparent. He even did this for the new generation, GM-influenced Saab 900 Mk2 launched in late 1993. Decades earlier, Carlsson defined the 93 and 96 via rallying. But it was Olof Landbü and Rolf Mellde who did the initial work from 1946 to 1948 on the 92.

As the first Saab car was developed into a wooden styling model and then the first metal-panelled prototype, a new name would join Saab in late 1946. Under the 92's skin there lay the influence not just of Gunnar Ljungström but also of Rolf Mellde, who had a passion for cars, motorcycles and boats: he later designed his own twin-V powered speedboat in what little of his spare time must have been left after all the Saab projects.

Mellde was a driven character. His grandfather August Johansson had built one of the first cars in Sweden as a one-off project and sold it to Lars Magnus Ericsson, the Swedish inventor and founder of the telecomms company. Mellde's father Evald had taught mechanical engineering. Young Rolf grew up surrounded by such thinking.

OLOF LANDBÜ

Olof Landbü (1918–1948) had been a successful Swedish pre-war rally and trials driver and had entered a series of national class reliability tests, the same kind of 'Trials' events so popular in Great Britain in the 1930s. After the war Landbü had won the Swedish National Trophy in 1946 with his colleague Bengt Carlqvist. Landbü started to build home-built trials 'Specials' as cars with cut-down bodies, giving lighter weight and more traction. He also began to modify DKW 2-stroke engines for use in these cars.

Rolf Mellde worked with Landbü in building three of the 'Specials' in 1947 and drove one in a trial. Gosta Berqvist, who was well placed as an employee of Philipson's, the Saab dealer, and Landbü drove the other two cars. Mellde was injured in a practice accident and was fortunate to survive.

When Mellde arrived at Saab, he found in Landbü a tutor and perhaps a bit of a mentor. Although Mellde had been working on engines and their design for the best part of a decade, the older and more experienced Landbü was perhaps more important to the early process of the Saab car's basic engineering and optimal driving set-up than commentators have generally realized. Having learned more of Landbü's contribution through the Saab Veterans Archive, it is only correct to further profile Landbü and his works, not least because of his tragic early death in 1948. Mellde assumed the lead test engineer role after his mentor died, maintaining Landbü's contribution to the 92's character.

Born in 1922, he studied thermodynamics at the Stockholm Technical Institute. His tutor was a racing driver and engine designer named Folke Mannerstedt, and this may have spurred his later interest in rallying. He then worked for several engineering companies, notably on a 2-stroke marine engine. Mellde even came up with his own car design, but he joined Saab instead and brought a tenacious and forensic engineering and driving focus to the new car's development. Handling, steering, suspension and road quality were all influenced by Mellde.

65

■ 92: SOUL OF SAAB

Classic Saabism on the go as the 92 spools up. This is the purist's Saab.

The famous Saab image of a green 92 at speed in a blur of green.

By 1946 Mellde was a young man going places. Articulate, intelligent, an aspiring rally driver and motorcyclist with advanced high-speed control skills on ice as well as tarmac, he had experience of setting up car engines, drive lines, suspension and steering. Mellde, who had been drawing engines since he was a boy, was the man who built Saab's competition department. Cars, motorcycles and engineering were his thing, as was driving.

The 92.001 and three styling development cars had already been built when Mellde joined Saab in late 1946 fresh from Swedish Army National Service. Yet he was instrumental in developing the car at late prototype stage. While we can credit the legendary Erik Carlsson with influencing Saab's dynamics from the 1950s, we should look to the somewhat obscured name of Mellde as a promoter of what were to become the Saab 92's handling traits and ultimately a Saab branding motif.

Mellde organized the first rally entries of the new Saab car in 1949–50, notably the Swedish national rallies and the Monte Carlo Rally. Driving the new 92 Mellde won the 1950 Rikspokalen Rally and the 1953 Swedish national rally championship. Mellde also drove the 92 with Bengt Carlqvist in 1950.

Saab's early successes with the 92 included winning the 1949 Östergötland Rally with a very early production car. A few weeks later, 92 chassis numbers 7 and 8 entered the 1950 Monte Carlo Rally and were placed 69th and 55th, respectively. Note that this was before Erik Hilding Carlsson came along and became the rally 'king'. The early contribution of Mellde (and also that of Olof Landbü) to the car, its evolution and rallying prowess, which was fostered by the nascent but not yet fully 'official' Saab Competition Department, should not be lost under the legend of the great Erik himself.

Female drivers who took Saab 92s to early 1950s rally successes included Greta Molander, Helga Lundberg, Margareta von Essen, Ewy Rosqvist and Ursula Wirth. Ewy Rosqvist would go on to fame as a rally driver for Volvo and Mercedes-Benz, and later became Baroness von Korff-Rosqvist.

When the 93 debuted (in late 1955 for the 1956 model year) with its revised engine and suspension designs, Saab scored second place in the gruelling 1956 Tour d'Europa Rally and then won the 1956 Great American Mountain Rally.

Rolf Mellde also developed the original Sonett in secret as a personal project with Sixten Sason and a small team. He drove Saab's motor sport and engineering departments, urged the company to seek a 4-cylinder, 4-stroke engine and created Saab's first research department. We can credit him with making the 92 and the 93 such fine driver's cars that were equally adept as rally and race car tools. Many Saab fans will be familiar with 'Mellde's Monster', the twin-engined, 3-cylindered, almost-V6 version of a Saab 93 that he developed as a one-off (see Chapter 4).

Engines were an area of focus for the 92, 93 and 96: from an initial transverse-mounted 2-stroke, 2-cylinder in the 92, to the 1956 revision that was the 93 and its longitudinally mounted 2-stroke, 3-cylinder engine, on to the 96 V4's 4-stroke, 4-cylinder Ford-derived V4 engine.

Back in 1948, to ensure reliability Mellde had installed Saab's new design of 2-stroke engine in old DKWs as development cars and won a rally and was placed in others using these test 'mules'. Thanks largely to Mellde's work, the 92's engine was well proven before launch.

It was Mellde (no shrinking violet) who risked much by going behind the scenes to lobby on behalf of the Ford V4 with no less a figure than Marcus Wallenberg's son, who rallied Saabs.

Mellde also created the rare, front-wheel-drive Saab Formula (Junior) single-seat racing car project at Saab in 1960. The next year Saab ran two such cars in a professional race series as the sole participating car manufacturer to do so. Of great technical interest, Mellde gave this car reverse-function coil spring suspension with springs working in tension, not compression. The rest of the engine and drivetrain components were straight off the Saab 93, but the gearbox was turned upside down to fit.

In an interesting outcome, decades later Mellde would work for Volvo and influence its cars, notably in terms of safety and the building of the 1980s LCP concept car, with its superb direct-injection, small-capacity diesel engine, which was developed from Mellde's concept. Widely honoured, Mellde was another Swedish engineering legend who came out of the Saab car process of the 1940s. Without his involvement Saab's rally story might not have been what it was.

INTO PRODUCTION

The 92 was a fine driver's car, steering and braking with wonderful feedback and accuracy. The column gear shift used was a touch ponderous, perhaps, but the standard of the day. A 'freewheel' clutch allowed the drive to disengage the gears and save fuel by coasting. Effectively, the

■ 92: SOUL OF SAAB

Maroon looked great on the 92 and 92B. Note the chrome strips over the wheel arches.

A 92B with all the aerodynamic shaping at the rear caught by the light. Note the larger rear windscreen.

transmission was allowed to 'run' faster than the engine by interrupting the drive train. This could, of course, lead to engine lubrication issues if the engine was left to run at idle speed on a long downhill descent for perhaps too long. Later engines had direct oil injection into the combustion stage of the 2-stroke cycle, which made the problem of pre-mix lubrication less of an issue.

One oddity is that there was no boot lid, so luggage had to be loaded via the main cabin doors. Amazingly, early versions of the 92 had no heater, which seemed especially mean for a car from Scandinavia. The dashboard design was very spartan and simple, and the tubular-framed deckchair-type seats might have come out of a 2CV were it not for their thicker padding and design motifs, which in turn echoed 1930s Bugatti design architecture. Indeed, 92.001 had a French or Italian feel to its interior furnishings, with salmon grey buttoned cloth and angled seat squabs, set in a sparse, simple room that was lightened by painted panels.

Saab set itself a high target when it started car production at Trollhättan, for at the same time the company was launching a series of civil and military aircraft and embarking on building its jet engine under licence from de Havilland of England. Saab cars and Saab aero engines were to assist each other in many ways.

A great deal of heavy engineering was required and forces of between 350 and 500 tons were required in the new pressing machines used to build the cars. These were sourced from America at considerable expense. Expert pressing and fabrication skills were also needed for the aircraft parts and engines.

Links with the British were to prove strong and old friendships were to be very useful. Several aspects of the tooling machinery required for Saab to build the 92, 93, 95 and 96 were sourced in Britain, including from Vauxhall in Luton and the aircraft and shipbuilders Vickers-Armstrongs of Newcastle and Weybridge, who were providing expertise. Saab was working with de Havilland on jet engine development and would later work with Standard Triumph, in consultation with Ricardo & Co. Engineers, for the new 4-cylinder engine for the Saab 99.

One question often asked is why Saab's production factory's main area was called the 'Winter Palace'. The answer lay in the fact that white paint on the ceiling began to flake and drop showers of paint flakes onto the workforce below in what looked like a snow fall, hence the nickname.

The early 92 metal bodies were welded up inside a wooden frame and then gas welded. Bodies were transported around the production area on trolleys or carts, but as production ramped up in the 1950s a proper conveyor-type car body assembly line was established.

There was close co-operation between the 92's design team and the tooling/build workers. Sixten Sason was not just the creative mind one might expect of a designer, he was also closely involved and had an understanding of the construction process. Sason, Ljungström and Mellde all worked closely with the 92's build team and this eased any develop-

SAAB 92 TECHNICAL SPECIFICATION

Production of 92 began 12 December 1949 after 1947 92.001 prototype

Engine	Transverse-mounted, 2-cylinder, 2-stroke engine
Cooling	Water with thermoisophonic circulation
Bore x stroke	80 x 76mm
Capacity	764cc
Compression ratio	6.6:1
Maximum power	25bhp (18kW) at 4,000rpm
Carburettor	Solex 32 AIC; other types tried include Autolite
Fuel	Mechanical fuel pump feed. 4% oil mixture by pre-mixing at tank
Transmission	Front-wheel drive; single-disc dry plate clutch; column change 3-speed gearbox and freewheel device; synchromesh on top gears
Suspension	4-wheel independent springing with transverse torsion bars front and rear; hydraulic shock absorbers with very strong semi-structural mounting plates
Steering	Rack and pinion with 5.5m radius
Wheels and tyres	15-inch wheels
Brakes	Hydraulic Lockheed system of drum brakes all round. Handbrake activated on rear wheels
Electrics	6 volts system
Bodyshell	Stressed skin monocoque with reinforcing beams in windscreen and door pillars; box-section sills and reinforced front bulkhead; Cd 0.35 in production trim
Dimensions	
Wheelbase	2,470mm (97.24in)
Length	3,920mm (154.33in)
Width	1,620mm (63.78in)
Height	1,425mm (56.10in)
Weight (net)	765kg (1,687lb)
Top speed	105km/h (65.24mph)
Price in Sweden at launch	Skr6,550

The essential elements of the 92, again in maroon. R. GUNN

92: SOUL OF SAAB

ment problems. Such was the spirit at Saab that it built the soul of Saab.

After the launch cars, Saab had settled on a production specification for 1950 involving a better-trimmed deluxe variant with a heater, engine thermometer, ashtray, sun visors, clock, bigger bumpers and painted wheel rims. The biggest external difference was that the grille was now chromium plated and not body paint colour. Twenty pre-production 92s were made: two were the base model and eighteen were the higher specification cars. Philipson the dealer wanted the deluxe version to be the sole model to introduce the Saab car brand, and at a price of Skr6,750, almost double Saab's price estimate of 1944.

SALES AND DEVELOPMENT

The 92 was advertised by Saab as some new form of family car coupé with sports car properties within its 'aviation'-inspired ethos. In Sweden the car came to be seen as something unique and yet not a 'prestige' brand. Overseas, however, the Saab brand soon came to be perceived as a quality and slightly upmarket entity.

Saab managed to make up to four cars a day and produced a total of 700 cars in the first full year. In 1951 chassis numbers ran from no. 701 to 1469. For 1952 new instruments by VDO were fitted, replacing fittings from the US company Stewart-Warner. For 1953 several modifications were made,

In the MIRA wind tunnel: note the smooth flow up and over the car – as intended.

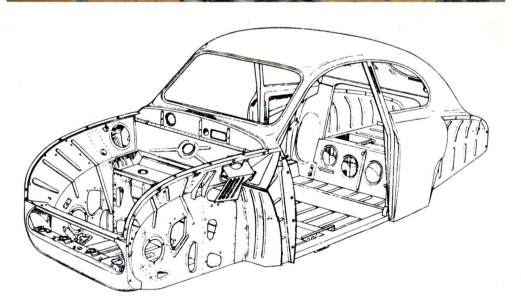

A 1949 drawing of the 92's monocoque shell and its various structural elements. Thick steel rods reinforced the A- and B-pillars. The shell had the highest torsional rigidity rating of any production car when new and for decades afterwards. *See* text for reference to Ljungström's related yacht hull and wing section designs.

SQUADRON LEADER ROBERT MOORE AND SAAB GB

The Saab 92 was introduced to Great Britain when Squadron Leader Arthur Robert Moore, who had spent nearly three years as a test pilot on the Saab J29 'Tunnan', decided to import his own 92 to Great Britain in the early 1950s. From that first move came the setting up of a Saab GB concession for which 'Bob' Moore would rise to managing director. But why did Moore import a 92?

Moore had joined the Royal Air Force Volunteer Reserve in 1939 and had a very active wartime role flying RAF fighters, including many operations over France and northern Europe. He was reputed to be the first RAF Hawker Tempest pilot to shoot down a Messerschmitt Bf109G, on 8 June 1944. He also had a go at an Me262 jet fighter deep over Germany in late 1944. He was awarded the Distinguished Flying Cross in July 1944 and a bar to that honour in February 1945 after his final sortie.

Moore's flying skills marked him out as a potential instructor and then test pilot: he undertook the test pilot's course at Boscombe Down (Empire Test Pilots School) in January 1945 and was posted to the RAF Development Unit Central Fighter Establishment. He was released from the RAF upon receipt of an offer to become a test pilot for Rolls-Royce on 1 May 1946. After a year at Rolls-Royce, Moore was approached by Saab in Sweden to join its test pilot unit. He accepted with alacrity since, despite walking away from the glamour of being a Rolls-Royce pilot, Saab had offered him an exclusive, *jet* development role. Saab was of course licence-building British jet engines for its own use.

The arrival of an ex-RAF, ex-Rolls-Royce test pilot at Saab did not go without some reaction, but Moore's flying skills and good manners soon won people over. Thus it was that post-war Moore had found his way to Linköping. As a Saab test pilot, he was involved in the development of the Saab J29 'Tunnan' ('the flying barrel' as its nickname stated). He piloted the prototype's maiden flight in September 1948.

Moore was a Saab fan to the core and he purchased his personal 92 in Sweden, then with his contacts and with the company's encouragement he established his own Saab concession in West London. Several years later he started Saab GB in time for the great 1960s car sales boom. He was director of Saab GB until 1973, and a man who was greatly admired and respected.

It was Moore who used British-resident Erik Carlsson and Pat Moss-Carlsson as the high-profile names to promote Saab in Great Britain. The wrestler Jackie Pallo became a Saab 96 owner, as did Eric Morecombe and Ernie Wise. Ex-RAF Second World War fighter pilot and later famous broadcaster Raymond Baxter soon became a Saab owner; the fact that Baxter and Moore knew each other and lived nearby in Berkshire was simply a coincidence, of course!

Moore created Saab GB's profile with class and style, recruiting well-known names. Saab GB's success continued to grow and it became one of the company's key sales outposts east of the Atlantic Ocean. The dashing Moore also owned a Saab Safir light aircraft and with his glamorous wife Georgie raced the Safir to several air race victories. Once again Saab's British connections were underlined: the 92, 93 and 96-series cars were crucial to the plot. Moore was a true hero and great man.[12]

One of Moore's Saab GB stalwarts was Roy Clements, who worked for Saab from the 1950s until his retirement in 1990 (as marketing director) and had a hand in specifying the British-supplied 93, 96 and 99 cars. He, like the other employees and dealers, enjoyed the Saab GB 'family' atmosphere and camaraderie under Moore's leadership.

including a rear window that was 53 per cent larger, a repositioned fuel tank and filler, and a proper external boot access.

It was in 1953 that such a modified 92 was first described in internal documents as the B series nomenclature, but it was not until the 1954 model year that the 'B' label was publicly launched after 8,000 original 92s had been manufactured. A more comfortable seat back for the front seats was quietly slipped into the mid-1953 specification.

Four new paint colours were added and a new carburettor from Solex (the 32 BI) boosted output to 28bhp. Extra chrome trim mouldings on the wings were fitted, together with the trademark plexiglass, window-draught shields.

The facia panel was also painted to match the chosen body colour, which significantly smartened up the interior. More powerful Hella headlamps replaced the weak sealed-beam American specification lights of the early cars. The piano wire starter handle cable, which often broke, was replaced with more durable and rather organic rope! At this stage the car had neither a starting key, nor a starter located between the seats. The inconvenient position of the battery under the boot floor was also changed to an engine bay location.

Saab Inc. and Ralph T. Millet

Now that it had a toehold in Britain, the Saab car was ready for the next stage: America. The first Saab car to reach there was a 92 privately shipped in 1951. More were to follow during 1953 and the Saab legend had become established by the time an official US concessionaire, Saab Inc., was founded in 1955. The 93 was definitely on its way: by 1958 Saab would be selling 10,000 cars a years in America and launching the Grandturismo 750 in New York surrounded by rally victory trophies.

It was again a connection with Saab's aviation division that led to expansion into a new territory. Ralph T. Millet was an aeronautical engineer and pilot with a qualification from the Massachusetts Institute of Technology (MIT). He was then Saab's aircraft and airframe parts supply agent in America, so he knew Tryggve Holm, the company's top boss. Millet originally had the idea of building Saab cars in America under licence, but that vision did not materialize. Interest in small cars was increasing in America and Millet thought that a 4-cylinder engine would make the Saab an attractive proposition, not least as an alternative to the VW Beetle. Millet was doubtful about the chances of the 2-stroke engined Saab, but he was persuaded by a meeting with Tryggve Holm in 1955 to go along with Holm's determination to send some 2-stroke Saabs to America to test the market. Millet would soon hire Bob Sinclair, who would go on to play a pivotal role in Saab's future, not least as a key figure in the realization of the 1980s 900 convertible.

In 1956, after Tryggve Holm and Millet had agreed on the plan, Saab shipped four 93s and an early example of the two-seater Sonett 1 roadster to America. Floor space was booked for a stand at the first International Automobile Show in New York. Such was the expression of interest in the Saab 93 at the show that within days Millet had decided to set up a company to import and sell Saabs in America. The 93's win in the Great American Mountain Rally against all-comers and much bigger engines was the icing on the cake.

In 1957 Millet's US Saab operation sold 1,410 examples of the new 93. By 1959, less than four years since importing the first cars, Millet was selling 12,000 93s in 1959 alone.

The 93s went down well, but Millet's worries about the 2-stroke were not unfounded. Perhaps Saab had not had the chance to long-term test the engine on long interstate

The early owner's handbook had this line-drawing style sketch of a car in blue – not green.

92: SOUL OF SAAB

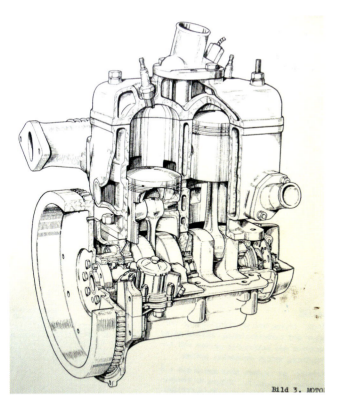

This is the original factory drawing of the twin-pot engine – no valves and not much power.

Saab's charming advice in its original owner's manual for wheel changing or maintenance was to prop the car up on wooden boards! It all depended on the quality of your wood.

On Swedish plates for display, this is Tony Grestock's early 92, looking somewhat frog-like.

■ 92: SOUL OF SAAB

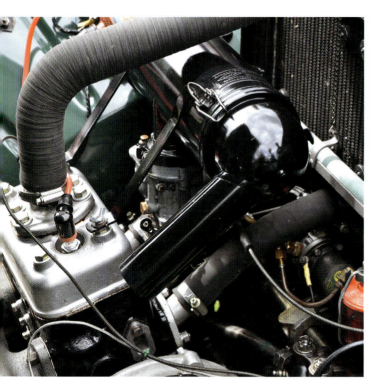

Transverse-engined, front-wheel-drive, two-stroke and all by 1950 – long before the Mini or other mass production front-wheel-drive cars achieved their fame.

The early 92 interior was stark yet stylish, as seen in this 1950 variant. Such original specifications would soon change.

Ken Dover's 92B captured in grey and shining metal.

INGVAR LINDQVIST: THE TRUE SAAB BELIEVER

One often forgotten name of Saab in America was the Swede Ingvar Lindqvist. He had a distinguished record with the Swedish Red Cross, which included rescuing wartime prisoners of war, and a notable United Nations operational record in the 1950s. After he married Patricia (née Tyrrell), they settled in 1956 in Culver City, California, where he established dealerships for European cars, notably an early Saab outlet. Lindqvist Motors on Sepulveda Boulevard was a dream of a Californian Saab garage, and Lindqvist was to become the other 'Mr Saab' in 1960s America.

Lindqvist raced a 93 GT750 as an amateur. He then raced a home-built Lin-Saab single-seat racer between 1959 and 1963, and created a part-Lotus, part-Saab single-seat racer in the early 1960s. His Saab-powered, Porsche-gearboxed 'Double-Ender' racer used the same glass fibre moulded body at each end. Was it back to front or front to back?

In 1969, up against Erik Carlsson and an official Saab rally team, Lindqvist and his co-driver Sven Sundqvist won the Baja 1000 main saloon car class in a new Saab 96 V4, beating famous teams and V8s to do it. In fact his 96 V4 had a lower specification than Erik Carlsson's own ex-Trollhättan rally department car. Erik had led the race, but coming out of retirement and having a bad back did not help on the Baja's dirt and rocks (for further details, see Chapter 6). Saab America Incorporated's dedicated and loyal PR boss Len Lonnegren, Millet and Carlsson had all lobbied for the support and funding to get Saab into the 1969 Baja 1000. Saab would also return the following year.[13]

Lindqvist would retire to his yachting hobby and remained a much-respected Saab enthusiast. He died in 2008 after more than four decades of Saab enthusiasm and belief.

highways at high temperatures, for in such conditions, with the engine set at near-constant speed, the 2-stroke cylinder/piston lubrication issue would manifest. A rash of broken engines was bad publicity, so Millet set up an engine repair centre and often simply installed a 'free' replacement engine under his unique 'lifetime' warranty for the 2-stroke engine for American customers. The scheme was created to limit any consumer complaints and image issues that might damage Saab. It was an inspired move. The customer loyalty and continued orders for Saabs far outweighed his costs. Eventually Saab would have 130 dealers across America in the period leading up to the car company's demise.

Danish Sales

From 1950 a Danish company, Nordic Diesel Auto AS of Copenhagen, began selling the 92 in Denmark and by early 1951 thirty cars had been imported. Not least of these was a 92 for Queen Ingrid of Denmark, who, like the Swedish Royal family (and the Dutch royals), soon had a penchant for the little Saab. By 1953 Saab had exported forty-eight cars to Denmark, out of a total of 330 export cars, and also exported some 92s to Morocco, which was a surprising destination for a winter-tuned car. In 1954 Saab's Danish agency was placed in the care of Leon Jorgensen as general agent until 1957.

Production Problems and the 92B

In 1954, as production was really ramping up, one of the three main presses, which was producing the 92's roof, malfunctioned. Lengthy and major repairs to the press-panel stamping machine were needed. This was the key heavy-force press and Saab had to temporarily fabricate major panels from other locations and presses. A store of one-piece 92 roof panels kept things going for a few weeks, but production was soon affected. Repairs to the heavy press required it to be shipped to Gothenburg for heat treatment and re-forging of its actuator beams, which had been bent in the incident. It had been an expensive error.

For the 1955 model year an electric fuel pump was fitted and in 1956 two new colours were added, bringing the total in the Saab palette to seven. By late 1956 Saab's first car had sold a remarkable 20,128 examples, of which 14,828 were of the B specification. But the car had been developed to

92: SOUL OF SAAB

a certain point and after five years of life some significant updates could be envisaged. The pace of development across Europe's carmakers was notable. Saab had to move on and the 92 would need to grow up a touch. Yet the basic ingredients had been set, for the little Saab was a joy to drive: responsive and tactile, it sent messages back to the driver through the steering and the suspension. The brakes and the steering had a communicative feel, and you knew what the car was doing, or about to do next: only the large steering turning circle was noted as an issue and this would be reduced in the Saab 93. Driving the Saab was an involving experience that was about to get better.

Design details: the early **Saab** badge and the 'slats' of the front grille are evident.

Following aircraft design techniques, the 92 had a very smooth skin surface to preserve boundary layer airflow from localized disturbance or triggers.

This view captures how far the 92's front wings overhung the wheels.

The 92 had a transverse engine with front-wheel drive long before better-known exponents of that configuration.

SJÖGREN: STYLE AND PUTTING ON THE 'GAS'

In 1959 Gunnar A. Sjögren achieved his aim of working for Saab. He was an established 'motoring noter', freelance designer and illustrator, who shared the passion for aircraft, cars, trains and boats demonstrated by so many at Saab, including Ljungström and Sason.

Sjögren worked for General Motors from early 1941 as a draughtsman and ended up in the advertising department. His design drawings were widely published in the Swedish motoring press, yet his first car was a Chevrolet!

He left 'the General' in 1954 and spent the next five years in a freelance career before joining the company he had long had in his sights: Saab. Starting at the Linköping technical office in 1959, he was initially involved in creating advertising materials for Saab cars, but his design ideas soon found their way into a higher profile inside the company. He advised on colour schemes, notably for paint and interior trims for the revised 93 and 96 interiors, and he would soon contribute design updates to the 93 and 96, and play a partial role in the design processes of the Sonett II and Sonett III.

He was always known by his signature initials GAS and this became his pen name. He wrote the book *The Saab Way* and recorded the vital details of Saab design history from 1949 up to 1984. Famed for his headgear (a beret), Sjögren was also known for his interest in nature, wildlife, philately, Scotch whisky and Viennese opera. GAS was perhaps less well known than the headline acts, but he was a vital contributor to the legend of Saab.

CLOCKWISE FROM TOP LEFT:

Red seats and a white steering wheel were early elements of Saab 'design' to emerge.

This example has the decorative branding 'SAAB 92' plinth on the dashboard. Sadly, these are now very rare.

Bruce Turk's US-specification 92B has a lovely two-tone interior and the wooden steering wheel. Pure Saab perfection.

The way that the highly raked A-pillar is swept from the front wing line up into the domed roof would surely have been the subject of an article if it had been designed by an Italian.

The original Saab 92 had Swedish values built in, but that did not mean it could not be improved. Ljungström and Mellde were keen to do better. By 1956 a revised Saab 92B had morphed into the 93. It was not just a facelift but a heavily reworked, re-engineered car with higher quality fittings and better ride and handling. It also gained a new engine. Perhaps it was the real beginning of widespread fame for Saab's amazing little aero weapon of a car. Saab's unusual story had, however, truly started in the 92. The spirit of Saab, the ethos of its engineering excellence, had begun to roll. The 93 was to prove even better.

1954: SONETT'S FIRST POEM?

As Saab was more than busy building the 92B, designing and production-prepping the 93, expanding the rally/competitions department and hiring Erik Carlsson, and making plans to further expand production volume, the ever-busy Rolf Mellde had a secret project on the go.

This involved using the new 3-cylinder engine from the 93 and various parts from the 92 and 93 to create a unique 'composite' contruction, chassis-less, ultra lightweight, open roadster of alloy and plastic/resin body type around a metal 'box' or 'punt'. Dreamed up by Mellde, the body weighed only 70kg (154lb) yet was very strong.

Mellde and Sixten Sason built a small-scale wooden model of the car they both envisaged and brought together a small team of dedicated Saab men in a barn at Åsaka, away from the factory and with very little funding. The key team members involved in this, the original Sonett, included Lars-Olov Olsson, Gösta Svensson, Olle Lindkvist, Arne Frick, Sven Fredriksson, Erik Johansson, Elis Olsson and the body construction technician Erik Nilestam.

MR WALMSLEY'S ARGENTINIAN 92B

Charles Walmsley has been resident in Buenos Aires for decades and his black 92B is a familiar sight both in the city and at local Saab gatherings. Another Buenos Aires Saab 92 resident is maroon – a lovely dark maroon. The sight of two Saab 92s speeding along through downtown Buenos Aires would be a moment to treasure.

Charly's car is one of the original batch of ten Saab 92s that were exported to Argentina. It was not new, but a previous owner had a Ljungström family connection, so it may have had an interesting specification. Despite mild renovation to keep it going over the years, Charly Walmsley's 92 is 95 per cent original and just reeks of Saab's brilliance. It is of course hugely valuable, but is used and driven as intended. Charly managed to secure two junkyard 92s from Uruguay as a source of 'original' spare parts, as he explains:

> I bought my 92 in 1972 when I was twenty-three years old and it has been a love-hate relationship with the amount of times I have had the engine out, but I love it like a friend. I talk to my Saabs, they all have names. The 92 is called Cucaracha (cockroach) and my 96 is Tomate (tomato). I bought two more 92s in junkyards for their donor parts, but some of these parts went to help a 92 in Uruguay.

Charly's 92 may have a special provenance because the wife of a previous owner was Monica Sjögren (née Ljungström). Strong circumstantial evidence suggests that she was Gunnar Ljungström's sister. If so, the car cherished by Charly Walmsley for nearly five decades is indeed special. Among the many vintage and veteran originals from across the years that may be seen at events organized by the Club de Automóviles Clásicos de la República Argentina is the exquisite 1950s Saab 92 of Buenos Aires. Still there and still going.

When Erik Carlsson visited South America in the 1990s, Charly Walmsley and Enrique Durhart offered to take him from Buenos Aires to Uruguay in Walmsley's other Saab, his red 96 Tomate. Erik later commented that the Walmsley 92 was wonderful and so was the red 96, driven by Walmsley with Durhart in the back.[14] (For more information on Saabs in South America, see Chapters 4 and 6.)

SAAB 92 PRODUCTION CAR BUILD FIGURES FROM 1 JANUARY 1950

Year	Cars
1950	1,246
1951	2,179
1952	2,298
1953	3,424
1954	5,138
1955	5,163
1956	680

(Excluding pre-production cars chassis numbers to 92.025, built prior to first production car built on 12 December 1949)

Sonett 1 was not to become a production item; six were constructed for test and competition development. Publicly unveiled on 16 March 1956 to rave reviews, it looked like Saab had an answer to the MG or the Alfa Romeo roadsters. Despite plans to produce 2,000 Sonett 1s a year using a slightly simpler pure-steel, rather than the alloy/resin body base, the project faltered, but much was learnt. Forces of caution inside Saab's management seem to have decided that problems finding a producer for the Sonett's body were insurmountable. Saab at this time was working flat out on the new 93 and new airframes. A decade later, however, came the production status Sonett coupés, which were based on the underpinnings and powerplants of the original Saab 95/96 cars.

Several private-venture Saab sportsters with lightweight bodies, Saab 2-stroke engines and with Saab 92/93 underpinnings were constructed in the USA, Uruguay and Australia in the late 1950s, but none made it to series production.

Total simplicity by Saab: the original badge.

The 'ribbed' door handle design was far from simple. This Sason-designed piece of genius was apparently inspired by cutlery and jewellery.

The 92 owned by Henk Ossendrijver in the outback of Western Australia, where many old Saabs still rest. H. OSSENDRIJVER

■ 92: SOUL OF SAAB

On the move, the curved beast gets going.

With its dedicated owner at the helm, the 92B makes its statement.

SAAB 92 MODEL RANGE DEVELOPMENT

1945–6   Sixten Sason's early sketches and Ljungström's plans of autumn 1945 result in the creation of the UrSaab 92.001 and pre-series cars into 1947. Rolf Mellde joins Saab design and development team in 1946: prototype designs result in 92.002, started April 1946. Completed car shown internally at Saab on 4 June 1946. Car registered in Linköping as E14783.

1947   Final Board decision to proceed with the Saab car on 27 February and ordering of further two prototype cars. Car 92.002 shown to Swedish press and cited as Saab 92 on 10 June 1947. Car operation moved to Trollhättan in November 1947.

1948   Early Saab 2-stroke engines fitted into DKW by Mellde and tested on the race track at Skarpnäck, Stockholm, in May 1948. Initial interest in Saab 92 project from South Amrican parties.

1949   92 production design set and car number 92.005 built and tested by June 1949 leading to definition of the Saab 92, public exhibition, and early production of the first twenty cars. Serial mass production run begins 12 December 1949 with first chassis numbers 1 through 700.

1950   First cars delivered 16 January; total of 1,246 cars delivered in 1950.

1951   Major series-production builds. First 92 exported to the USA.

1952   New German VDO instruments fitted in place of earlier Stewart-Warner instruments.

1953   92B launched as first cars with boot aperture, larger rear window, and relocated fuel tank from chassis number 5301. Early plans to import SKD-type Saab 92 to South America fail as regulations stifle the contract.

1954   Further revisions as B/2 specifications. 10,000th Saab car delivered 6 March. New 93 presented on 12 December. Upgrades include changes to carburettors, new ignition coil and numerous trim and specification changes. New engine and gearbox plant opened in Gothenburg.

1955   Electric fuel pump fitted. New colours offered. New model Saab 93 facelift on production line but with 92B base model production to continue. Several 92s sent to the USA, to be followed by 93s in 1956.

1956   Last 92B cars built in late 1956 into early 1957 to a total of 20,128. The new 93 model becomes the defining Saab car with new frontal styling and major revisions to specifications, including the new 3-cylinder engine. First Sonett revealed. Saab Motors Incorporated founded in the USA. Saab wins Great American Mountain Rally in New England.

The 92 profile: Saab was aiming for something quiet with that green paint.

CHAPTER FOUR

93: ESSENTIAL SAAB

With the 92, Saab had not just won its gamble, it had triumphed. Slowly the car evolved and was improved. Minor improvements were made and even a Golde-type full-length sunroof would become available. Sixten Sason came up with several cabin trim improvements as 1951 rolled into 1952, but money was tight at Saab and the 92B series would take a while to appear. Gunnar Philipson, the dealership chain owner, told Saab what his customers wanted to add to the 92 and the idea of the 92B (and then the 93) was further reinforced. The 92 slowly turned into the 93. The changes were really worthwhile and not just the usual styling tweaks and a new range of colours that the terms 'facelift' or 'Mk2' would mean at some carmakers.

Vast amounts of money had gone into making the aircraft company's first car. Thanks to intelligent innovation in engineering and design, the little car captured both the motoring press and the public. Demand was growing and all of Saab's spare aeronautical production capacity was focused on the car part of the business. Post-war shortages, however, were still limiting factors: Saab wanted top-quality British steel and no compromises were to be made for the thick-skinned car. Saab needed 1,600 tonnes per year, a trifling amount that, as Tryggve Holm often pointed out, America cold churn out in a few hours.

The 92 was not perfect and there were aspects that could have been done better with more time and experience. The Saab team, restless and enthusiastic, did not sit on their laurels. Before the end of 1955 the thoughts that had been buzzing around the design team's heads for more than a year were realized in a developed version of the original car, first through the 92B and then the bigger revision, the Saab 93.

First announced in December 1955, the early production 93 model cars were produced alongside the 'run out' 1956 model year 92B specification cars, which were still on sale at the end of 1956.

By this time, Saab Motors Incorporated had been founded in the USA after the success of the early 92 imports. Now the 93 was sold through an official Saab USA subsidiary: the adverts for the 93 ran with the curious slogan 'Look, Ma, NO VALVES!'

Ralph Millet was making huge strides up against American domestic muscle and iron in the form of large, lazy, low-compression, low-torque lumps of engine despite the Saab only being a two-stroke. The locals soon learned that the buzzing bumble-bee Saab went like a startled porcupine.

Saab had been busy working on ideas for the revised car both in Europe and the USA. All the things that buyers had previously noted and asked about were acted upon, and then some added style was thrown in. Launched on 1 December 1955, the 93 had been announced on paper in August during the summer break, the traditional, quiet summer news period. Highlights were:

• New engine
• New gearbox
• Revised styling
• New suspension
• Better trim and more luxury-type practical fittings in the cabin

The changes to the car over the 92B were far more dramatic than anyone had expected. Only the centre and rear body really remained unchanged, and even that had undergone styling surgery, more notably at the front.

Underneath there was a new engine, but it was not a 4-stroke engine as Saab could not afford to design its own. Tryggve Holm, the senior Saab director, seemed wedded to the concept of the 2-stroke even as the fashion for the cost-effective engine began to fade across Europe. There were,

A Saab 93, then owned by dedicated Saab enthusiast Chris Hull, shows off the revised frontal design that Sason created to take the car upmarket.

■ 93: ESSENTIAL SAAB

'Quality, precision, elegance': so stated the Saab strapline for marketing the new 93 series. This was still the era of delightfully illustrated brochures.

Non-politically correct advertising like this was reflective of its era. The Swedes had not then fully embraced their more recent social science nuances... The car, of course, is the star.

More elegance: Sason's badging for the 93 was all-new for the Saab image of the late 1950s.

750 GranTurismo GP866 looks fantastic in the correct red hue and with the rally-type lamp fitted to the roof.

however, a new gearbox and major changes to the suspension: even the suspension load paths into the bodyshell had to be changed from the 92's set-up.

'ITALIAN' FRONT BUT GERMAN ENGINE

Externally there was a stylish new frontal 'face' to the car, an 'Italian' front styled by Sixten Sason after yet another sweep through the design houses and motor shows of Northern Italy. Inspired by Turinese style (and perhaps a touch of the later Voisin Coupé), Sason drew up a new frontal aspect and grille design inspired by an Alfa Romeo or Lancia shape, flanked by chrome bars and twin headlamps that really gave the car a new presence, a much stronger image. It was not a copy, but a new look with hints of other influences. This was perhaps less organic in design terms than the 92's frontal design, but it gave the car a level of international elegance and sophistication that many admired.

The addition of chrome strips over each wheel arch and more elaborate bumpers might today be considered as 'bling', but in 1955 it brought a touch of brightness in contrast to post-war European austerity design.

The styling panache was somewhat diluted when Saab added the 'Klimator' winter heating device to its car. This required a radiator blind that ruined the style of the elegant grille, but it did allow warmth to be quickly generated for the engine and heater. The price of the 93 at launch was, due to a new tax regime and rising manufacturing costs, more than Skr8,000.

Of great note was the fact that, suddenly, Saab's car no longer had a transverse-mounted engine. It retained front-wheel drive, but lurking under the bonnet was the new 3-cylinder, now longitudinally mounted. The reason for the change was that DKW, the company that had inspired the 92's engine design, had bounced back with a pretty little two-door car powered by an efficient and torquey 3-cylinder engine. Suddenly, having set a trend, Saab had competition from the company it had admired in 1945.

Despite changes, the 93 retained the highly aerodynamic form of the 92 at the rear. Note the heavier-gauge bumpers.

Saab hit back with its own new, larger engine, but one that would not lie across the engine bay. The basic design principle remained the same: the valve-less 2-stroke cycle with oil added to the combustive mix at 3 or 4 per cent. The engine, based on an original design by Dr-Ing Hans Müller, was flexible and revvy – spinning and wailing up to 38bhp at 5,000rpm. Best of all, the torque figure exceeded the horsepower figure by creating 52lb/ft of torque at 2,700rpm. Mounted at a 30-degree inclined angle, with a radiator providing water cooling placed at the bulkhead, the new alloy-headed, iron block motor actually had a smaller cubic capacity at 748cc than Saab's earlier 764cc engine, but more bhp and more torque.

Saab spent money on a three-bearing, single-row crank with expensive roller-bearings for each con-rod. By avoiding a forged or cast construction, the shaft could be built from machined parts. This was exquisite engineering. No wonder the little 3-cylinder was (almost) unburstable from the crank/con-rod standpoint. Josef Eklund was the lead man alongside Ljungström in developing the new 3-cylinder engine and the 93's new gearbox. Among the small team of less than twenty engineers working on the 93 was Dick Ohlsson.

Key design highlights to the engine included:

- Iron cylinder block and upper crankcase cast in one piece
- 3-cylinder head of light alloy material
- Valve-less construction
- Three-bearing crankshaft counterbalanced
- Carburettor used pre-warmed air
- Carefully designed pistons and cylinders improved combustion 'swirl' process
- Special attention paid to exhaust/manifold flow and pressures to minimize losses
- Engine has only seven main moving components: one crankshaft, three connecting rods, three pistons

Müller's engine was a development of ideas he had been working on for some time. It may even have had a pre-war origin in a scheme with Heinkel lineage for possible use in a scooter or micro-car. First Müller and then Saab further refined it, adding an anti-vibration shaft as well as care-

GP866 well deserved its prime position in Erik Carlsson's Saab memorial convoy.

fully designed block construction to reduce harshness and vibration. Working with Ljungström, who designed the new ZF-built gearbox, the first 3,000 engines were built under contract in Stuttgart by Ernst Heinkel's company, which was itself once an aircraft maker, because there were production capacity issues in Sweden.[15]

Saab's new engine factory in Volvo territory at Gothenburg would soon produce the new engine. With its radiator unusually mounted behind the engine at the bulkhead, a fan with a long driveshaft was needed to create engine bay airflow into the radiator. Saab owners soon decided that this was an 'overhead fanshaft'. A water pump and thermostat were also fitted for the first time.

Saab spent money on developing the suspension. The 93 now boasted front coil springs, hydraulic telescopic dampers and some clever locating arms where unequal-length wishbones with coils mounted above them let the driveshaft and CV joints function.

At the rear the torsion bar had gone, replaced by a cleverly located rigid U-type axle with rubber mounts and short trailing arm levers and coil spring function. All this meant that the handling and ride quality in terms of spring and damper rates, and the resulting roll and rebound characteristics, were transformed to a new level of comfort. A tighter turning circle with better 'feel' through the steering was also evident.

Other major improvements included:

- 12 volt electrics
- Better heating and ventilation
- Tubeless tyres
- One-piece chrome bumpers
- New seats with foam rubber cushioning
- New gearbox design with clutchless shifting on 1st and 2nd gears, and revised freewheel device
- Interior camping bed conversion kit marketed as 'bedable'
- Interior cargo box liner for rear seat
- Safety fuel tank between rear wheels

■ 93: ESSENTIAL SAAB

Bruce Turk's US specification 93. The addition of chrome, whitewall tyres and extra kit captured the attention of new customers despite its 3-cylinder engine. B. TURK

BELOW: **This very rare image shows off the 93 on white-wall tyres and with the bonnet/hood removed for easy access. Saab's brochure illustration department was always a centre of excellence.**

BEHIND THE WHEEL

The new gearbox had a short length, achieved by the gear drive passing through just two gearwheels on the main shaft. For the 1957 model year, the 93 with its very comfortable and strongly framed new front seats was fitted with two-point safety belts as standard, a major innovation in the marketplace. Three-point (Nils Bohlin-type) belts would soon follow.

Saab now had a class act of a car with real buyer 'showroom appeal'. Throw in some chrome strips, whitewall tyres and a cigarette lighter, and the little car was all the more acceptable as an alternative to home-grown metal in Detroit, New York, Los Angeles and, significantly, on the USA's eastern seaboard.

The little twin-pot 92 had been a hard-riding, hard-charging car that might be described as a high-speed sledge when driven on mud, ice and snow. The steering was direct but a touch ponderous in turning circle, the suspension firm and the ground clearance very good. To say the least, with all that weight up front and the hard suspension, the 92 understeered, to put it mildly. Yet the 92 was a great driver's car. Saab soon added a few items to make life more palatable in the 'basic' Swedish market vehicle: but there were areas for improvement, hence the 92B and then the 93.

You step 'into' the 93 rather than sitting upon it, but more luxurious trim in the cabin allied to a brighter late 1950s colour palette evoked a less austere invitation to drive. Yet floor-hinged pedals still evoke a 'classic' feeling.

The engine fires up with a startling burst even when cold, and the new torque figure, which exceeded the horsepower figure by creating 52lb/ft of torque at just over 2,000rpm, is immediately obvious. The torque figure of the three-pot was greater than its hp figure.

You have to learn the 93's 2-stroke technique, and frankly the later four-speed gearbox car is easier to live with. But leap in, rev up, power away and steer – that is the stuff of the Saab sensation and the technique of the 93: use the engine, its revs and the gears, and the car comes alive. Ignore the clock, go for the power and use your left-foot braking technique. The little Saab is just pure joy.

There is a Saab 'stroker' technique to be learned in driving it, but once mastered this is a car of wonderful ability, a car with soul and a sense of fun that really does make you smile. Here was driving finesse, and with the correct technique this car was surprisingly fast. The Saab had such character.

Classic Saab advertising: a well-known and much loved archive shot of the 93.

Pale blue looked great on the 93, as this Saab legacy image shows.

93: ESSENTIAL SAAB

Erik Carlsson had a hand in the 93's dynamic development. For his rally 93s he had a 1½ spring section removed from each unit, which lowered the car, reduced roll and understeer and made it faster. It was Erik's secret weapon that few people knew about for some time. He also removed the anti-roll bar from his later 93 and 96 rally cars. This made them more reactive, 'twitchier' and easier to 'flick', but you had to know what you were doing, which Erik surely did. The uninitiated might get caught out by 'snap' handling reactions in a car without an anti-roll bar and riding on cut-down springs.

Carl-Magnus Skogh joined the Saab Competition Department in the mid-1950s as Erik Carlsson's co-driver, and together they won the 1956 1000 Lakes Rally. Skogh would go on to rally fame for Saab before he moved to a great rally career with Volvo and its 4-stroke engines in the 120-series.

SAX-O-MAT

Also for 1957 came the Saxomat (actually branded and badged as Sax-O-Mat) automatic clutch as an option. This Fichtel & Sachs device was an early form of mechanically controlled semi-automatic gearbox and had been designed in Germany and used in the Borgward Isabell, Hansa 1500, Auto Union 1000, Ford Taunus, Trabant and Wartburg, and also in the Lancia Flaminia and Fiat 1800. Opel used the device in its car under the 'Olymat' name. A derivative of the mechanism, with a revised gear-change solenoid-activated system, found its way into the NSU Ro 80. Porsche reinvented the idea as the 'Sportomatic' for the 911 and, despite all expectations, it worked quite well.

Saab deployed the gear change in the 93, but intriguingly re-launched an electronic version of it in the 1994 Sensonic-equipped new generation 900 model.

The Sax-O-Mat 93 had no clutch pedal: instead a servo clutch and a centrifugal clutch operated respectively to activate and then disengage the gears via a weighted mechanism and a vacuum valve.

Even though many cars of the 1950s were equipped with four-speed gearboxes, Saab stayed loyal to its tough three-speed gearbox. Somehow with the engine's flexible torque and pulling ability, which now gave a top speed of 118km/h (70mph) and a 0–60mph time of just under twenty seconds, this meant that only having three gears was not the handicap one might have expected. Overtaking performance and times through the gears were excellent, the car could be stoked along with great verve even in a Swedish winter when Saab's aircraft-style carburettor heating was needed (this device could be deactivated for the summer).

If all these changes were not enough, Saab then tweaked the 93 even further for 1958, creating a 93B. Sason added more chrome, a one-piece front windscreen with bright trim, and a new windscreen wiper design and sweep pattern. The old-fashioned external turn indicators on the door pillars were also deleted and new indicator lamps fitted front

Brighter blue seen in recent years in Sweden. Imagine still driving about in this. In the author's opinion, this blue 93 is the tops.
R. MORLEY

Another wonderful Saab legacy image from the company archive, complete with the Afghan hounds that kept appearing in Saab adverts. Note the twin side-stripes, lamps and wheel embellishers.

and rear. From a mechanical standpoint, the oil-to-fuel ratio for the combustion chamber was reduced from 4 per cent to 3 per cent. In the cabin Saab raised the rear seat base (children had complained that they could not see out due to the low seat height). Clearly this was a car company that listened to its customers.

EKLUND, THE 'GURU'

The only cloud on the horizon was not the fault of Saab, its head of production Svante Simonsson, Ljungström himself, Müller the engine designer or Saab's expert engine man Josef Eklund; the issue lay in the concept of the 2-stroke 3-cylinder engine, which in the course of its combustion and cycle action exposed the internal engine surfaces to bore and liner wear, particularly if left standing or if badly lubricated.

Josef Eklund was Saab's man on the spot in Germany to manage the development and production of the new engines in Stuttgart and then back in Sweden. Eklund had grown up next to heavy engineering around his father's gravel and transport business and his first post-war employment was at the famous Albin engineering company after he graduated from the Gothenburg Institute of Technology. He joined Saab in November 1953 as a gearbox designer and would rise to become leader of the engine development laboratory, a department that included his fellow engine man Olle Lindkvist. Paul Broman was the department's foreman and the 1950s team included Alvar Andersson, Arne Gustavsson, 'Lille Bengt' Törnqvist, Bengt Ullström, Tore Jonsson, Dick Ohlsson and Olle Johansson, who became a test engineer and had a penchant for American V12 engines. Åke Järkvik also joined the engine lab team during this early period.

Eklund was, like Ljungström, a yachtsman and meticulous. He is a bit of an unsung hero to those outside the Saab 'circle', yet was a vital figure in the success of the Saab 93 and 93 2-stroke. Eklund had to re-engineer parts of Müller's engine design due to excess pin and bearing wear. There were problems to solve as the 3-cylinder engine's development had not been without problems, and the development of a new gearbox would require solving engineering challenges related to vibration, wear and noise. One example of Eklund's skill during this development period was the creation of a clever internal oil feed for the gearbox via hollow shafts.[16]

New tooling and steel presses were needed as production expanded and the car was developed. Bengt Åkerlind was the plant production manager who oversaw these elements of the factory's expansion. Many cast housings or casings, such as that of the gearbox, were manufactured by German companies.

Curiously, a common shaft off the engine drove the generator and the water pump, today referred to by some American 2-stroke restorers as a 'waternator'.

Despite the new 3-cylinder engine's behavioural foibles, which were less likely to become apparent on engines used on a daily basis, the 93 was a massive success and sales fig-

SAAB 93 TECHNICAL SPECIFICATION

Introduced 1 December 1955 alongside 92B run-out model

Engine	Longitudinally mounted 3-cylinder, 2-stroke valveless engine
Cooling	Water cooled with pump circulation
Bore x stroke	66 x 72.9mm
Capacity	748cc
Compression ratio	7.3:1
Maximum power	33bhp (24kW) at 5,000rpm
Maximum torque	7kg m (68Nm) at 3,000rpm
Carburettor	Solex 40 AI; other types also used, notably Amal on the GT750
Fuel	Electric fuel-pump feed
Transmission	Front-wheel drive with single dry-plate clutch; column shift 3-speed gearbox with freewheel and synchromesh on top two gears
Suspension	Coil springs and hydraulic shock absorbers on all 4 wheels with rigid rear axle; independent front suspension
Steering	Rack and pinion with 5.5m radius
Wheels and tyres	15-inch wheels
Brakes	Hydraulic drum brakes all round
Electrics	12 volts with 33Ah battery capacity
Bodyshell	Stressed skin monocoque two-door with reinforcements as per Saab 92. C_d 0.35
Dimensions	
Wheelbase	2,488mm (97.95in)
Length	4,010mm (157.87in)
Width	1,570mm (61.81in)
Height	1,470mm (57.87in)
Weight (net)	787kg (1,735lb)
Price in Sweden in 1956	Skr7,500

The Le Mans Classic historic Saab entry 93 in all its glory. R. GUNN

Chris Partington was here! The Le Mans Classic car's 2-stroke as tweaked. R. GUNN

ures shot through the roof: more than 13,969 were sold in 1958 alone and Saab sold its 50,000th car in 1958. In 1959 17,778 Saab 93s were sold. Torsten Nothin, an original Saab chairman, retired in 1958 and was replaced by Erik Boheman. Royal patronage continued with Prince Bertil of Sweden ordering a 93 to replace his 92, and later a Saab 93 750 Granturismo in the national colours of yellow and blue.

750 GT

In April 1958 Saab surprised the motoring press and the market by showing a sporty version of the 93B. This was a car with twin carburettors, 50bhp and a special tuning kit option to raise output to a heady 57bhp SAE, or a touch less at 55bhp when expressed as DIN. There were extra driving lights, sports stripes and an interior with padded seats that could be adjusted to more than a dozen settings. A classy steering wheel with three alloy spokes and wood rim looked the part, as did the fitting of a Halda Speedpilot timing chronograph device on the dashboard. Two paired chrome stripes were added to each side of the car, making it look longer. Grippy but soft Pirelli Cinturato radial tyres were fitted as standard; later a switch was made to longer-lasting Dunlop SP tyres. Before long Saab was also offering the rather less crucial fitment of chromed hubcaps.

The GT had the 'Carlsson-spec' preferred twin-fuel pumps as well as twin Solex carburettors (some owners fitted the Amal type), a 9:1 compression ratio, and larger brakes discs were also fitted. Saab sold more than 500 GT750s in its vital American market.

Just like the standard 93, the GT750 needed to be stirred along and changing gear at high revs required a technique to be learned; the unburstable little engine had to be kept revved up beyond 4,000rpm in order to keep its pace going. Once mastered, this high revving method of driving meant that the Saab could keep up with larger engined and much more powerful cars. The resulting sound and noise level were best described as unique.

What caused this new model to appear? The answer lay in the fact that Saab had begun to build its profile in the USA and Great Britain. The GT750 and the later GT850 were designed to raise the cars' abilities alongside the company's marketing profile. Saab were learning. Furthermore, by now Saab had a massive profile in the world of rallying, overseen by Rolf Mellde, and the name of Erik Carlsson was becoming legend. The Granturisimo 750 was a great way of marketing Saab and all it stood for.

Rallying was to be the key. Rolf Mellde, winner of the 1952 Swedish rally championship in his 92, was despatched across the Atlantic to oversee a competition campaign that delivered strong results and huge publicity gains. Entering the Great American Mountain Rally in thick November snows on the eastern seaboard, a 93 driven by Bob Wehman and

93: ESSENTIAL SAAB

Louis Braun won the three-day rally. Mellde was sixth and another 93 was seventh. The 93s won their class and the team award. The abilities of the 93 and the engineering within it were proven to an American public sceptical of small European cars, let alone ones with 2-stroke engines. Saab as a brand in the USA was born and 250 examples of the 93 would be quickly sold in America off the back of such a profile.

The Granturisimo 750 sold 605 examples, of which 546 were exported to the newly expanding American market, where Saab had now taken control of imports and set Ralph Millet up to head the company. The 750 GT, or the 'Granturismo 750' as it became known, was created to frame Saab's image as it stormed to success in America and sales of Saab 93s increased off the back of its reputation.

Saab were quick to react and readied a revised version of the 93 for the dawn of a new decade. After minor trim and specification changes in the 1959 model year, the 1960 model year Saab 93F was announced on 7 October 1959 in the Hotel Palace, Stockholm. This car had front hinged doors at last (hence the 'F' for Front), and a smartened-up interior with (one) headrest and new door-mounted armrests. There was even more exterior chrome seen as rear wheel arch splash guards. The cooling system capacity was increased. The ultimate version of the car was the 93F GT 750 'Super', which first appeared as early as April 1958 at the New York Motor Show – which meant it was around far earlier than many realize.

The 93F itself was a huge success, but it was perhaps an interim event, buying Saab some time while behind the scenes it prepared the Saab 96 as a new car, not just a facelift. The GT 750 was something more and offered 50bhp (SAE)/45bhp (DIN). A special tuning kit soon increased that to 57bhp or 55bhp (DIN).

The 93 GT 750 was perhaps a stopgap, but it was to be reincarnated in 1961 in the new Saab 96 bodyshell with the 748cc '750' engine. Curiously, the 96 GT 750 had the new bodyshell but retained the interior and trim of the 93 GT 750, including the minimalist rear seat. A four-speed gearbox helped stoke the stroker along. The Halda Speedpilot, seat belts and extra lamps were all still fitted to the sports version of the Saab.

SPORT 850

By February 1962 the GT 750 had morphed into the new 'Saab Sport', complete with badging that stated such. This car had the triple-carburettor 841cc or '850' engine with oil injection via a separate oil tank of 3 litres capacity. The four-speed gearbox, new trims and a wonderful array of round dials across the facia made the Super Sport 850 something special. Yet by 1963 penny-pinchers at Saab had substituted a modified 'stock' 96 facia (but with two round dials) and deleted the Speedpilot device: confusingly, the Saab Sport was the 'GT 850' only in the American market.

The later GT 850 or Super Sport, however, really did bring changes to the car's sporting character. The GT 850s were touching 60bhp. All that was needed was

The US specification 93. Princess Beatrix of the Netherlands drove a similar-looking car around Amsterdam.

773 XUR at rest. The 93 needed very little embellishment.

Saab's new dual circuit braking sytem (announced in 1964). The Super Sport/GT 850 also evolved with the new long-nose styling of 1966. To further confuse things, the Saab Sport/GT 850 became the 'Monte Carlo' in many markets, notably in America. By this time the oil-mix in the combustion prcess was down to 1.5 per cent from 3 per cent.

Even more model-confusion became apparent when the US and Swiss markets received a 96 and a 95 with the 'Special' tag added to define their specifications. These had the separately lubricated engine of the Monte Carlo but without the sporting trim.

A few front-hinged-door-type sporting Saabs were reputedly made. In the main the rear-hinged door 93 to 96 series, in the forms of the GT 750, GT 850 and Monte Carlo, offer us rare and very special versions of the standard car. Add in the short-lived 96 V4 Monte Carlo and you have a range of Saabs that were appealing then and even more appealing now: each type has its followers. It ahould be noted that the 96 V4 Monte Carlo was a trim-derivatve not a tuned-engine derivative in the manner of its GT-series predecessors.[17]

The noted Saab GT-series guru, driver and owner Bruce Turk, reminds us that the GT-series 750 and 850 cars were built in randomly chosen batches on the production line and therefore their chassis numbers (or 'VIN') have little or no pattern or indicative basis. Bruce also advises that Saab held batches on site for a bit, so the year of registration may not necessarily match the year of build.[18]

DENMARK

The story of Saab's exports took a turn closer to home in Denmark. Saab had exported cars to Denmark very early with a handful of 92s sold from 1950 onwards. Between 1957 and 1963, however, Saab was shipping semi-knocked-down (SKD) cars the short distance to Denmark by trailer and then by special train wagons, for final completion and assembly. These were essentially fully trimmed, painted, boxed 'kits' of cars that could be put together without the need for massive factory infrastructure.

For the Danes, the attraction of building cars on home soil would be 10 per cent lower purchase tax and cheaper labour rates. The Saab car could be sold for a good 'local' price in Denmark. After selling 29,711 Swedish-built cars in Denmark in the previous year alone, during the second half of 1957 Saab changed its general agent in Denmark to a company named Automobilforretningen ICI A/S, established in the Copenhagen suburb of Glostrup.

By February 1958, after a pre-trial run of one car in December 1957, the first fully painted SKD car 'kits' were arriving on a regular schedule from Trollhättan to be built up in Denmark. The only significant specification difference was the use of French, Kleber tyres.

Twenty-one people were employed and at the height of operation fifteen cars a day could be produced. Only 140 cars were produced in the first year, however, due to a series of local tax and regulatory issues, but by 1959 Saab Denmark had made 740 cars. In 1962 the Glostrup plant pro-

Epic Saab badging: 'Saab GranTurismo 750'.

Saab made much of its sporting success and 'GranTurismo' branding. This is from an original Saab advertisement.

Another view of the Saab in an America setting. Note the extra bonnet vents – chromed up and looking great.
B. TURK

93: ESSENTIAL SAAB

In the end days of Saab, two of its luminaries drove restored 93s in historic events to gain profile. Both cars were of earlier split-screen type.

duced 3,776 cars, mostly 96s with some 95s. Advantageous tax rules in Denmark also helped create the Saab 95 van, because blanking out the windows of the estate car made it subject to less tax. So was born the rare 95 panel van, built exclusively in Denmark.

By 1963 Saab had sent more 'cars' to Denmark, albeit as kits, than Saab had exported to the USA. Denmark was Saab's nearest yet biggest export market. At one stage in 1963 Danish-built Saabs were being sent back to Sweden for sale: a total of 995 entered the Swedish marketplace after storage near Skåne in barns and greenhouses!

Yet the story ended abruptly. Tax changes for 1963, the rise of the European Free Trade Area (EFTA) and another new Saab plant in Mechelen, Belgium, where locally welded completely-knocked-down (CKD) cars were created, meant that the advantages of re-constructing Saabs in Denmark disappeared overnight. The last batch of 1,250 cars was sent to Glostrup between January and June 1963. In total 9,630 SKD Saabs were assembled in Denmark between 1958 and 1963.

Making Saabs in Denmark ceased, just as making Citroëns at Slough, close to Saab GB's headquarters, would also end. Saab had CKD agreements in Belgium with Brondeel and IMA. The main Belgian plant was IMA's in Mechelen, where Saab made 276 of the 93 model and 2,348 of the 96 model. In the 1970s a further manufacturing agreement with IMA at Mechelen resulted in 1,500 Saab 99s from SKD kits and 23,321 cars as CKD, giving a total of 24,821 Belgian-built Saab 99s.

In 1962 Saab also entered into a two-year SKD agreement with Chrysler at their factory in Rotterdam, where 570 Saab 96s were locally produced for the important Dutch market.

The 92, 93, 95 and 96 proved a huge hit in the American market and a great alternative to the VW Beetle. The sight of Saab 96s in the Manhattan traffic became a normal event. Conditions on the eastern seaboard, with cold winters and twisting roads like rally tracks, were ideal for fostering the legend of these early Saabs. The handful of 92s imported in the early 1950s really had sown the seeds of something bigger. Way out west, away from Saab's eastern enclave, Saab 'strokers' were buzzing around California.

SAAB 93 PRODUCTION FIGURES, 1955–60

Year	Production
1955	457
1956	5,640
1957	9,847
1958	13,968
1959	17,778
1960	5,041

Saab frontal design from the 93 to 96.

Inside Chris Hull's two-stroke red rasper – that drilled-spoke steering wheel is rather special.

Chris Hull's stunning 93 split-screen seen at Goodwood – as invited. Note the unusual windscreen wipers. Well-known Saabist Chris Hull has owned many classic Saabs and currently has a pair of 93s. The other one is black.

MELLDE'S 'MONSTER'

Mellde, forever thinking ahead, had the V4 project to keep him busy in the late 1950s. Yet he also wanted to know if the concept of front-wheel drive could handle higher power. There was also the possibility of attempting to get into the world record books for engines with smaller outputs. In the late 1920s Alvis of England had built about 150 front-wheel-drive cars, some of which were fitted with a supercharger and raced at Le Mans. Alvis had also patented the idea of pairing two engines together and using a single output driveshaft. Was this possibly where Mellde took his inspiration from?

The problem of transferring power to the front wheels via short, high-revving driveshafts of equal or unequal length,

93: ESSENTIAL SAAB

ABOVE AND BELOW: **Rolf Mellde's amazing six-pot 93 'Monster'.**

101

and the resultant need to control torque, was not the only problem. A large engine meant more weight over the front wheels, which would lead to a greater dynamic understeer effect. Mellde tried to reduce the weight of the car, even fitting a lightweight resin-plastic bonnet held in place by leather straps.

Mellde was now working with a few members of his engine team, which by now included Hugo Bock, Sigvard Gustafsson, Olle Johansson and Kjell Knutsson, who was made lead performance engineer and was responsible for Erik Carlsson's rally car engines. In 1959 Mellde took a standard red 93 and began tinkering with the engine. Could he join two Saab 3-cylinder motors together? How would the gearbox accept its drive source? Some form of complex gear transfer mechanism was needed. Josef Eklund was in on the project with a handful of others including Ingvar Andersson, who worked with Kjell Knutsson. According to Eklund, it was Knutsson who was the main hands-on mechanical engineer behind the resultant 'Monster'.

Mellde had the idea of joining two 3-cylinder engines together in terms not of actual engine blocks, but in terms of a shared power transfer mechanism. The two 3-cylinder units were to be coupled via a spiral-cut conical bevel gear connecting device, a form of inertia coupling. The combined output of the two engines would be 138bhp (103kW). This would give a weight ratio in a Saab 93 of 7.7kg per hp. This engine, with its two 3-cylinder blocks mounted together, was placed transversely across the engine bay to become the world's first transverse straight-six engine. It also had two distributors and an intriguing and complex gearbox and clutch amalgamation. The over-thick sill panels were drilled out with many large circular holes to reduce weight (and also strength).

The issues of vibration, revolving torque forces, conical driveshafts, opposing engine torques and the complex engine bay mountings needed to tie down the structures were significant issues that would require internal Saab funding to solve. Sychronizing the two throttles was no easy task as they had to be closely matched, and the gearbox input shaft speeds would also need reducing to avoid over-revving and consequent destruction.

Test drivers of the converted, red 93 'Monster' were Sven Olsson, Carl-Magnus Skogh and Rolf Ebefors. Ebefors went on to be a tuner for the competition department and in 2010 hepled restore the original Mille Miglia 93 at the Saab museum prior to its run in a 2011 Mille Miglia re-enactment.

The Monster was tested at Såtenäs airfield and achieved straight line speeds of up to 198km/h (123mph), with one reputed run of more than 200km/h. Sadly neither run (the fastest then ever achieved in an engine of such capacity) was officially recorded to the strict FIA world record rules, and transmission failure ended the mandatory second or return run required by the record rulebook.

The Monster was further tested at the Gelleråsen race circuit in Karlskoga. Massive understeer and strong torque steer were evident on the twists of the circuit. In the end it was the transfer of power from two engines into a single gearbox that proved the Monster's undoing: the gearbox transfer device broke and ended the experiment. Nonetheless, Saab's engine design team had learned a great deal about high-power, front-wheel-drive applications.[19]

Even by 1959 the little Saab had made its international mark yet again. Next the 93 would turn into the 96, but before the new body of the 96 came to the market Saab pulled another surprise out of its toolkit: the Saab estate car as the 95. First marketed in 1959 as a two-tone beauty, the estate model was the first real departure from the origins, toolings and skeleton of the 92 and 93.

SAAB 93 MODEL RANGE DEVELOPMENT

1955 New model Saab 93 announced in December 1955, but with 92B base model production to continue at order of Tryggve Holm, Saab's CEO.
First 93 chassis number 25001

1956 Five colours for 92B and trim upgrades from 93 fitted, notably bumpers. Last 92B cars built very late 1956 into early 1957 to a total of 20,128.
The new 93 'Italian front' model becomes defining Saab car with new frontal styling, major revisions to specifications with new 3-cylinder engine: also adds new interior, gearbox and coil-sprung suspension.

1957 93 with revised 12-volt electrical system. Two-point safety belts fitted at front as standard equipment and export market option. Sax-O-Mat automatic centrifugal clutch system offered from Spring 1957.

1958 93B announced for 1958 model year in late 1957 to lead Saab line-up. Eleven major modifications to the 93 specification, including new larger and curved one-piece windscreen, new indicators, self-mixing fuel dose. GT750 GranTurismo announced in New York to complement early US sales. GT 750 defines new Saab competition potential in production car.

1959 93B in full global sales. Larger brakes, better seats and a new air filter appeared across 1959. 93, now defined as 93F, launched 7 October 1959. Saab 95 estate announced late 1959 for 1960 model year. Larger, new factory opens on Trollhättan site.
Saab takes over the dealerships AB Nyköpings Autofabrik (ANA).

1960 93F fully launched to include new front-hinged doors, larger engine cooling capacity, new colours and interior trims. GT750 increases export sales and is soon set to continue in new 96 bodyshell.
Saab 96 2-stroke announced for 1960 but is delayed. 93F continues for some months until 96 takes over completely.
Total production of all 93 types reaches 52,731 cars at termination of production with 20,272 exported. Sales by model: 93 (11,759); 93B (29,830); 93F (11,142).

The 93 in profile.

CHAPTER FIVE

95: ESTATE CAR SAAB

Volvo had marketed its first estate car in the Duett. German and British carmakers were starting to produce estate cars, or estate car conversions of vans. Americans also hankered after such a car as the 'shooting break', while, just to confuse things, the French called an estate car a 'Brake'. In northern Europe the term 'Combi' or 'Kombi' would become familiar for an estate car. Curiously, the closest competition to a Saab estate car in 1959 was the DKW 'Universal' estate car.

Saab was still in some sense a smaller brand on the world's stage in 1955, whereas DKW had a high profile. While Saab would expand and endure, however, DKW would disappear, like other great German car names such as Adler, Lloyd and Wanderer.

Saab had designed its new car for the 1960s, the 96 model, as an updated and reshaped 93, but it was encountering delays. Several components, however, were ready and waiting by late 1958. A new 841cc engine and a four-speed gearbox had been planned and tooled up. Front-hinged doors, designed for the 96, were brought prematurely to the 93 to keep it going until the truly revised 96 was ready. There were also other revised and improved items ready on the shelf, so Saab's design team thought, why not use them?

Many customers, both in Sweden and abroad, had been asking for more carrying capacity, a bigger rear seat and a larger boot. The ability to carry cargo and people was vital in rural communities and to growing families. Saab gathered

The famous early Saab 95 image of 1959. Note the chrome trims on pillars and very effective two-tone paint livery.

95: ESTATE CAR SAAB

Well-known Saab enthusiast Ian Meakin in his delightful 95, seen in 'battleship' grey.

together all its inventory of unused parts and also those new or revised mechanical items. Sixten Sason put his design skills to work and very quickly Saab had a new model, a proper estate car or wagon with family appeal. It was also popular with farmers and tradesmen, spawning a rare panelled van variant. So was born the Saab 95 'estate' car. The Saab numbering system following on from the still-born Saab 94, otherwise called the Sonett, gave us the 95.

The 95 was trialled in March 1959 with twenty pre-production cars released and the model was formally announced in May 1959. It did not enter production until late September as the 1960 model year car, yet by December 1959 only fifty-five cars had been built. The early cars featured a two-tone blue and white paint scheme designed by Sason to make the most of the car's long side panels and Kamm back rear-end. These first few 95s had rear-hung front doors. The lovely chrome trims on the roof pillars and wings were sadly removed as early production ramped up. Expanding production rates saw the 95's early move from a specialist production line at Linköping to join its fellow Saabs at Trollhättan.

The longer, taller, slightly wider (at the rear) body and longer roof panel, allied to floorpan re-engineering and strengthening, resulted in an increase in weight over the standard 96 body of 101.6kg (224lb), roughly the weight of one extra burly Swedish male passenger. This affected the already lethargic through-the-gears times of the performance and speeds.

Of significance, the 95 was equipped with the new 841cc engine before it went into the 96. The 95 was also fitted with the first four-speed gearboxes and therefore had some technical novelty. The 95 was eventually fitted with a V4 engine in 1967.

Since the four-speed gearbox designed for the 96 first found its way into the 95, Erik Carlsson grabbed a 95 for the Monte Carlo Rally of 1961, finishing fourth in an estate car.

One change between the 95 and the 96 was a revision to the rear suspension design with the addition of a lever-arm type shock absorber of greater strength to take the higher body loadings. The tyre size on the 95 was also larger at 5.60 x 15. An extra 100mm was apparently hidden in the 95's wheelbase, a fact long argued over by Saab fans.

■ 95: ESTATE CAR SAAB

> **KEY SAAB 95 TOOLING AND SPECIFICATION FACTORS**
>
> - Use of Saab's new 841cc engine
> - First use of Saab's new four-speed gearbox
> - Revised rear suspension
> - Fold-out rear cargo space seats to create seven-seater
> - Revised rear floorpan tooling with resited fuel tank and spare-wheel well
> - 100mm increase in wheelbase
> - 500kg (1,100lb) payload ability on reinforced rear cabin floor
> - Increase in weight over 96 body of 101.6kg (224lb)
>
> Early cars suffered wake vortex dirt accumulation at the rear, so in 1961 an aerodynamic vane was added to the rear windscreen as an 'air-wiper'. This 'blade' cut the airflow and directed some over the blade and some under the blade down onto the rear end, which 'infilled' the low-pressure wake vortex and not only stopped dirt being sucked upwards, it also 'wiped' the window once a certain velocity was achieved. A rear wiper was also a quick fix for static cleaning before you drove off!
>
> V4 engines were fitted from the 96 V4 and 95 V4 joint launch in late 1966 for the 1967 model year. Later 1970s 95s were upgraded with the new Berglof-designed Saab safety seat from the 99, numerous cabin and trim upgrades, and '5mph' impact-type cellular bumpers from 1976, alongside many late 96 V4 trim items.
>
> A curious late-life tooling change was made in 1976 when the rear-facing foldaway seats in the 95's rear cargo cabin were deleted and the spare wheel moved to a position below the floor. This added more rear-seat legroom.[20]

Again, as with other Sason themes the car had a touch of the American styling trends, yet looked European at the same time. Some observers thought that from the rear the car had hints of the Chevrolet Nomad. There were vestigial 'fins' off the rear wing line and early prototypes carried chrome B and C pillar embellishments. This and the two-tone paint scheme were soon dropped and the 95 assumed a less transatlantic look as a result. The first pre-production cars also had the rear-opening doors that Saab was eager to delete from the 93 and the upcoming 96. What on earth was the point in persisting with them for the 95, argued the planners, so by the time main-series production began the 95 had front-hung doors and benefited from the forthcoming revised engine and gearbox, and an array of improved and refined trims and fittings.

An often ignored tooling change took place for 1961 when the corners of the rear side windows were reshaped in the steel pressing (and the resultant glazing) with curved radi-corners; this reduced stress and fatigue in the steel and made both of the twin side windows the same size, thus reducing build costs (on the very early 95s, the square-cornered rear side window had been slightly larger by a tiny amount).

The 95 could carry an excellent payload of 500kg (1,100lb) of cargo. This was a significant amount for a small estate car, enhancing its appeal as a commercial or farm vehicle and as a van. The strength of the body and the thick 18-gauge (1.214mm/0.0458in) steel of the roof panel allowed such a large payload ability. Saab used thick 14-gauge steel (2.03mm/0.089in) in parts of the chassis, which was certainly expensive engineering.

You could use your 95 as a van (and van-type versions with window blanks were first produced as commercial vehicles in Denmark), or turn your 95 into a camping car. Just three 95 vans were exported to the British market. Saab GB used a 95 van as a service vehicle. It is of note that that vehicle was fitted with right-hand drive and has recently been the subject of a significant recent restoration. The substantial way in which it differs from the standard 95 makes it the grail-Saab to purists and aficionados.

With its strong hull and floorpan reinforcements, allied to new rear side panels and roof pillars and its new top roof panel, the 95 was also a safe place, even for those in the back seats. A rear-facing seat suitable for two children was built in, with suitable box-section strengthening beams in the rear floor to protect the occupants of this rear-facing seat, yet the seat folded into the floor to revert to cargo area in a five- or two-seat 95 configuration. Here, early on, was an American-style seven-seater available for Europe. All but the later 95s offered this rear-cabin seat option.

The Saab 95 became a fondly regarded member of many car-buying families in Europe, the USA and Canada.

The 2-stroke 95 was slightly heavier, yet it was still a Saab. It did not feel as slow through the acceleration range as its

95: ESTATE CAR SAAB

Ian's car has some interesting on-board facilities to complement the round-dial dashboard.

A view of a later 95 interior with the strip-type speedometer.

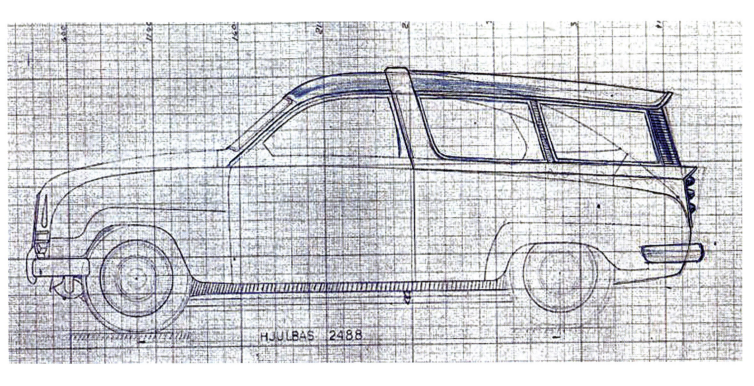

An early engineering drawing for the 95's revised bodyshell.

■ 95: ESTATE CAR SAAB

The classic Saab legacy shot of a chromed-up 95 from late 1959 for the 1960 model year.

Fast back or flat-back. The two differing bodies.

Side-by-side to compare just how different the estate looked from the standard two-door shell.

timings suggested: you could really hammer the new 3-cylinder engine and the more you revved it, the smoother it got! Top speed was just on 110km/h (70mph). Noise levels in the 95 cabin, however, were also a touch higher due to resonance in the cabin space. Like the 96, the 2-stroke could run on low-grade 82 octane petrol and had to have its oil mix correctly sorted. Slow driving in a lightly laden car might get the fuel consumption up to 8ltr/100km (35mpg), but in normal use, laden with family and kit or cargo, the consumption was less generous at around 9.9ltr/100km (27.8mpg). If you drove it like Erik Carlssson even less mpg and range was soon a consequence.

By 1964 the 95 had been upgraded to a more De Luxe offering with chrome wheel embellishers, the new Saab dual-circuit brakes and a new emblem to the rear. As with the 96 De Luxe that came along, the export markets had the most deliveries of the upgraded models. To some Swedes, the 95 was and should remain a spartan, austerity wagon, not a comfort-class cruiser.

By 1968 the 95, fitted with the new generic Saab 96/95 long nose design, was exported to the USA with a 95 V4C tag and some of the old fittings of the Monte Carlo model 96. Perhaps Saab had a big box of spares that needed using up, which would be typical of Trollhättan!

The 95's longer roof and Kamm back with a sharp rooftop separation point for the airflow aided the aerodynamics of the more boxy shape. The rear window, however, was in a turbulent void of air and Saab did not want to fit a rear wiper. Instead it designed a roof-mounted aerofoil wing or blade that redirected some of the airflow down onto the rear windscreen to effectively brush it clean with the power of the airflow's passage. This rooftop device was the 'air-wiper' that is now seen on many estate-type cars, but it was a Saab idea in 1960.

A very rare 95 from the late 1960s was the American specification car known as the 'Shrike': one version of its revised, detuned engine got as low as 816cc. The year 1968 was the last in which a 2-stroke was fitted in either a Saab 95 or 96. The V4 1.5-litre now ruled and by 1971 the V4 1.7-litre was being installed in the American specification export 95 and 96 only, although this was in a lower-compression tune. Rectangular headlamps were now fitted, except in the USA, which had round lamps in unique frames.

From August 1975 Saab built a batch of 95B models with the 1976 model year specification but without the detuned 1976-type engine. Then in the first days of 1976 it switched

Early 95s had the lovely grille that had come in with the 93, but not with the Saab emblem cast in as seen here. This one has been retrofitted.

to the new engine as standard fitting for the Swedish market only: Swedish 95s were detuned to 62bhp (46kW) to meet local emissions rules, but export market cars retained the 65bhp (48kW) rating. The 95L model tag was introduced in 1976 to identify De Luxe models.

Heated windows and new mirrors, colours, seats and other items were thrown at the 95 despite its age. Twin carburettors were now fitted, which reduced fuel burn by a paltry 5 per cent but did add a few more horsepower. Saab's abandonment of the potential 95 replacement meant it had little to offer in this market sector other than a well-specified 95 based on a car dating from the 1950s, yet one which remained safe, strong and, with the V4 engine, eminently capable.

In 1977 the 96 cars were given the new high-backed seats from the 99 model designed by Björn Berglof. In an odd move, Saab witheld these from fitment to the 95 for more

95: ESTATE CAR SAAB

SAAB 95 ESTATE PRODUCTION FIGURES, 1959–78

Year	Units	Year	Units
1959	55	1969	9,407
1960	1,634	1970	9,367
1961	3,182	1971	7,603
1962	3,377	1972	8,121
1963	4,475	1973	7,991
1964	4,380	1974	559
1965	8,290	1975	5,140
1966	7,243	1976	3,364
1967	7,223	1977	2,168
1968	11,478	1978	470

Another Saab legacy shot from the archive. Note the steel back to the rear passenger seat.

95: ESTATE CAR SAAB

This famous conversion looks like it could have come straight from Sason's pen. Simon Coleman's 95 'Ute' now wears more conventional paintwork, but it looked great in oily-rag hue.

than a year before making them standard 95 kit in late 1977. The addition of a twin-stage Solex carburettor was noticeable in 1977 models.

The 95 was removed from the Saab model line-up in 1978, two years before the final 96s were built and sold. The last 95 was manufactured on 23 February 1978. By this stage 110,527 examples of all types had been manufactured at Trollhättan (and intitially at Linköping) since the 95's very slow start in 1959. The 95's best year was in 1968, when 11,478 were built.

Only the Saab 98 concept car, a long-bodied, sloping tail 'combi wagon-back' prototype briefly proposed in 1974 by the Saab design centre, offered a hint at a replacement estate car. This Envall-designed device, originally known as project X-14, was not built beyond a few test-body cars and it would be more than two decades before Saab produced its next estate car. The sole survivor of the sadly terminated Saab 98 rests in the Saab Museum in the unlovely hue of Sienna Brown. Take a look at a later Audi 100 sports estate or any of the 'sports-back' or sports-hatch estates of the 1980s and you can see what an opportunity Saab threw away from a pioneering position. However, we have to admit that the Saab 99 three-door Combi Coupé (especially as a Turbo) was a much better car than a 98 V4 could ever have been facelifted into via the 98 project design.

SAABO

Saab also designed a delightful little caravan named the 'Saabo' for a launch in 1965. This was an attempt to produce a lightweight, modern twin-berth caravan to be towed by small cars, specifically (but not exclusively) the Saab 95. Moulded in resin plastic, aerodynamically chamfered with curved edges for less drag and fewer crosswind problems, weatherproof and insulated, the Saab caravan made its contemporary British and American caravan competitors look like the antediluvian, coachbuilt panelwork dinosaurs that they were.

95: ESTATE CAR SAAB

ABOVE: **An older 95 with a revised 95 in beige fitted with the 5mph impact-type bumpers.**

LEFT: **Detail in the design: the 95 rear lamp motifs.**

Saab kept the 2-stroke version of the 95 (and 96) on the market even after the V4 arrived, priced at just Skr560 less than the V4-powered model. A brand new 95 V4 cost Skr13,350, and surely only a hardened Saab enthusiast would still purchase the 2-stroke models – but Saab still marketed the 2-stroke in America.

As an example of the Saab development effect, in 1966 Saab sold 29,766 of the two-door 96 2-stroke and 7,243 of the estate version. In 1968 Saab sold 37,633 two-door 96 V4 models and 11,478 of the V4 estate. During 1968 only 28 2-stroke 96s were registered in Sweden, while a few American market 'strokers' lingered from 1967 into 1968.

The 96/95 2-stroke died at the end of 1968. The total number of Saab 95 estate cars built was 110,527.[21]

SAAB 95 MODEL RANGE DEVELOPMENT

1959   Early 95s had rear-hung front doors. 95s initially built at Linköping. Unique trims and rear side window treatment. 95 estate gets four-speed gearbox before 96 and is noteworthy in the Monte Carlo Rally in the hands of Erik Carlsson
First few 95s (only) with two-tone paint

1960   95 series fully launched 17 February 1960. Revised rear side-window trims

1961   Aerodynamic work on 95 estate leads to rear 'air-slicer' spoiler on roof. 95 production moves to Trollhättan

1962   New colours. Seat belts are standard fit

1963   New cast in-grille emblem. Minor trim changes include 'horn' ring steering wheel

1964   New diagonal-spilt system brakes: new rear badging, round-dial instruments

1965   Revised tail lights. US and Swiss markets see 95 'Special' badging and specification (including rev counter) and used the 55bhp engine from the Monte Carlo model

1966   New longer nose panels and revised grille

1967   95 V4 launched. Very rare US-market 'Shrike' 2-stroke editions in 95 models (also 96) with either the separate-oiler engine or the later pre-mix type continue. Shrike had lower hp rating at 42bhp after the original 55bhp 'Special' edition and its engine were discontinued

1968   Larger windscreen aperture. All 95 2-strokes discontinued

1969   US-legislation headlamps and trims fitted to US models. New safer, collapsible steering column

1970   Revised cabin trims and colours. All-black coloured dashboard-finish introduced. Finnish factory opens with Finnish-built 95s from chassis number 50600001

1971   Revised nose with rectangular headlamps (but not on US cars). 95s get side strips. 1.7-litre low-compression V4 engine for US market only due to emissions legislation

1972   Electrically heated front seats. New colours

1973   New colours and trims

1974   New black grille colour and revised badging

1975   Strengthened gearbox casing. Use of black trim on windscreen wipers

1976   '5mph' impact cellular-type bumpers fitted (from Saab 99). Retooled floorpan increases space in rear cabin and removes spare wheel from under rear seat to a new side locker. Year number plate raised in setting

1977   Black trim to side windows. L-model trim badge and specification. Electrically heated rear windscreen

1978   GL trim and badges. Revised 68bhp engine available, with 'V4 Super' badging. New front seats from 99/96 now fitted to 95. Last 95 built on 23 February 1978: a total of 110,527 Saab 95s had been built

AN OWNER'S VIEW: ALEX RANKIN

My ownership of a 95 started when I placed a factory order for a new generation 900 in 1996. The main reason I ordered a Saab was its good safety record and quality of build. So, having started my Saab owning journey with a new and up-to-date car, a decade later I found myself looking to the past and bought several first-generation 900s, each time adding to my collection. It wasn't long before I began to get interested in the original Saab 2-stroke, particularly the short-nose early cars. I didn't want a project, I wanted something good to go, something that could be used as soon as I bought it. My ideal car was to be a Saab 96, a car from the early 1960s with the 849cc 3-cylinder engine. I soon realized that finding one was going to be a challenge as few if any seemed to come up for sale. Then, while pursuing the Internet one evening, a 95 estate caught my eye in what I think is one of the best colours: white. It was one of the last short-nose cars from 1964, which also had my preferred round-dial facia design.

It was, however, left-hand drive, but to be honest, in my mind this was a bonus, because it meant it was an actual Swedish car, a car that had travelled most of its miles on Swedish roads and had been owned by real Swedes, a perfect combination.

The first thing that struck me was how easy it was to drive, and how willing the engine was to rev. It really seemed to love full throttle and the noise was sublime, there is nothing on earth like it! The handling was also far better than I expected, and the free-wheel just added to the enjoyment, as gear changes were just a matter of lifting my foot off the throttle, flicking the tiny column gear stick and planting my foot hard down again. The seats at first glance looked really small and uncomfortable, but I quickly found the opposite; they are actually very comfortable indeed, and of course the 95 is a full seven-seat car, as it has a 'dickie' seat cleverly concealed in the boot floor that simply lifts into place. I'd owned the car for about three years, and really couldn't fault it, even though it still had the original drum brakes on the front; I just adjusted my distance from the car in front and paid very close attention to the road ahead to anticipate any need for sudden braking. I was caught out once and had to do an emergency stop. Surprisingly the car pulled up quite quickly with no real drama.

The 95 is a great car to drive and really communicates to the driver. I think it is a very 'connected' car and the original engineers certainly succeeded in their remit.

Although I'd originally wanted a 96 saloon I found the estate quite a handy car, regularly making trips to the DIY store or garden centre. The load space was exceptional for such a small car and the suspension seemed to be unfazed by the extra weight; the performance really wasn't affected that much. I loved my three years as a 2-stroke owner, but it's a car that needs to be used on a very regular basis. Sitting idle doesn't do the 2-stroke engine any favours. I was constantly worried about corrosion forming in the bores and possibly on the crank and con-rods (being a 2-stroke there is no separate engine oil function), which may or may not be true, so I reluctantly sold it to a man from Belgium, where I believe prices are higher: he obviously thought my UK car to be a bit of a bargain.

95: ESTATE CAR SAAB

Alex Rankin's ex-Tony Grestock 95 was rare in its white hue and totally classic look.

A 95 V4 in white looking the part with chrome/steel bumpers.

The Boffey-owned 95 in a classic Saab paint hue. Note the enlarged bumper over-riders for the model year specification.

Saab 95 in classic profile displaying the sharp top edge to the end of the roof.

95: ESTATE CAR SAAB

A V4 at rest. Note the stiffening and crush ribs in the front wing inner pressing – typical Saab design care.

Extra rear seats and footwell reinforcement on show.

Adding the 'air-wiper' aerofoil to the trailing edge of the 95's roof really did keep the rear end clean.

117

■ 95: ESTATE CAR SAAB

Precious cargo, but Saab beefed up the rear end to protect these passengers.

You could always buy a Volvo! Saab 95 in classic Verona Green shows off the difference between the marques' respective design philosophy.

Final era rubber-bumpered 95 in lovely beige.

95: ESTATE CAR SAAB

The ill-fated 95 updated as the '98'.

95 profile in Saab beige.

119

CHAPTER SIX

96: DEFINING SAAB

It was 17 February 1960 and once again the men of Saab had been busy. Constant development and refinement was to produce another heavily revised version of the original Saab car. After the 92, the 93 and the 93B/F, for 1960 Saab had reached the new 96, a truly international class car. Announced for the 1960s sales boom, the Saab 96 was a thorough reworking of the ethos. At Tryggve Holm's continued insistence, quality was still to the fore, but so for now was the 2-stroke engine.

The under-the-skin panels and tooling remained basically unchanged in the main body of the car, but many new tooling and pressing efficiencies were introduced at the rear and in the floorpan. Front-hinged doors had already been worked into the later 93F, so that tooling problem was already solved. The pretty nose styling would remain untouched for some time.

Hugo Möller was the chief toolmaker and under him the production department started to reassess the 93's body in 1957 for an update that had been suggested by Sason and other senior executives. By the time the project had been approved and the money agreed by the Saab Board, 1957 was more than half gone. New toolings, new presses and major design and styling updates created the 96. Sixten Sason and Möller worked together on engineering and design sketches, which also incorporated the new rear end and higher roofline, with new rear side window designs. Gunnar Ljungström took a daily inspection tour of the new car's progress and contributed to reworking the design.

Tore Svensson, Gösta Svensson, Dick Ohlsson, Magnus Roland and Karl-Erik Ståhlgren were key names in the development team tackling the 93 and, specifically, the 96. Ohlsson

96 Sax-O-Mat on the fly with owner Arthur Civill at the wheel. Today a semi-auto Saab is a rare item.

The nameplate that says it all.

had joined Saab's engineering/design department in 1953 alongside Josef Eklund, and would not retire until 1990 having even contributed to the 'new-age' Saab 9000. In 1967–8 Ohlsson and Ståhlgren would spend time in England to work with the Vickers Company on the test bodyshell and new steel presses and toolings that Vickers were creating for the later 96 V4.

In 1958, however, the department was so short-staffed that extra draughtsmen were brought in to assist on the first 96 (2-stroke) project. Stig Norlin with two designers, Ove Pärsson and Rune Fredriksson, joined the project to help create the 96 in just under three years. Norlin would go on to create the famous Saab 'cellular' self-repairing 5mph bumpers, which were fitted to the 96 V4 and the 99 in the 1975 and 1971 model years, respectively.[22]

The 96 was instantly identifiable by the new Sason-styled cabin and boot with new internal structures and a larger fuel tank. A wrap-around rear windscreen, the reshaped rear side windows and a 25cm (10in) increase in cabin width were all significant improvements. The rear window was 117 per cent larger. The aerodynamics were even better, with Sason taking the opportunity to better preserve the airflow around the rear end and down the tail into a Kamm-style spoiler at the boot lid as a sharply edged horizontal fence. A pair of clever, low-drag air extractor vents on each rear C-pillar quickly removed stale or humid air from the cabin and assisted with vortex control and sidewind stability.

The 96 replaced the 93F on 17 February 1960, yet the 2-stroke GT750 was given the new 96-body in late 1960 and then given the 841cc engine in 1963 to create the 96 Sport as a further niche model for the performance enthusiast. Yet there were 93-type cabin and trim fittings to the GT and Sport models (soon to gain a 'Monte Carlo' tag). This was definitely a curious marketing mixed message designed to appeal to the Saab purist niche. We can assume Tryggve Holm preferred a 2-stroke 96 'GT' or 'Sport'. The 96 V4 Sport was also briefly available.

The 93-series frontal styling had been very popular and was retained for the new 96: Saab had no intention of changing something successful. In fact the project to develop the 93 into the new car had been called 93C; calling the car the 96 was a later decision.

By 1961 the 96 had quietly been fitted with a 'key' activated starting system to replace the old 'starter-cord' that had hung incongruously under the 92 and 93 dashboards for a decade.

Saab's new car factory extension, built on the existing Trollhättan site, opened in 1959 and allowed an increase in production numbers. Alongside the improvements to the 93 series, the launch of the 95 and then the newly restyled and re-engineered 96, the Saab car was now a class act on the international stage. That early 92 series had been continuously improved into the 93, and now Saab could offer something really special in the 96 in the global, not just Swedish, marketplace.

Every new 96 off the production line was subjected to a proper test drive and a test run of the engine. Rolf Mellde managed to create a near 100-strong staff of quality inspectors and rectifiers. Under Tryggve Holm's chairmanship, Saab spent Skr50 million on improvements (including Eklund's new engine laboratory) and factory expansion (more than 36,000sq m of floor space) for the 1960s. Its new factory's target was to build 60,000 cars per year by 1963.

AMERICANS AND OLD SAABS

Ralph T. Millet was the man who imported Saab 92s into America in the mid-1950s and then created Saab in 1960s America. Robert Sinclair was the doyen of Saab, or maybe the scion of Saab in its later American existence. When he started working for Saab Motors USA Inc. in the early days, he carried a spare engine in the boot of his Saab because his hard-pressed, high-mileage 2-stroke often broke down on long interstate trips. Sinclair is said to have worked his way through five engines.

America was and remains a huge Saab sanctuary and we must mention the Saab Club of North America, the Vintage Saab groups and give particular credit to Saab racer and restorer Tom Donney, his Saab collection and his new Saab museum at Sturgis, South Dakota. The man is a Saab saint and typical of the passion it instills in people, who are all different, but who all love their Saabs. It was Donney who took a 96 and a Sonett to the Bonneville Salt Flats in Utah and set crazy speed records. We owe him much.

Bruce Turk is another big-time American Saab supporter and driver. Bruce is the founder of a movement, a deeply felt American Saabism. He is also closely associated (as President Emeritius) with the Vintage Saab Club of North America and to the linked Vintage Saab Racing Group, which has framed what you can do with old Saabs.

Turk's addiction to old Saabs is a commitment that many admire. His barn is full of Saabs such as a 93B, a 96 2-stroke, other 95 and 96 types, not to mention his stunning Sonett collection, and demonstrates one man's utter love of old Saabs. He drives his 96 'stroker' rally car with the sheer elan and pace of a true Saab rally professional.

Tom Cox of Woodstock, Maryland, is a typical East Coast Saab enthusiast. Tom owned a 96 V4 and a Sonett, and became a founding part of the esteemed Vintage Saab Racing Group with Randy Cook and Ken Payne, after which he drove around for years in an 'oily rag' 96 two-stoke. The car has now been restored to its original beauty by new owners in Virginia, making it one less 'oily rag' old Saab 'stroker'.

The Vintage Saab Racing Group makes sure their Saabs are driven as intended. The Saab 93, 96 and the Sonett were a big hit with American enthusiasts in the 1960s and 1970s, and more recently Chris Moberg has collected numerous Sonetts on his Sonnet Ranch in Maine. George and Stefan Vapaa of Wilmington, Delaware, have done much to tune and tweak

LEFT: **Classic proportions of the 93 GT850. Note bonnet/hood side vents. Some confusion can arise between the 'Sport', GT850 and 'Monte Carlo 850' labelling from 1962 to 1966. Chassis identification plates for the GT850 categorically carried a US-market 'Sport USA' sticker. Officially, these 'Bullnose' Sport cars were not imported into the UK at the time. Later 'Longnose' types did appear in the UK, however.**

old Saabs (including the Quantum Saab) and keep the flame of Saab alive – as did Bud Clarke in California. Other names associated with old Saabs and Vintage Saab historic racing in America have included two residents of Orwigsburg, Pennsylvania, Mary Anne Fieux and Charles 'Chuck' Christ, who both compete in the 1960 93F, a hill climb star, that Chuck has rebuilt to replicate the 93F that his father Joseph originally raced in the 1960s.

The late James Orr was an SCCA competitor for years. Reinertsen Motors Inc. of New Jersey has raced old Saabs in professional and amateur classes from the 1970s onwards. Willie Lewis raced a 96 V4 in the Barner Saab Pro-Series and that car went on to Len Schrader of South Carolina, who restored the car to racing condition from 2006 and has taken it to the Lime Rock Park Vintage Festival in Connecticut.

Chris Mills is well known for his Spirit of Saab website and also the New England Saab Association. The New York Saab Owners Club, which was active from 2002 to 2010 with about fifty members, might sound surprising but it is an example of how Americans took Saab to their hearts.

Saab's profile in America was launched when Bob Wehman and Louis Braun won the Great American Mountain Rally in late 1956 in a Saab 93 'stroker'; this greatly increased the awareness of the brand in America. It is often forgotten that Rolf Mellde was sixth in the same event in another 93, having persuaded the notoriously parsimonious Saab to cough up the fare to get from Trollhättan to the United States.

America also saw the 'kit-car' Saab, the Quantum. Designed by Walter Kern, the Quantum project offered Saab 93/96 owners the chance to fit their car's mechanical parts to a lightweight glassfibre body for a racing series. The Quantum MkI and Mk2 used Saab 93 components; the Mk3 turned to the 96 for its parts, notably the suspension.

America was also home of the unique Saab GT 750-engined Elva 'copy' known as 'Brand X', which was actually recognized by the Elva Registry. This car was created and built by the dedicated Saab enthusiast Joseph Christ. The activities of the Californian Saab dealer Ingvar Lindqvist have been discussed earlier in Chapter 3.

Despite Detroit iron and the great marques of America, Saab of all the 'imports' remains close to the hearts of its US enthusiasts. The Saab addiction crosses all boundaries and state lines, securing the name's place alongside MG, Alfa and Porsche.

Viewed from above, the wind-cheating form remains sublime and so full of character. Early GT850s had aluminium external side trim strips but Saab changed to chrome strips when steel to aluminium decay occurred between the two metals.

Inside the GT850 it was all dials, gauges, red trim and special seats. Bob Abels was a famous GT850 owner, and his utterly original car now resides in the UK with Robert Crawford as one of two original, unmolested GT850s – the other being Neil Ryder's car seen here.

(continued overleaf...)

AMERICANS AND OLD SAABS (continued...)

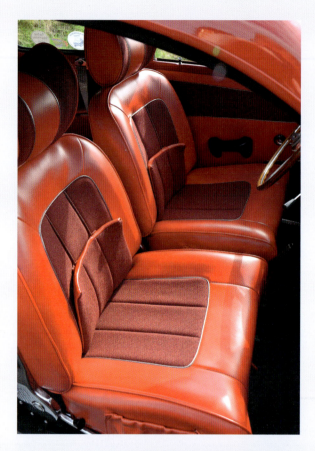

ABOVE: **Luxury sport in the US specification with red trim, lumbar cushion pads and twin headrests (not just one). Disc brakes at the front really aided driver confidence. This car had real comfort and real Saab style.**

ABOVE: **Gran Turismo 850 badging: the chassis plate states 'Sport USA' as per Saab's decision, due to American rights issues of the name 'Sport'.**

RIGHT: **The uprated three-pot GT850 carried the two-stroke engine in the 96 in a unique niche. Replacing the GT750, the GT850 or 'Sport' then latterly gave way to the short-lived 850 Monte Carlo, then the four-cylinder 96 V4 Monte Carlo type. A separately lubricated 841cc engine, with added zest, was the key to the car. The trims, wheel-type (five-stud) and many other modifications were apparent.**

96: DEFINING SAAB

Saab shot of a high-spec early 96 2-stroke.

'The ideal car': the French/Swiss 1960s brochure cover.

■ 96: DEFINING SAAB

Neil Ryder in his stunning and award-winning 1963 Gran Turismo 850, as a 96 two-stroke US market 'Sport' with the unique American market 'GT 850' nomenclature.

Up to the end of 1960 a total of 13,700 new Saabs were registered in Sweden, which *Vips: Vi på Saab*, Saab's in-house publication, described as 'a sensational increase of 44 per cent over the previous year. No other car manufacturer achieved this.'

Saab took over the AB Nyköpings Autofabrik (ANA) sales dealerships in September 1960, which gave Saab direct outlets to the public who clamoured to see the new car. Not only did Saab increase its sales in their home market, 11,000 new cars were also exported, which was 1,500 more than in 1959. The new 96 sold 5,200 units in the vital American market in 1960.

Key names of the 96 project development, engineering, production and sales story in the early and mid-1960s included Rolf Mellde, Tore Nilsson, K.-G. Karlsson, Bengt Åkerlin, N.-G. Nilsson, Svante Holm, Hans G. Andersson, Arne Rydberg and John Engström. Per Gillbrand, known by many Swedish fans as 'Turbopelle', and Olle Granlund would later engineer the V4 into the 1966 V4 for the 1967 model year.

A revised 2-stroke engine was found under the 96's front from 1961, and before long it was joined by a four-speed gearbox. The larger engine capacity had the effect of raising the top speed to 125km/h (77mph) and greatly improving the overtaking performance. In 1961 disc brakes were introduced, followed in 1963 by Saab's diagonally split safety braking system. These were major improvements to the car's global appeal, not to mention its rallying abilities. For

Smokin' stroker scuttles away. Note the narrow-slot rear window type.

Classic interior. A wooden wheel seems a must on a 93 or 95 stroker.

The lovely two-tone interior of the Sax-O-Mat specification car.

96: DEFINING SAAB

the model years 1961 to 1964 Saab made annual tweaks to the specifications of the 96 and 95. In 1964 this included the launch of Saab's gear stick and ignition key locking mechanism, which prevented key withdrawal unless the gear lever was in reverse gear.

A stylish new instrument panel with round dials really spiced up the previous Saab interiors, but in the 1960s the 'strip' or thermometer design of speedometer was substituted. A sunroof and the semi-automatic Sax-O-Mat clutch using a three-speed gearbox remained options.

For 1963 the Saab aircraft-type logo was to be seen 'cast-in' to the main latticework front aluminium grille. By the end of 1963 Saab had sold 100,000 96s, of which 4,117 cars were sold in the United States – and in that year Erik Carlsson won the Monte Carlo Rally again.

The early 96s kept the Italian-style front, but by 1965 the 96 would have the new longer nose, which curved downwards in a clean arc of wing line. This car was known in-house at Saab as 'Project Emilia'. There was even a vestigial under-bumper front spoiler to control air pressure under the car. It would be more than a decade before other production cars, even the aerodynamic Citroën GSA, would sprout the same techniques. The 96 was probably the most aerodynamic mass-production, small to mid-size car in the world in its era, in fact its C_d 0.35 shamed even 1960s supercars.

COLOUR BLIND?

A new range of cabin trims, patterns and colours for the 96 was created by Pierre Sager Olofsson. Key exterior paint colours introduced for the 96 were Polar White, Arctic Blue, Ocean Blue, Midnight Blue and Saab Green, followed by Glacier Blue and Savannah Brown. Then we had the wonderful Toreador Red. In 1964–5 Yellow and Olive Green were added, then Hussar Blue, Black and Silversand.

Bright Sunset Orange, Alabaster Yellow, Opal Green, Topaz Yellow, Solar Red, Caroline Blue, Chamotte Brown, Dorado Brown and Antelope Brown would all become later colours for the 96 and 96 V4. Tyrol Green and Verona Green were very popular for British Saabs as the 1970s era of Saab gained momentum. The less said about 'hearing aid' Saab 'old-age-pensioner' beige the better, although Savannah Beige (Savannbeige) has become a cult colour for some enthusiasts.

ABOVE AND BELOW: **How to restore a Saab to its rightful glory. The Arthur Civill-owned Sax-O-Mat makes all the right moves.**

RIGHT: **One of the 93/96's best points was the truly massive boot. And you could fold away or remove the rear seatback to carry cargo, or sleep.**

BELOW: **Posing for the camera, the lovely Sax-O-Mat car captured the essence of Saab.**

96: DEFINING SAAB

All the elegance of the aerodyne form seen on the move. Note the single arc of the unbroken curve from scuttle to boot lid.

Metallic paints such as Acacia Green and Aquamarine Blue would not be seen on a 96 V4 bodyshell until the late 1970s, although the sometimes troublesome Cardinal Red metallic and Silver Crystal metallic both debuted as early as 1975.

SOUTH AMERICAN SAABS

Saab had been selling aircraft in Brazil, notably the Saab S90 Scandia airliner, so it was natural for the car division to open a sales franchise in that country. As early as 1950 Saab appointed a Swedish company, Janer AB, to act for it in São Paulo and Rio de Janeiro. Saab was soon to ship six 92s to Brazil, where it would also undertake hot-climate and rough-road development of the car and get some off-the-record, safari-style rallying practice.

Strict government import tariffs and currency regulations meant that importing more cars was to become impossible as they would be priced out of the market. The only way to sell Saabs in Brazil would be to build them there. By 1952 Saab was talking to the Brazilian company Vemag SA about using its light engineering and vehicle assembly plant in São Paulo to construct 92s from kits that would be shipped in crates. The two parties agreed that 1,000 Saabs could be built from 1953, rising to 5,000 per annum by 1958. The agreement was confirmed in written letters of discussion on 1 October 1953.

Despite much planning and a basic draft agreement, the idea was stopped in its tracks by the detail and delays of trying to meet new government restrictions in Brazil, which were introduced just as the Saab deal was about to materialize. The full contract was drawn up as far as the final stage, but was never signed.

It seemed as though Saab car production in South America was not going to happen, but then an approach came from Uruguay. As early as 5 May 1947 interested parties in Uruguay had heard about Saab's intention to launch a car and written to Saab asking if it could represent the company in setting up an import agency in Montevideo. This was just under a month before Saab announced its 92 prototype in June 1947.

Further approaches were made to Saab from various interested Uruguayan companies eager to sell cars. During

URUGUAYAN SAAB-AUTOMOTORA PRODUCTION

Saab 96 including 2-stroke and V4 as SKD	243
Saab 96 including V4 as CKD	65
Production total	308
Saab 95 including V4 as SKD	20
Saab 95 including V4 as CKD	50
Production total	70
Later Saab 99 two-door as CKD	100
Combined Uruguayan SKD/CKD all model production total	**478**

a sales tour of Brazil and Argentina with the new Saab S90 Scandia airliner in 1949, Saab met with ten representatives from these potential South American partners, notably from Uruguay. Due to demand in Sweden and northern Europe, and shortages of raw materials in a post-war environment, the idea of selling or even building CKD Saabs in Uruguay came to nothing. Saab, however, did not forget how keen and how early into the fray the Uruguayans had been. In 1952 ten Saab 92s were shipped to Uruguay and eighty were shipped to Peru. Several found their way to Chile, Venezuela and Argentina, where legend has it a handful remain lost, awaiting their chance to become 'barn finds'.

A decade later, in 1963, Saab's export manager Göran Hagström found himself talking to the Uruguayan company Automotora Boreal SA of Montevideo. This time it would happen, the small Saab with the big heart was about to touch the people of Uruguay, who in turn would come to love 'their' Saabs.

After discussions in 1963 Saab entered into an agreement with Automotora, which was already selling BMWs to a local market that included many Germans, for the Uruguayan company to build 2-stroke Saab 96s from semi-knocked-down (SKD) kits. These would arrive ready painted, with all major components boxed and crated ready for reassembly. In February 1964 the first SKD components, enough to construct twenty-three cars, arrived for assessment by the import control and tariff authorities. From that assessment were set the rates and costs for SKD Saabs in Uruguay, Saab's most-distant SKD/CKD market.

The key men in Saab's Swedo-Urguayan operations were Brynolf Holmqvist and Göran Hagström for Saab, and José Arijón Rama and René Irion for Automotora. Assembly of the SKD factory facility continued into June, and by December 193 2-stroke 96s had been built and sold to eager customers. In the following year only fifty examples of the 96 were sold, but twenty of the 95 estates were made in Uruguay from SKD kits and sold.

Automotora wanted to show what it could do, and Saab wanted to make the cars cheaper. This could be done by moving to completely-knocked-down (CKD) production, in which basic panels and items were shipped from Sweden, and Automotora then welded up the complete cars and painted and trimmed them. The possibility of reduced import taxes was also raised by sourcing some locally procured components. On 5 April 1966 Åke Jonsson, the Swedish Ambassador, attended a formal ceremony at the Automotora factory on the occasion of the first truly locally built Saab car. This was the first time Saab had undertaken full CKD production outside Europe and is an often overlooked chapter in Saab's history.

The build quality and paint finish of the Uruguayan-built cars was very high. Saab's local men set high-quality goals and Automotora was similarly minded. Late in 1966 government and policy issues in Uruguay caused a temporary halt in production, but all turned out well and by mid-1966 Automotora-Saab was churning out 96 V4s, much to the locals' delight. This delight was also manifest in the form of a highly active local Saab competition department and rally entries (*see* Chapter 8).

Further Uruguayan state intervention in tariff and policy agreements saw more interruptions in production, but after political changes in 1967, and a visit to Sweden by Automotora's management, CKD production of 96s and 95 V4s resumed. By 1969 Automotora wanted the new Saab 99 and pushed for a contractual agreement regarding CKD supply from Saab, but the company was struggling with production capacity and supply demands, and the possibility of the Saab 99 starting a South American life was postponed. At the same time Saab was embroiled in its merger with Scania, to create Saab-Scania in 1969.

By January 1970 the first two-door Saab 99 CKD crates were on their way to Uruguay. Automotora had agreed with

1962: SAAB IN HONG KONG

The impact that Saab's rally successes generated worldwide, especially the Monte Carlo Rally victories, is well demonstrated in an article that first appeared in 1962 in the Saab house magazine *Vips: Vi på Saab*.[25] It was written by Lennart Cedrup, Saab's Far East market correspondent, and illustrated with his own photographs, the first of which shows 'a Chinese lady, with a carrying pole over her shoulder, [stopping] for a while to admire the new Saab in the showroom of Continental Motors in Kowloon', which was run by General Manager James Wong.

The deal to sell Saabs in what was then the British Crown Colony followed on from Saab sales concessions being set up in Thailand, Singapore and Malaysia. The Hong Kong agent China International Motors Ltd was controlled by a number of leading Chinese businessmen based in Hong Kong, while the company's managing director was Geoffrey Binstead. Saab sales in Hong Kong started on 12 August 1962.

Saab that seats, electrics, glass, carpets and even the paint would be locally sourced by Automotora. Like the the Uruguayan Saab 96s, the 99s were unique, not least because by 1969 Automotora was building CKD BMWs and selling Alfa Romeos in Uruguay: it was possible for Saab 99s to emerge from Automotora's factory wearing a coat of a BMW paint shade. Even a Saab in Alfa Blue might have emerged.

By the early 1970s the story of Saab's high-quality manufacturing in Uruguay was finally over after nearly 500 cars of the 96, 96 V4, 95 and 99 types had been produced.[23]

Saab appointed an official concessionaire in Quito, Ecuador, and as early as 1962 Saab's representative there, Marco Baca, rallied a GT750 in the Circuito del Valle, an Ecuadorian speed trial and he won. Baca's brother also entered the event in a standard-specification Saab and finished fourth. This was great publicity for Saab as it expanded in South America. Sightings of an old Saab in Ecuador, Mexico, Venezuela, Chile and Peru are rare but still possible. In Argentina and Uruguay, however, Saab still reigns.

Although small in scale, the story of the South American Saab 93s and 96s once again captures the energy and internationalism of the Swedish company and its little cars that ranged across the world. Saab still has a dedicated following in parts of South America. Club Saab Uruguay was founded in 2008 with Alberto Domingo as its President.

In Brazil a 96 850 Sport Monte Carlo was formerly used by its owner Luis Cezar Ramos Pereira, but has more recently found ownership in a private collection.

The strong classic car movement in Argentina extends to enthusiasm for Saabs. The long-running Saab Club Argentina remains active and its members run two very smart Saab 92s and up to a dozen 93s, 96s and 96 V4s. The two 92s, one in black (Charly Walmsley's car) and one in dark maroon, can still be seen running in Buenos Aires.

The sheer level of enthusiasm for Saab found in this corner of the world is a vital part of the Saab story, past and present.

OTHER EXPORT MARKETS

Saabs were sold in Thailand from 1961. A small concession known as SS Motors was opened as one of several businesses run by Sampow Sirisambhand (hence the 'SS' name) and his brother Armorn. SS Motors' showroom was at 217 Smutprakam Road.[24]

For the 1965 model year, announced on 19 August 1964, more power and a revised cooling system were added. The different cooling system was accommodated by the new longer nose styling of the 1965 model year cars.

In some countries, notably the USA and Switzerland, a 96 'Special' was marketed. These cars had the sports-tuned engine from the Monte Carlo variant minus all the additional trim items carried by the Monte Carlo 850 and its forebear, the GT 750.

One small but significant tooling change across the 1966 cars was the use of top-hung pedals, which replaced the floor-mounted lever-arm type pedals that been introduced with the 92.

The 96 was very popular in Norway as a 2-stroke and later as a V4. Rural Norway in winter was a sensible place for a Saab 2-stroke with decent rough-road abilities. Top Norwegian Saab dealer Oddmund Barmen is generally regarded as the driving force behind rural Norwegian Saab sales near Nordfjord from as early as 1962 when he sold his first 96 2-stroke. He became an official Saab dealer in 1967 after persuading AS Autoindustri in Oslo to grant him the official

96: DEFINING SAAB

ABOVE: **24 NPO** is well known and has received attention from ex-Saab GB expert Chris Partington. Now owned by David Lowe, this 'rasper' is the original thing. Blue on blue, and original!

RIGHT: **Sports seats and two-tone touches to the interior make this car.**

133

AN OWNER'S VIEW: CHRIS REDMOND AND HIS 'OILY-RAG' 96

My 1963 Saab 2-stroke is a 1964 model year car. The distinguishing features that show it to be a 1964 model year are the 'Saab plane' motif, which has moved from the front leading edge of the bonnet to the grille, and the dashboard has circular VDO gauges replacing the long 'strip' speedometer and square temperature and fuel gauges. This particular car is pearl grey and quite rare in the UK: I've only ever seen one other. It can appear a light blue colour in certain lighting.

The car has, to my knowledge, never been completely restored, but it's had many localized repairs and paint when required. It's a car that's been used for many years by its previous owner as a daily driver. In keeping with the spirit of a classic car that is used daily it has not been restored and is what is referred to as an 'oily rag classic', only receiving repairs where needed.

In keeping with the rally heritage of the 1963 Erik Carlsson victory at the Monte Carlo Rally, the car is adorned with numbers and a period rally look. This suits its rough and ready appearance, which proudly displays the battle scars of many years of enjoyable driving. The car has an 841cc single-carburettor, with a three-speed transmission; it certainly takes some driving around the South Wales Valleys where we live, working the small engine for every accent whilst carefully managing every ascent and descent with the drum-brake system. It's an exhilarating drive and as much fun as any high-powered more modern Saab.

Chris Redmond, who plays a key role in supporting the Saab club scene in the UK, is also obsessed with Saabs and owns several of differing types. This is his superb 96 looking very real in its patina of history and enthusiasm.

This Saab 96 is part of a small collection of Saabs, some of which are under restoration, such as two 1973 95 V4s, a 1975 99 GL Super and a fully restored 1985 900 T16S. The 900 T16S was the first car that I completely restored from scratch after rescuing it from a Saab specialist who was going to scrap the car. It is a very well-known car in the UK: I also have other 'modern' Saabs to keep the classics company.

I've been driving Saabs for thirty-plus years. My Saab affair started with a fascination for aircraft as a young child attending air shows with my uncle. We used to love the slightly unusual shape of the Saab Viggen compared to all the other fighter jets. This interest in aircraft, coupled with an obsession for cars, was passed down from my father. Saab's early 1980s advertising campaigns featuring their cars and fighter planes sparked my interest in the classic 900. Like many other 'Saabists' I have now owned nearly every model and find it extremely difficult to sell any – another 'Saabist' trait!

Here in the UK we have a very healthy Saab community with lots of local enthusiasts' groups. I currently run Dragon Saab, a regional Saab group in Wales with the help of a fabulous group of friends. At the time of writing I'm the Chairman of the Saab Owners Club of Great Britain, an honour I could not have imagined all those years ago when I became interested in this Swedish marque.

Redmond's car, HAS 170, just reeks of the Saab aura and Saab history. You can almost smell it from here.

96: DEFINING SAAB

Saab concession for Nordfjord. This led Barmen to team up with Hans Erik Lund to form Barmen & Lund AS as a dealership in 1968.

RECUTTING THE DIAMOND

The 96 had been developed through five years of annual upgrades, but Saab knew that the next update had to be more comprehensive because it was not as economical or as fast as its rivals, and it was still a somewhat smokey 2-stroke. Saab had increased production by enlarging the factories at a cost of nearly Skr50,000,000, and annual production was approaching 50,000 cars. Behind the scenes, however, a battle, perhaps subconsciously, for Saab's stability and security, its very survival, was taking place.

By 1965 Saab had been tweaking the 96's 2-stroke to produce more power and less smoke for several years. The car was faster and had a triple carburettor. The Saab engine laboratory under Josef Eklund carried out a series of advanced studies into cylinder heads, bolt torque, piston behaviour and gasket design during the early developments to the 3-cylinder engine. These resulted in a novel approach to controlling the 3-cylinder engine's behaviour, creating a reliable cylinder head/gasket regime that did not warp, leak or fail. Further studies into piston behaviour saw Saab fit a plexiglass window into the side of an engine block to allow the team to observe piston and combustion behaviour by spectroscope and to solve an early problem with an internal engine issue where the fuel feed and piston pins failed. The problems were solved using chromium-plated piston rings and modified connecting rods.

The result of all this work by 1965 was Saab's 841cc, 44bhp (SAE) 3-cylinder with a new hydraulic clutch that replaced the cable-actuated type: also added was a new fuel pump. But the effect of this further tweaking of the design was an unwanted increase in fuel consumption to the point where a reputation for being a touch fuel-thirsty was being created. This was effectively the ultimate 2-stroke engine, a new modified unit with triple-carburettors and a higher power, while oil mixture decreased from 3 per cent to 1.5 per cent, which reduced the emissions. With its liking for fuel, however, the car's sales figures fell in the important Swedish domestic market. Total sales in 1965–6 declined from 48,500 to 37,000, a drop of more than 10,000 in one year, reflecting the poor fuel consumption. Soon that sales figure would dive further.

This is the Saab emblem as woven into the rear-seat trim – what a Saab touch.

Bruce Turk's amazing rally-spec 'stroker', which he drives with the talent of a true rally professional. B. TURK

SAAB 96 2-STROKE PRODUCTION FIGURES, 1959–68

1959	3
1960	19,391
1961	29,858
1962	32,513
1963	35,899
1964	39,113
1965	40,226
1966	29,766
1967	The 96 with V4 engine was introduced; 2-stroke cars were sold in the USA as the 2-stroke 96 and 95 Shrike for just over a year into 1968. The 96 2-stroke Monte Carlo became the V4 Monte Carlo
1968	Only 28 of the 96 2-stroke were sold in Sweden

The later Saab badge, as applied to the famous 'ear'-type air extractors, was rather 'designer' in its day.

Saab 96 in Sweden on Swedish plates. The real thing. R. MORLEY

■ 96: DEFINING SAAB

ABOVE AND BELOW: **White seems to suit the car almost as well as red or blue. This 96 is near-perfect from all angles.** R. GUNN

GORDON BEDSON'S AUSTRALIAN SAAB

For reasons that seem more commercially than design related, Saab was slow to expand its Asian sales of the 93 or 96. A few Dutch-owned 96 2-strokes were privately imported into Indonesia, but private imports into Australia were even rarer.

Australia's very high temperatures and long-range driving might have been expected to cause trouble for the 2-strokes, but little evidence for that exists. In July 1961, however, Saab imported into Australia two right-hand-drive 96 2-strokes (reputedly from the Hong Kong outlet) to test the local market reaction. The cars were registered on South Australia State plates and given to the motoring press. Intriguingly, the Saab local offer was for a 100,000 mile warranty on the 2-stroke engine. The motoring press in Australia loved the 96s, but the truth was that import taxes and local costs pushed the price up so far that the 96 was uncompetitive against home-grown Holden and Ford cars. Saab walked away before dipping its hand into the Australian market once more nearly a decade later, focusing on the Saab 99.

There is, though, an interesting tale of an Australian Saab 96 personal import before Saab gave it a go. Gordon Bedson was an English engineer who had worked for the Bristol Aircraft Company and then for Vickers Aviation at Weybridge/Brooklands as a chief project engineer on the Valiant four-jet bomber, which was developed in the 1950s as part of the British V-Bomber force. (Vickers was also responsible for the Viscount, Vanguard and VC10 family of world-class airliners.)

Bedson was an engineering marvel with a strong interest in aerodynamics: when not working on jet bombers, he designed single-seat and two-seat racing cars (including the Formula Three and Formula One class 'Kieft' types respectively), the ultra-light Frisky 'Sprint' sports car, which ran in the 1958 Monte Carlo Rally, and hatched a plan to build an Australian-made sports car using Saab parts.

Through contact with Australian industrialist Harold Lightburn, Bedson became involved in a plan to use the 2-stroke Saab GT750 engine and Saab running gear in a space-frame steel-tube chassis and glassfibre body as an affordable Australian 'specialist' car. Saab in Sweden were actively involved in the idea with an eye to Saab handling potential global sales. The car might not have been a Sonett 1, but it was a daring private enterprise. The body styling was highly professional and aerodynamic, looking as if it had come out of a major styling studio in Europe or America. It was said to be Bedson's own work.

Sadly the Saab-Lightburn-Bedson car died at the hands of various alleged internal machinations at the Australian end. Bedson is reputed to have been very sad at the outcome of his business liaison with the 'Lightburn Affair', as it has since been called.

Bedson went on to design light aircraft in Australia. Of more significance to the present subject is that he was one of the first (perhaps even the first) to import a 2-stroke Saab 96 into Australia for his personal use. The Saab's aerodynamic body and clever chassis-hull really appealed to his engineering mind. Bedson imported a 96 in the very early 1960s and also imported spare 96 components for the car project with Lightburn. Given Bedson's curriculum vitae with Bristol and Vickers, not to mention some famous motor racing luminaries in the 1950s, Saab in Trollhättan took Bedson very seriously. Tragically it was to prove a dead end and Bedson was

The very clever cabin-air extractors. More Saab design genius.

■ 96: DEFINING SAAB

The later interior was very modern indeed. Only the 1960s-style steering wheel hints at a lady with a past.

The controls were kept simple and to the minimum.

140

96: DEFINING SAAB

The longitudinal 2-stroke of Eklund design, with its Muller and Heinkel DNA, seen up front in the 96 'stroker' with the radiator to the rear.

killed in 1984 flying one of his airframe designs, the Magra.

Bedson's 96 2-stroke, however, which he raced in Australia, opened the door to Australian perceptions of Saab. Official Saab sales and distribution in Australia would take more than another decade to become reality.[26]

TUNING THE 'STROKERS'

The 96 might have arrived for 1960, but there were still plenty of 93s for sale and in use, not least in motor sport. The new 96 retained the 93's engine, so it was logical that the tuning measures for the 93 could also apply to the 96.

Below we survey the origins of what you could do with the 3-cylinder engine.

In the modern context, historic Saab rallying often focuses on the 96 V4. Yet as early as 1957 Saab's Competition Department was revealing just what you could do to the little 2-stroke 'triple' to get more power and faster rally stage times. Of course, tuning the engine in its later GT750 and GT850 guises is a well-known art, but back in 1959–60 there were several relatively inexpensive routes to more power for your pound (or krona, or dollar).

With more than 100bhp per litre, here was the engine that could get to massive revs and would only 'burst' if you did something wrong. Engines with modified specifications could be purchased direct from your local Saab national concessionaire, notably in the USA, and ranged in cost from three figures in your local currency to a full-competition race or rally engine into four figures, equivalent to more than $1,000. This was the 'GT Super' package, which was ordered direct from Saab in Sweden and comprised a complete engine that was given five hours of dyno-testing, before being despatched for local delivery to the Saab owner in a state ready for fitment.

Somewhat more affordably, however, Saab would also sell you a tuning kit at the remarkably low price of $148 in 1960.

Going for the 841cc engine gave more power, but the engine head and various combustive improvement parts from the GT750 would not fit the 841cc engine, so perhaps it was true that the smaller 750 offered more scope for engine tuning. More power could be extracted from the smaller engine because more could be done inside the head and with the pistons. Erik Carlsson insisted (to the author) that, although the 841cc could be tuned to nearly touch 70bhp (at 68bhp), the 750cc engine could be tuned to 65 or 66bhp, so there was not much in it, except that the smaller engine gave you more 'zing'!

Erik's Tweaks

Erik's preferred rally and race car 'secret' is worth reiterating: he had springs on his 93 and 96 rally cars cut and lowered (1½ spring cut per coil), and he removed the anti-roll bar. These measures made the car quicker, lighter, more reactive and much easier to 'flick' (Erik's technique for getting the tail out on a front-wheel-drive car with inherent understeer), and it was also easier to set up and power through a bend that did not require a so-called 'flick' (although you might end up on the car's roof, of course, which is why he was sometimes known as 'Carlsson på tacket', 'Carlsson on the roof', in a reference to a character named 'Karlsson på tacket' in three books by Astrid Lindgren).

Erik and others always advised the Saab engine tuner to 'never' try to modify the transfer ports in the 750cc engine and avoid any attempt to polish them. It was also vital to use a Saab-specification high detergent oil (Castrol-type) in order not to lay contaminants in the vital transfer ports.

The Saab modifier needed to remember that the triple-engine has no valves. The compression ratio was one thing, but the 'closed' and 'open' ports are dictated by the mov-

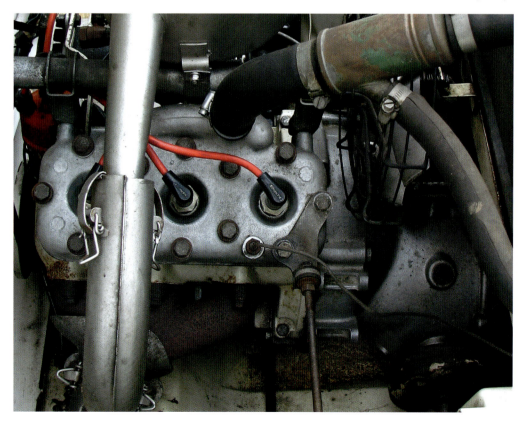

Close-up of the engine.

KEY TUNING/COMPETITION SUGGESTIONS FROM SAAB

Engine 750cc and 841cc dependent on relevance of modification. Modify intake ports (porting/polish) and polish transfer ports but not in GT750 engine. Modify head and gasket. Modify cyclinder. Modify cylinder head roof shape. Fit GT-series crank and counterweights. Enlarge ports on outside of block and avoid changes to contours inside the head. Carburettor changes and upgrades were available from Solex, Weber and Amal. Avoid damage to vital oil transfer ports inside engine. Increase crankcase compression (and transfer port pressure) by fitting circle-web crankshaft (to either type of engine). Porting, timing and compression ratio changes are all more feasible with the smaller 750cc engine. Clutches might be best left as Fichtel and Sachs originals, but a later Highgate diaphragm type was also to become available. Competition grade clutch linings were also available, but any hint of incorrect tolerance might upset the mechanism. A larger capacity radiator was also suggested for competition use

Tyres Fit Pirelli Cinturato for ultimate roadholding and grip due to their design, but use Michelin X for longer lasting and straighter-type circuit performance. Pirellis fitted by Saab to the GT750 as standard road-going specification

Wheels Reinforced wheels (a Saab sports parts catalogue item). Also available for standard steel wheels were reinforcing gussets with ten radial braces to be externally welded/fitted and with six reverse side parts also to be fitted to brace the rim

Brakes Saab offered ceramic pads (made by Bendix) in 1960 for less than £75.00. Ferodo-type brake pads of better grade were also offered

Suspension Fit Koni shock absorbers. Note that Erik Carlsson's cars and those competing at Lime Rock Park reputedly had lower/cut springs. For race circuit use only you could copy Erik Carlsson's secret and remove the front anti-rollbar, but be warned that this is anecdotal reporting of a reputed action and no liability for the resulting consequences can be implied nor given herein

Body Replace non-structural front and outer-rear wing panels (fenders) with lightweight glassfibre replacement panels, but do not alter main heavy-gauge steel body monocoque. Take care over using glassfibre replacement door skins without full roll cage with side braces fitted. Fully glassfibre replacement doors remove enough weight to 'add' approximately 5bhp, according to experts, but such doors offer little side-impact protection. The Saab can be lightened by removing the heater, rear parcel shelf, rear seats, trim panels, carpets, and the use of plexiglass in rear windows. Fit alloy skid plate to protect gearbox casing from impact and shattering

Cabin Competition 'padded' seats were 30lb (13.6kg) heavier than the standard seats, but much more comfortable. Strangely only the passenger/co-driver/navigator seat included a headrest. Fit Halda timing devices and a wood-rimmed and alloy-spoked sport steering wheel

Owners were given clear instructions to add the oil to the fuel, but the time of the 2-stroke was over for mainstream cars and Saab knew it.

96: DEFINING SAAB

The revised 1965 car with new nose, bigger windscreen and more chrome.

ing position of the piston and the resultant 'fixed' or static (sealed) mechanically set gaseous compression, then by the changing (unsealed) compression or pressure ratios as the piston moved across the respective ports, which were crucial to the engine's design and output. The 93's 841cc compression ratio (standard of 7.3:1) is set by design and mechanical action as the 'swept' volume, but this is different from the actual volume of the moving piston as ports are either opened or closed across the full volume of the cylinder head by the valveless compression and exhaust mechanism. So the volume according to the position is either a 'short' cylinder (with a compression ratio of 5.1:1) or the 'long' cylinder position ratio of 7.3:1, depending on the position in the 2-stroke cycle of the actual piston(s).

The 750cc engine had differing internal sizes and volume and therefore differing compression ratio(s) at full or long setting and at the part or short setting of the piston.

For the 841cc engine, the modifier had to remember the vital point in terms of altering the timing of the ports, up with the transfer ports and down with the exhaust ports. Exhaust temperatures on both the 2-strokes could get very high and some racers using these engines fitted exhaust temperature gauges to each cylinder to monitor this crucial indicator. This was a bit like the exhaust gas temperature (EGT) on a large piston engine or jet engine: the EGT was vital as a telltale sign of trouble afoot.

2-Stroke Tune-Up with Tom Donney

From 2-stroke to V4, Saab's dedicated engine tuners in-house at the Saab Sport and Rally Department at Trollhätttan came up with series of tweaks, modifications and improvement packs that an owner could apply to 'their' 93, 95, 96 or V4.

As described above, early in their career the 92 and 93 'strokers' were subject to engine tuning and improvements to brakes and suspension for rallying use, both by privateers and as part of official works campaigns. Adding different brake pad compounds, roll cages and so on was one thing, but fitting revised engine parts, different carburation and tuned exhaust manifolds could eke out a few extra bhp, or more psi per compression ratio for each pot.

Changes to bore, carburation, head, pistons and combustion were all central to coaxing more torque out of the little engine. Just as with the later problems with the V4's gearbox, the 2-stroke engine had a couple of known areas of wear and failure: one of note was that seals could break down, allowing oil and sludge to escape beyond the cylinder and the crankshaft seal, pumping out oil under pressure at both ends. Also evident was a reduction in compression due to piston and cylinder wear. If your 2-stroke was down to 80psi for one or more of its 'pots', then there was trouble internally. Oil seal failure and main bearing 'rumble' signalled what some call 'time bomb' issues.

The standard, healthy 2-stroke compression measurement should be over 100psi per cylinder and nearer 110psi for a later engine. The later 3-cylinder GT750 and Monte Carlo engines with their improvements should have at least 120psi across their pots as standard, if not a touch more. Triple-carburettor engines should breathe better too.

Saab 2-stroke guru Tom Donney, who runs his superb new Saab Museum at Sturgis, South Dakota, where he also restores Saabs, is an example of a globally respected expert who is quite happy to add modern technology to the 2-stroke engines:

> Technology has moved on since Saab's original old school engineering, so why not use it when restoring or tuning such an engine. We can get over 130psi, in fact up to 140psi per cylinder across all the cylinders consistently by using modern techniques and modern piston technology. My Bonneville record stroker engines were doing 122mph with about 135psi compression per cylinder. It is all about how you utilize your head design.

Tom takes the old original Saab 2-stroke heads and blocks and applies lateral thinking with many clever tweaks that make the engine run with even more verve. Donney advises that old pistons are best replaced with modern, advanced metal-compound, two-ring types (he uses the Wiseco make). He also uses ceramic coatings and domed heads. Choice of cast or forged pistons depends on requirements.

From the 2-stroke's original era to today, some people have skimmed 4mm off the head, which as Donney and many others know can lead to the original head casting warping, resulting in consequent compression reduction and other problems beyond gasket failure. A habit developed of skimming between 2.5mm and 4mm off the block instead. The head then required extra clearance for what would now be pistons that stood proud of the block. If head-skimming by 4mm, a 5mm clearance had to be engineered into the head for piston clearance. A different gasket requirement becomes obvious.

Old 'flat-top' pistons could be replaced with a domed type: recessed piston pockets are part of the tweaking process and through such techniques improvements in intake swirl/duration can be achieved. Numerous carburation choices were also the focus of tweaks to Saab's 2-stroke

X-ray view by Saab of the 96.

The famous team who 'made' Saab and its original car (from left to right): Svante Holm, Tryggve Holm, Gunnar Ljungström, Sixten Sason and Rolf Mellde.

BRITAIN'S UNIQUE SAAB 96 '60'

The early British market was denied the Saab Sport specification 96 (unless you imported a left-hand-drive example), because the right-hand-drive Saab Sport did not exist early on. So Saab Great Britain decided to create a domestic British market 'Special'.

In this, a standard Saab 96 2-stroke engine was taken apart at Saab's British head office workshop and fitted with a new machined crankshaft. The inlet ports were repositioned slightly lower, with the exhaust ports being raised upwards. Changes were made to the metal composition in the valve stems and also to the valve seals. The timing and carburation were improved and a free-flow exhaust manifold and system was fitted. As a result the engine 'breathed' better and the combustion process was also affected. This increased the standard engine's 45bhp rating to a stunning 60bhp rating – hence the term Saab 60 for this special edition car. A 15bhp gain was a significant return for the work done.

The suspension was lowered by using shorter coil springs (x 1 coil lower) and stiffer adjustable dampers. Expensive and very grippy new technology Pirelli Cinturato tyres gave a notable improvement to the handling dynamics, but they did wear out rather quickly when the car was driven as intended. Of interest, the new four-speed gearbox first seen on the 95 model was retrofitted in place of the standard 96 three-speed gearbox. Curiously, no changes were made to the original-specification speedometer with its three-speed gear markings, but a tachometer was fitted. Each revised engine bore its modifier's code of 'ML' and a number. Only one such engine block is currently known to be extant.

A special '60' numerical badge was applied to the rear valance of the 96; this was reputedly ordered from Porsche GB and came off the 356 (it certainly matches that official Porsche number badge). The Saab 96 60 cost £750 new, exclusively from Saab GB.

The model was uniquely available in Great Britain from March 1962 for one year and commemorated the Erik Carlsson Monte Carlo Rally profile. Of significance, Erik drove a Saab 60 in a 1962 autocross 'mud-plugging' publicity race and it was this car that John Bloxham purchased for use in autocross in 1962–3. Influenced by the exploits of Erik's wife Pat Moss in a Healey 3000, Bloxham would rally a Healey, but later he would also rally a Saab 96 V4, registered as LUK 3K (see Chapter 8).

96: DEFINING SAAB

ABOVE AND BELOW: **When Saab was creating the new 99, a 96 was cut up as a 'mule' to test the 99 in disguise. This is how it looked.**

'twins' and 'triples' with the standard type being replaced by the likes of Weber, Solex, Zenith and Dell'Orto.

Skimming (milling) the block height also changes the gasket requirement. Boring the cylinders and adding wider pistons also require other consequent changes in the head before you bolt it down. Such changes are fairly simple to make when restoring an old Saab block and head combination. Donney seems to prefer to focus on re-engineering the head and chamber roof, and also adding aluminium parts and ceramic coatings. Reshaping the contours of the head's combustion chamber roof requires rather more expertise.

The use of modern seal technology, notably at the crankshaft end, can also make a big difference to the 2-stroke in terms of performance and longevity.

If you are in any doubts about such tuning effects on the 2-stroke, watch a modern, tuned 2-stroke on a rally stage, or see Tom and Patti Donney race a mewling, rasping 'stroker' at speed up Canyon Road, Sturgis, under its higher compression ratio after a 'blueprinted' engine rebuild.[27]

The late Bertil Sollenskog owned a tuned-up 1966 96

Monte Carlo and it held the Bonneville Salt Flats record and the Ohio Mile title. Bertil broke the then existing class record at Bonneville in 2011 with a two-way average of 110.187mph. In late 2014 he reached 112.642mph. Tom Donney set further records with the car, including three new records at the Ohio Mile in 2013 and a speed of 107.6mph in the J/Pro classification. This car had fuel injection and numerous tweaks.

THE SHRIKE AND THE LAST OF THE SAAB 'STROKERS'

A lesser-known sideline of the Saab story, except among Saab enthusiasts and experts, is the 'Shrike' specials conceived for the 96 (and 95) American market. In 1967, with V4-engined cars in production, it was decided to offer the now very rare 'Shrike' 2-stroke as a 55bhp 'Special' edition with a unique engine specification.

Two versions of the Shrike specification are known with the engine having slight technical differences: these centred on the choice of either the separate oiler engine or the later 1969 model year pre-mix type. The 'M'-type 'Shrike' had a single-carburettor 42bhp 841cc pre-mix engine, while the 'L'-type used oil injection and offered just over 50bhp. These cars were of basic specification but with a number of US-specific trim changes, such as one-speed wipers, use of a generator, drum brakes and all-round vinyl seat trim.

The last run of the Shrike idea evolved into the final US market 2-stroke in 1968 and saw its displacement slightly reduced to 820cc (and even a rumoured 795cc) due to the ever-present emissions problems and an exemption for any engine under 850cc.

The Monte Carlo 850 had survived into 1967 with separate lubrication engine specification, but was eclipsed by the lesser-known Monte Carlo V4 by late 1967. Even that, however, was fading by 1968 – after all it was not a true 'performance' Saab with a more powerful engine, it was a V4 with more trim.

From 1950 to 1968 Saab had built a total of 320,000 cars with 2-stroke engines. The 96 had had a massive effect in 1960 when its introduction had caused a great rise in sales of the car despite its 2-stroke engine. The dramatic collapse five years later, when sales of the 96 tumbled from 40,226 in 1965 to 29,766 in 1966, could not be ignored and was a warning that the 2-stroke had had its day and had been kept

The new 'face' of Saab for the mid-1960s.

An early advertisement for Saab in Great Britain.

The 'New' Saab 96 as advertised for 1965.

on for too long. Without the effort put into the V4, which was now waiting in the wings, Saab may have been in deep trouble very quickly. The glitz, glamour, chrome and bling of the 'soft-metal' Ford Cortina, the superficial charms of the Vauxhall Viva, and the delights of the British Motor Corporation's personality-disordered marques and cars, soon to become British Leyland, were now tempting the mainstream motorist. Even loyal Saab buyers, once safely in the Saab niche, had become frustrated.

Fortuitously, with the writing on the wall, there was also the new V4 badge upon the front wing of the Saab 96. V4 was for survival, not just success. Who cared if it was a Ford V4 not a Saab V4 ...

■ 96: DEFINING SAAB

A superb 96, 500KNX, brought up the rear of the Carlsson memorial convoy in 2015.

SAAB 96 2-STROKE MODEL DEVELOPMENT

1960 New Saab 96 and 95 series fully launched 17 February 1960. The 42bhp-rated 96 features new rear styling with revised side windows and rear windscreen. Saab Great Britain Ltd formed.
Early 95s (only) had rear-hung front doors. 95s initially built at Linköping.
95 estate gets four-speed gearbox before 96 and is successful in the Monte Carlo Rally driven by Carlsson. The 42bhp-rated 96 features new rear styling with revised side windows and rear windscreen. Major cabin design and trim changes. 841cc engine launched and GT850 specified. Saab GranTurismo 750 finally gets the body of the new 96 850cc, which had been available on standard model 96s for some months, but retains 750cc engine. GT850 Saab Sport created

1961 New key-activated starting mechanism and new cabin trim headed a 42 per cent sales increase in domestic sales of Saab car. Aerodynamic work on 95 estate leads to rear 'air-slicer' spoiler on roof. 95 production moves to Trollhättan

1962 96 refined with minor trim changes and three-point seat belts as standard in Sweden. Saab Sport 841cc with 52bhp supersedes GT750 in 96 shell and has three carburettors, disc brakes at front and separate oil tank

1963 100,000th Saab 96 manufactured

1964 Twin-circuit split diagonal 'safety' braking system introduced across range. Four-speed gearbox across range in all markets. Sax-O-Mat still a rare option on three-speed gearbox (only). Round-dial instruments across range

1965 New lower-line longer nose styling with pressed-steel mesh-type front valance. New cooling system; radiator repositioned ahead of 44bhp engine. Top-hung pedals now fitted. 96 Saab Sport now named Monte Carlo 850 (with 55bhp) in the USA. Svenska Aeroplan Aktiebolaget becomes Saab Aktiebolag, registered 19 May

1966 Major engine specification changes reduce oil mix in 2-stroke from over 4 per cent to 1.5 per cent. Triple carburettors on standard engine. New trims, brightwork. 'Specials' marketed as model-hybrids in USA and Switzerland only, with older separately lubricated engine from the Monte Carlo 850 model but in standard 96 trim specification. Three-speed gearbox deleted

1967 V4-engined cars announced, but 2-stroke 96 continues as lower-line model. Sales steady but slow due to high cost ratio in comparison to new V4. Very rare US market 'Shrike' 2-stroke editions. Monte Carlo 850 survives into 1967 with separate lubrication engine specification, but is replaced by the lesser-known Monte Carlo V4 by late 1967

1968 Final year of 2-stroke 96 and 95: the 92–96 range sold a total of 320,000 units from 1949 to 1968

Saab 96 in profile.

CHAPTER SEVEN

SAAB 96 V4: CONTINUOUS IMPROVEMENT

After several years as a so-called 'second-tier' Saab behind the purists' choice of the 92, 93 and 96 2-strokes, the 96 V4 has now finally (and rightly) been recognized for the classic Saab that it truly is. Admittedly it is not an original 'Stroker', but what is also true is that fitting the V4 engine and the significant engineering and design upgrades across all aspects of the 'new' 96 V4 (and 95 V4) created a superb car that is now better appreciated.

In the world of today's enthusiasts, you chose your tribe and will be respected for that, and no judgements should be made. If you are a 2-stroke purist, great, but the V4 should not be ignored as a true Saab. After all, the twin-pots had engines of DKW and Heinkel provenance, so why castigate a Saab with a engine that came from Ford? Saab did not make its own engine, and that was Saab's responsibility. The solution to a lack of such an engine was Saab's, so why attack it? Purism can be taken too far.

After all, a Saab is a Saab, or at least it was until, depending on your view, it arguably became a GM, or a Subaru, or hybridized platform-sharer of a chassis. Even then, the team at Saab put effort into 'Saabizing' such devices to varying degrees.

An example of the recent dedication of the 96 V4 enthusiasts was that a batch of newly minted laminated windscreens for post-1968 V4 models (with the larger aperture) was commissioned by the Saab Owners Club of Great Britain

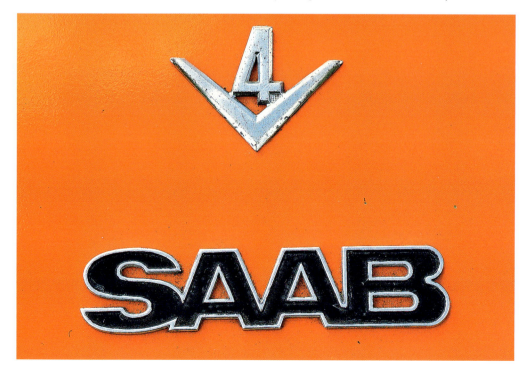

V4 for success!

SAAB 96 V4: CONTINUOUS IMPROVEMENT

Saab advertising displays the bigger windscreen.

and one of its stalwarts, Alistair Philpott, a devoted 96 V4 owner, and delivered at viable cost.

The V4 was transformative for the 96. It was rugged and reliable, and despite Ford's original reluctance, leant itself to careful modification and a very significant increase in horsepower and torque without major problems, providing certain criteria were met and observed.

The V4 for Saab was a long time coming and the 4-cyclinder Saab nearly did not happen. Was Saab right in being welded to the idea of the 2-stroke, or was it that Tryggve Holm seemed determined that the small 2-stroke engine in a small Saab should be the sole arbiter of the true Saab ethos?

Holm was actually correct in one sense: Saab had begun as a basic Swedish car, not an upmarket item. Keeping true to Saab's self was a worthy aim, but the world of motoring had moved on. Smoky 2-strokes and 'buzzing' power was no longer enough. Later events were to prove that Tryggve Holm's fears of abandoning the small car idea were well founded, however the subsequent record and opinions show that his reputed insistence on sticking with the 2-stroke as Saab's sole power source was an error in both marketing and driving terms as the sector's standards improved.

Saab needed to join the 4-stroke, 4-cylinder world if it was to survive, and a 4-cylinder engine did not necessarily have to mean the end of a small Saab. Among the many people within Saab who were working hard to convince the management of the need for a new engine, two of the most influential were Gunnar Ljungström and Rolf Mellde.

Rolf Mellde, whom we first met in Chapter 3, was now Saab's engineering/technical director. He was also a strong

SAAB 96 V4: CONTINUOUS IMPROVEMENT

One of these V4s has had the fashionable retro front conversion to the original late 96, employing new front wings and some under-the-skin work to create the early V4 nose design.

character who was utterly focused and, more often than not, correct in his opinions. If anyone knew how good a 2-stroke engine could be, it was Mellde. Conversely, he also knew the limitations of the type, and by 1960 he was convinced that Saab's engineering and design ethos was being hampered by its engine choice. It was Mellde who started to look at a 4-cylinder engine, even though it was reported that Holm had banned any such investigations.

At some professional risk Mellde and a few of his colleagues, including the test engineers Kjell Knutsson and Ingvar Andersson, apparently set up an unofficial 4-stroke engine research group. From 1962 onwards the members of this somewhat clandestine unit were quietly looking at creating a small 4-cylinder engine with a capacity of about 1.2 litres, not just for the 93's derivative, the 96, but also for a completely new Saab. It is reputed that Mellde even hosted design meetings in his own home. More openly, he sent a letter about the need for a better engine to Ljungström and Svante Simonsson, then Saab's production chief.

The journey towards a 4-cylinder engine was slow, but the expansion of the engine department that came from this would ultimately lead to Saab's Turbo years. Key names of the engine development team under Mellde and Eklund included Ingvar Andersson, Per Gillbrand, Olle Granlund, Bertil Ilhage, Kjell Knutsson, Olle Lindkvist, Lars Olov Olsson, Dick Ohlsson, Bertil Pedersen and Lennart Rosen. Nils-Gunnar Svensson was hired by Mellde in 1965 to work on developing the 2-stroke and joined the others on the V4 development team. They would soon evaluate a range of engines from competing manufacturers, and the links that they forged with Ricardo & Co. Engineers would influence the engine of the Saab 99. Before that happened, however, there was the story of how a Ford V4 engine found its way into the Saab 96.

V4 FOR POWER

In the early 1940s Sixten Sason drew up a design for a radically configured, steam-powered car. The obvious question was why? Odd as it may seem from today's perspective, by the 1950s steam power as an energy source for cars was under serious consideration. Sason had been early to the idea in 1940. Soon even Ford and GM in the USA were spending part of their research budgets on steam studies. Steam offered lots of torque, but for a car it was an engineering nightmare. The threat of explosion and the need for a pressure chamber were major issues, yet Saab looked at steam as a motive power source.

Inside Saab's aircraft division, under its technical director Tore Gullstrand, the thought of powering an aircraft by steam was neither weird nor eccentric; it was simply the extension of an idea that the German engineer Alexander Lippisch had considered in the 1930s. So it seems that precious time and resources were spent inside Saab researching steam power. The automotive division's engineering department were aghast. What they wanted was a small, efficient and, above all, tractable and perky 4-stroke engine with which to go rallying, and to power a new Saab.

Ljungström was working on refining the 2-stroke principle and trying to cure the problem that it needed lubrication within the piston and cylinder action. Although abandoned as a research idea, it had spawned thoughts of a V-angled 2-stroke. In later years the orbital cylinder cycle concept would make more of this research theme. By the late 1950s research had indicated that Saab should be looking for a V4 engine. Mazda had been investigating the twin-rotor Wankel engine, which would power the NSU Ro 80, while Citroën's own research would later result in the single-rotor M35 and twin-rotor GS Birotor. Saab looked at all the options, even the Wankel rotary concept, but thankfully rejected it.

The introduction of stricter emissions regulations in the 1960s, notably in California, made the search for a cleaner, leaner-burning engine even more urgent. Saab needed a new engine and Mellde and Josef Eklund started looking. Engines from various European carmakers, including the Fiat group, VW, Opel, the British Motor Corporation (BMC) and Ford, were tested to see if Saab could buy an off-the-shelf engine and save itself millions in development costs.

Several engines from other marques were considered. The big Volvo B18 was really too heavy, but there was always the excellent British design of the Standard Triumph 1300's engine or the free-spinning alloy unit in the Hillman Imp – at least that was small and light.

Svante Holm joined with Rolf Mellde's select team to take a good look at the 1089cc V4 engine of the Lancia Appia, with its cylinders set at an angle of 10 degrees, and at the different but very peppy 848cc BMC A-series as a transverse installation. Intriguingly, the Lloyd Company of Germany was still extant and Saab installed an 897cc 45bhp unit from the Lloyd Arabella in a 96 test car – as it also did with the Lancia and BMC units. By late 1964, however, Mellde knew he needed power as torque *not* just power as combustion volume.

Saab owner's manual from the mid-1960s.

SAAB 96 V4: CONTINUOUS IMPROVEMENT

The face of the V4: the low-line front with rectangular headlamps has its appeal.

The BMC, Lancia and Lloyd engines were not robust enough to offer development potential when it came to increasing the internal combustion pressure or modifying the cylinder heads. Mellde's team, which included engine men Olle Granlund, Per Gillbrand and Lennart Rosen, and other key technical engine/chassis team members such as Hakon Sörgardt, Rune Ahlberg and Kjell Knutsson, all knew what they were looking for and the BMC A-series was not it!

Olle Granlund and Per Gillbrand had recently jumped ship from Volvo to join Mellde at Saab (ironically, Mellde would later travel in the other direction to join Volvo). Granlund and Gillbrand were to bring with them vital knowledge of engine design, especially of turbocharging gained from working on truck and car engines, and reinforced the 4-stroke gang at Saab.

After testing each of the rival engines for more than 400 hours, only one engine met Saab's requirements and Saab very quietly purchased some units of the new Ford V4 alloy unit for further evaluation. Mellde knew that, even if Ford USA showed little interest in its own V4, the Cologne-built Ford V4 was strong, extendable and likely to be reliable in extreme conditions as found in Scandinavia. It was a short, square, stout little V4 and had a reasonable torque curve. Mellde was considering ways of adding more capacity as power output and torque, and is reputed to have told his colleagues that 'we could beef this up'.

The Ford engine was smooth and not so heavy as to upset the 96's balance. Saab thought it could probably be 'tweaked' to make it even better. One thing was for sure, if Saab were to compete, not least on domestic soil against the new 4-cylinder Volvos, it needed an engine and quickly.

SAAB 96 V4: CONTINUOUS IMPROVEMENT

Another view of the American-type 96 front end, which some people prefer.

Mellde approached Ford to see if the fairly new German V4 engine from Ford's 'Cardinal' project might be available for Saab. He had now identified the V4's 'over-square' 60-degree V4 with 1498cc as being ideal. This differed from the British Ford V4 known as the 'Essex', which was less robust. Ford's plans to sell its German V4-equipped Taunus model in the USA had been cancelled. Ford Germany had spare engine-building capacity and it made sense to recoup some costs by selling a version of the engine to Saab. But the go-ahead had to come from Ford HQ in Dearborn.

Mellde made a trip to America under the cover of attending a technical conference for the Society of Automotive Engineers. Saab's top team apparently had no idea what their man was up to. In a bizarre coincidence, Ford had reputedly been testing their new V4 engine in a Saab 96 2-stroke body as early as 1961. Apparently the Saab was deemed a good cover story for what was then a very small engine for Ford America and Europe. This seems almost as strange as the tales of General Motors testing a Maserati-engined Citroën SM in Detroit, but both reports are thought to be reliable. Ford's boss in Dearborn was prepared to hear Mellde out and did not have a problem with the idea in principle.

Mellde was still not home and dry with the 4-stroke for Saab and it is said that the internal Saab invoices for the V4 project investigation costs were made to a fictitious company name in order to distract from what was going on.

Ford gave the Saab deal the code name 'Daisy', whereas Saab called their end of the project 'Operation Kajsa'. Following further negotiations at the top of the Ford management structure in Dearborn, and also in Germany and the UK, after some delays Ford approved Mellde's request. A five-year licensing agreement was suggested. Although the engine was to be seen in the front-wheel-drive German-made Taunus 12M and 15M, Saab would have its own version. Ford had agreed, the problem was that Tryggve Holm had not. Despite his campaigns to maintain the quality of Saab's cars while expanding the factories and upping production, and pushing the company into its great American experiment, which had yielded so much, Holm still had a 2-stroke blind spot.

Mellde now had to reveal what he had been up to and how far he had reached in his 'research', as he framed it: this even included hiring a private workshop for his team to test the V4 – off-site. He made a presentation to Svante Holm and the Saab directors, but still Tryggve Holm said 'no'.

Could Tryggve Holm not see that Saab might falter if the 4-stroke engine was rejected? It was at this point that Mellde risked everything, even his career and professional reputation within Saab: *somehow* he had to win for Saab's sake. Tryggve Holm had done great things at Saab, but he seems to have erred with his refusal to move Saab quickly on to the 4-stroke engine.

For Mellde to challenge Holm, the boss, over Saab's adherence to the 2-stroke would have had serious professional implications, so Mellde boxed clever. He approached Marcus Wallenberg's son, Marc, and he in turn worked on his father. Wallenberg was the senior shareholder in Saab, and everything changed when Wallenberg Senior advised Tryggve Holm to pursue a 4-stroke future. Mellde had won a battle that had far greater implications than many people realized. Mellde's team really had saved Saab and opened the doors to a new era, a new dimension. Mellde deserves much credit for this.

Mellde had influence with management: he had set up a V4 development unit inside Saab, had the 96 lengthened a touch at the front end to accommodate the new engine and even sent Gillbrand to Italy to test the V4 engine and its 96 installation in secret. The scheme was funded by Saab, but how many at the top of Saab knew about it?

Gillbrand told everyone he was taking a leave of absence to manage the family paint supply shop. In fact he ended up in Italy, with his wife and young son, at 28 Via Sirmione in the town of Desenzano del Garda, working in a secure garage behind the gates of a house rented from Giacomo Acerbi. Here he experimented with the installation of a Ford V4 engine in a Saab 96. Gillbrand was there for more than four months, tinkering with the engine and the car, driving thousands of miles around the local roads. Mellde drove another V4-engined 96 down to Italy and joined Gillbrand in touring the local roads and adjusting the car. Long nights in the garage fettling the engine set-up must have made the locals wonder just what was wrong with the strange Swedish car.[28]

For the project to succeed secrecy was vital: Saab also had to ensure that its new suppliers did not let the cat out of the bag. If the public found out that the 2-stroke 96 was doomed, Saab would be left with a lot of unsold cars. Fewer than a dozen people knew about the Saab V4 and it is to their credit that the level of secrecy stayed that way for a year, even after Mellde ordered several engines from Germany and sent Saab staff to fetch them. Was it possible that Josef Eklund was kept in the dark for a bit, perhaps to avoid putting him in a difficult position? Mellde and Eklund were typical of Saab's finest, doing what they knew best even if top management said to do otherwise. Going against orders actually saved Saab.

The Ford V4 seemed well suited to the 96's temperament, It was an engine that revved easily, if noisily, and could be kept 'on the cam' – spooled up and ready to deliver its torque. Saab softened the valve springs in their version of the engine, which further reduced the risk of over-speeding and lowered vibration. In fact valves were to be the V4's only real issue: if not properly maintained, the valves' stems could stretch and the valve seats fatigue, leading to poor sealing and lower compression. It was necessary to look out for a rise in tappet noise in hard-driven engines. Fitting the correct type of oil filter was essential to ensure appropriate oil flow and return. As with all front-wheel-drive cars, gearbox noise would soon indicate an underlying issue.

The V4 engine had a balancer shaft, and the camshaft's fragile, fibrous gear wheel was an area that required later modification (notably by means of a Rolf Jensen-type steel-alloy blend wheel, which is now a rare item). Simple steel timing wheels are now the answer.

Saab fitted heavy-duty driveshafts that lasted for many miles, unlike certain other European front-wheel-drive car manufacturers.

These issues were often related more to use and maintenance than to 'pure' design problems; thankfully the early V4s were reliable, which was more than Saab's customers had experienced with the 92 and 93 engines in their early production forms. The robust V4 was ideal for the 96 and complemented its character. With its vibration counterbalance shaft and proper engine mountings, the V4 could be made to offer levels of smoothness approaching that of a straight-blocked 4-cylinder engine. Meeting ever-

SAAB 96 V4: CONTINUOUS IMPROVEMENT

A beige V4 with roof rack and wing mirrors typifies the 96 workhorse of the early 1970s era.

stricter emissions rules did however mean that Saab later had to lean off the fuel mixture and compression, which weakened throttle-combustion response times.

Another issue relevant to all of Saab's engines, from 2-stroke to the turbo 4-cylinder, was to be that of head gasket sealing and reliability. In the extreme arctic temperatures that were the Saab's natural environment, cylinder heads, engine block, liners and many metal components could behave at varying rates according to air temperature, the temperature of the component and the operating temperatures around the engine and engine bay. An engine starting and running from extreme cold was likely to heat up at different rates in different parts of the engine, which could lead to gasket failure, leakage and other problems.

During the development of 3-cylinder engines for the 93 and 96 models, Josef Eklund's engine laboratory men had to carry out many experiments to assess and achieve the correct performance from such vital engine components. Simply over-tightening the cylinder head bolts was not the Saab way or the answer, and special experiments were tried to find a solution. One included using fluid dye and special gaskets to assess the performance and integrity of the engine

Here the much larger rear windscreen size/aperture is very obvious, being cut up into the roof.

159

SAAB 96 V4: CONTINUOUS IMPROVEMENT

More Saab V4 advertising stock.

The new interior was clean and yet rather too calm. This type of steering wheel was very short-lived.

bolts, block and cylinder head gasket. This led to the adoption of a special cylinder-head bolt analysis by which their torque/tension and tensile strengths could be calibrated and then added to an assessment of their angle of action. Using these techniques, their clamping or pulling forces upon the cylinder head, block and gasket could all be calibrated to a degree previously unknown.

This work by Saab was both highly advanced and a precursor of later studies in this field. The Saab team also studied piston temperatures and expansion rates within the cylinder to refine further the 3-cylinder engine's performance.

These early innovative experiments by Saab's engine laboratory resulted not only in the larger 850cc Saab engine with twelve cylinder-head bolts, they also contributed to its record of not suffering from gasket or cylinder-head problems in normal use. When it came to altering the valve tensions and cylinder-head loadings for the new V4, Mellde, Eklund and the team had a wealth of experience to draw upon from their 2-stroke days.

Over time the issue of the balancer shaft and wear in its bearings would arise in the V4, since bearing wear could damage the teeth of the fibre timing gear and make the lack of water pump, fan and alternator somewhat obvious. On a very bad Saab V4 day you could always find shattered fibres

SAAB 96 V4: CONTINUOUS IMPROVEMENT

Big bumpers (off the 99) and revised trims modernized the V4 into a late dotage as a dowager duchess of a Saab, yet one that had a turn of speed. This one is a daily driver for owners Andy and Sheila Deans.

This interesting V4 blue beastie has it all: big bumpers, sunroof, rear deck spoiler, driving lamps, mud flaps and is left-hand drive. It lives in Scotland and travels afar with its dedicated owners.

from that cheap original equipment timing wheel in the oil and filter. Most 96 V4 owners would soon need to hear about the metal or alloy timing gear wheels available to replace the fibre timing wheel.

To stop the new V4 with its greater power and heavier engine weight, Lockheed swing-caliper front disc brakes were fitted, along with the, by then standard, Saab dual-line split-diagonal safety braking system.

The front of the 96 had to be redesigned to house the little V4. Longer pressings for the inner and outer wings, new engine mounts and cross members were needed for what was effectively a new, longer nose. New tooling, jigs and small presses were sourced in great secrecy from Chausson of France and Vickers of England. Such was the pressure of time that a Saab team went to the Vickers plant in Newcastle and brought the new tooling presses home on a North Sea ferry to Gothenburg, and then by road to the factory.

In August 1966 specially chosen employees were called in for some overtime during the summer break. Their secret task was to collect unsold 96 long-nose 2-stroke cars from the Trollhättan airfield storage compound and fit the first batch of V4 engines to already complete 2-strokes. Argument over the exact number of 'converted' cars has endured, but numbers between 100 and 600 have been cited: certainly there were hundreds of unsold 96 2-strokes languishing in the compound. The converted cars were sold as 'new' V4s and V4 badges sourced from Ford dealers in Sweden, Germany and even the UK were hastily stuck on their flanks. You can identify a very early V4 by these badges, which were also used on the British Ford Corsair and the German Ford Taunus.

After the summer break, Saab got its act together and V4 production cars streamed off the line. An earlier than usual announcement was made about the coming model year: the Saab 96 would have V4 power and the reaction was huge.

The 1.5-litre capacity V4, pushing out 73bhp (SAE)/65bhp (DIN), transformed the Saab. The vital 0–60mph or 0–100km/h timings were under 15 seconds, top speed was well over 70mph and approaching 150km/h. Fuel consumption when carefully driven could be 40mpg and the magic metric fuel usage figure of less than 7ltr/100km was achieved, but an average figure of just over 30mpg was more realistic. Overtaking performance in the vital 30–50mph sector was good, with that sprint taking 11 seconds, a vast improvement on the 2-stroke's 20 seconds.

Early V4s had engine blocks with 'Ford' cast into them, but later engines were lacking such markings. That the V4 would be modified to 120bhp and more was a piece of Saab magic that had not yet been achieved.

The V4 version of the Monte Carlo appeared, but it was a short-lived marketing idea that was available for less than three model years and was a trim special, not a performance special. For the 94 V4 a revised interior was announced, including strange detachable, in-car wastepaper baskets – plastic rubbish bins that hung from the seats or cabin footwells.

THE V4 EFFECT

The effects of the V4 on Swedish domestic sales and the world market were dramatic. Once word got out about the 96 V4's abilities, the sales figures rose steeply. A sales increase of more than 40 per cent simply from fitting a new engine to an existing car may be a unique record.

Saab invested heavily in an advertising programme across Europe and the world to promote the new car. Advertisements showed the handling and safety benefits, with headlines that read: 'Saab 96: the plane-makers contribution to safer driving' and 'Saab 95: for the professionals'. There were endorsements from Stirling Moss, which was an easy win for Saab since his sister Pat was married to Erik Carlsson. Safety was emphasized in Saab's advertising, with one British advert quoting *Motor* magazine of 17 August 1968: 'The Swedes are precise and meticulous engineers with probably the strongest bias in Europe towards safety in both its primary and secondary forms.'

In France the 96 was advertised as the ideal car ('La voiture ideale'), and indeed to many the new V4 Saab was ideal. Old purists still loved their 'stroker' Saabs, but the V4 was much more capable as a family car or for everyday driving.

The rally victories of the 1960s also helped create the Saab legend. The free publicity generated when Saab won the 1971 RAC Rally outright as well as the team prize – with Stig Blomqvist/Arne Hertz in first place, Carl Orrenius/Lars Persson third, Per Eklund/Sölve Andreasson sixth and Seppo Utriainen/Klaus Lehto tenth, all driving 96s – was worth millions.

Canadians liked Saabs as well, especially in the snow-bound provinces, but official imports of Saabs into Canada did not take off until 1975. The 96 V4 had been seen in the Canadian Winter Rally of 1969 when John Crawford and Waller Drafft drove over the border from the USA and came 9th in class and 15th overall. Quite a few Canadians went the other way

SAAB 96 V4: CONTINUOUS IMPROVEMENT

Purple Saab and pre-impact bumper too.

A well-used V4 at rest. There were many ways a V4's performance could be improved.

BJÖRN BERGLÖF

One of the less-remembered names of the 96 story, Björn Berglöf, worked in various roles at Saab from 1964 to 2008. One of these involved working on the interior design from the 96 to the 99. He is said to have been responsible for the defining Saab high-backed orthopaedic 'safety' headrest and seat design seen in the Envall-revised 99, the 900 and the late-model 96/95. Berglöf later became a key figure in the Saab motor sport department.

SAAB 96 V4: CONTINUOUS IMPROVEMENT

into the USA to purchase 96s in the late 1960s.

In Great Britain, Saab's second most important export market after the USA, the 96 V4 was launched at a price of £801 (the 96 2-stroke had been £742), and the V4 soon rose to £1,350. The 96 was advertised under the slogan 'Go Swift Go Safe Go Saab'. Saab GB Ltd moved from 207 Regent Street, London, and to 6 Wellcroft Road, Slough, Buckinghamshire.

One of the oddities of the 1967 marketplace was that the safe, sporty Saab 96 V4 cost the same amount to buy in Britain as a Wolseley 1100. This bizarre comparison demonstrates a marked improvement in Saab's market position in the UK, where Saab had been charging over £500 more for a 96 2-stroke Super Sport than the cost of a new Cortina 1600 GT, which outclassed the Saab in performance, if not strength.

1967 AND A MICHELOTTI RESTYLE?

Given the ever-important need for higher volume production to make Saab more financially viable, and given the slow start to 99 production – Envall's restyling of the model in 1971 would save both it and Saab's viability – the company looked to the 96 in early 1967 for any possible updates that might cheaply refresh or 'facelift' the car.

Saab turned to the self-effacing but hugely influential Giovanni Michelotti of Turin. Michelotti was a designer stylist whose pen touched a host of cars from a Triumph to a BMW to a Nissan/Datsun, yet did not always receive the design credit. Saab told Michelotti that he could make minor tooling alterations to the nose, tail and certain outer skin panels, but that the main body toolings and pressings, such

Somehow the later headlamp design and revised frontal treatment looks just right here as a green **V4** throbs away. It might not be a 'stroker', but it is still a mighty fine **Saab** original variant.

SAAB 96 V4 TECHNICAL SPECIFICATION, LATE 1968 FOR 1969 MODEL YEAR

The Saab 96 replaced the Saab 93F in February 1960 using a revised body and updated technical specification. The Saab 95 production specification was introduced in December 1959 with the bigger engine of the 96 2-stroke. The 841cc V4 engine was introduced in 1967.

Engine	
Configuration	4-cylinder overhead valve engine built on licence from Ford Motor Company Taunus 15M German model. 60 degree V-configuration longitudinally mounted
Cooling	Water cooled
Bore x stroke	90 x 58.86mm
Capacity	1498cc
Compression ratio	9.0:1
Maximum power	73bhp (54kW)
Maximum torque	12kg m (117Nm) at 2,700rpm
Carburettor	Autolite C8 GH 9510g; Weber alternative offered
Fuel	Cam-driven fuel pump
Transmission	Front-wheel drive: single dry-plate clutch with 4-speed full synchromesh gearbox with column shift. Freewheel device fitted
Suspension	Coil springs and hydraulic shock absorbers at front: rigid rear axle. 95 estate has lever-arm shock absorbers to rear
Steering	Rack and pinion with 5.3m radius
Wheels and tyres	15 inch 4J rims: radial tyre option of 155 x 15
Brakes	Diagonal-split safety system with front discs and rear drums
Electrics	12 volts 4Ag battery capacity
Bodyshell	Stressed skin monocoque with carry-over reinforcements from earlier shell. Revised rear body with larger windscreen and wider rear cabin. Improved aerodynamics
Dimensions	
Wheelbase	2,498mm (98.35in)
Length	4,200mm (165.35in) (Estate 4,300mm/169.29in)
Width	1,580mm (62.20in)
Height	1,480mm (58.27in) (Estate 1,490mm/58.66in)
Weight (net)	890kg (1,962lb) (Estate 955kg/2,105lb)
Top speed	147km/h (91.34mph)
Price in Sweden in 1968	Skr14,785 (Estate Skr16,560)

as the roof, pillars, sills and outer panels were to remain untouched. If needed, changes could be made to the lights.

For a small fee, by August 1967 Studio Michelotti had drawn up a 96 with a modern, chrome-grilled front, revised front wing/fender line and some minor nips and tucks to outer skin panels along the car. A slightly 'squarer' effect was applied to the 96's ellipsoid shape. Saab decided not to proceed with this restyle and instead used its in-house team to refresh the 96 with a new grille, trims and light designs. Soon the Saab 99's 'impact' bumpers would be grafted on as well as other items off the 99. So ended the possibility of a Michelotti 96 refresh for the 1970s. The 99's impact-type bumpers were kinked to fit its nose styling, and that looked even more obvious on the flat-fronted 96.

SAAB 96 V4: CONTINUOUS IMPROVEMENT

AN OWNER'S VIEW: MIKE PHILPOTT

My love affair with the 96 V4 started back in the 1970s. My best friend was a mechanic in the local Saab dealership and persuaded me to look for one after driving all sorts of stuff that kept breaking down. They were not easy to come by in those days, but I managed to find an unusual car in that it was a 1965 long-nose 2-stroke 'Sport' that had been professionally converted to a V4.

Some 2-stroke owners would call this sacrilege, but it is ironic that Saab made this model as the 96 V4 Monte Carlo. My converted 96 was a fantastic car and felt very special. It had retained its 2-stroke gearbox, so the top speed wasn't so high but, along with its twin-choke Weber and Saab sports exhaust, got there quite quickly. It was enormous fun to drive. The done thing in those days was to throw away the hub caps, paint the wheels black, bolt four Cibie Oscar lamps on the front, then fit a rev counter. You were instantly Erik Carlsson or Stig Blomqvist. Oh, and in Toreador Red, of course.

There was very little on the road that could keep up with a V4 due to its speed, handling and outright stamina. If anyone did manage to get past they were immediately chastised by the four Cibies! Apart from being fantastic to look at and drive, its rarity also made it feel special. I was living away from home by then and I knew only one other guy in the area with one and he was twenty miles away. If we met another owner on the road we would automatically pull over for a chat. What other car had that sort of following?

A succession of V4s furnished our household over the coming years until I moved onto the other Saab models. Even then there has always been a V4 in the stable, some as daily runabouts, others as 'show' cars, and others just workhorses for towing our caravan and big heavy trailers. These cars did it all.

Many years ago we tried to record all the 96s that we had owned and gave up at over a hundred. There have been more since. This included ones that I rebuilt with some minor accident damage or mechanical problems, one 'works' replica rally car, a grass-track racer and others just for parts. I have also promoted enthusiasm within our family by giving one to each of our granddaughters, which they still have.

These cars have also proven to be really reliable and we have had very few issues with them. There have been just two main concerns: the gearboxes can be a weak point as they were originally designed for the much lower output 2-stroke engine; and secondly, some parts of the bodywork and floorpan can suffer badly from rust. We have had a few that were actually past any sort of repair. Other than that, there really isn't much to worry about. I have only ever changed an engine once.

Having owned many V4s I am now down to just one in the stable. It is, however, the best one ever: a 1976 Souvenir, number 122 of the last 150 right-hand-drive 96s to be made. Finished in Cardinal Red metallic with a red interior, she

ABOVE: **Saab fitted this dashboard plaque to the numbered special edition.**

LEFT: **Mike Philpott's very special 'Souvenir' edition of the last of the line British 96 V4 series. Mike and his son Alistair have restored and run many Saabs of various ages. That black grille for the 1970s really did update the car's appearance.**

is truly stunning and has still only covered 42,000 miles (67,590km) from new. She's more or less totally original, other than some paintwork around the front end when a plate glass window fell on it! She is also quite standard apart from a twin-choke carb, Jetex sports exhaust, electronic ignition, electric fan, Saab 'Sport & Rally' steering wheel and super-rare Saab 'Sport & Rally' reverse rims. I plan to keep this one for ever.

We have attended many events and meetings with her including the Saab International meeting in the Netherlands a few years back. That was a great trip. In 2022 we are hoping to take her to the Saab Festival in Trollhättan.

I have been fortunate and privileged to have owned almost every Saab model over the last nearly 50 years, from 2-strokes to the last new-generation 9-5 and a Sonett. The 96 V4, however, is my favourite by far. Why? I guess because it has everything. Stunning looks, real character, it is superbly comfortable, sounds awesome, is fantastic to drive, handles like a dream, is safe as houses and so different: a beautiful thing, I just love them.

RIGHT AND BELOW: **The interior is true of its era. The Saab 96 and 95 eventually were fitted with the new 99's high-backed front seats, but not in time for the Souvenir edition.**
Three decades later the Saab shape still stands out.

Mike Philpott's car has had some of the tweaks that make a V4 more useable.

SAAB 96 V4: CONTINUOUS IMPROVEMENT

Giovanni Michelotti was the famous designer of many cars which never bore his name. This was his late 1960s very effective re-skin proposal for a 96 update with minimal tooling changes required – which Saab decided not to pursue.

The ever-present US emissions issues saw the new V4 1.5-litre high-compression engine with a 'base' of 73bhp (54kW: 74PS) being replaced in 1971 by the low-compression 1.7-litre engine of 65bhp (48kW: 66PS). US sales of the 96 and 95 V4 came to an end at the start of the 1975 model year.

RALLY CAR AND ROAD STAR

The V4 was a huge step for the 96 on the rallying stage and the engine modifications for rallying were soon reverse-engineered into the production 96 V4 as either improved specifications or optional accessories for the owner to purchase and fit. At the least, the road-going privately run 96 V4 would benefit from a Weber twin-choke carburettor (with something called an S&R manifold set-up, a sports exhaust and electric fuel pump or two). If you could afford a regular supply, there were also Pirelli Cinturato tyres, which had a compound that the 96 V4 suspension set-up seemed to like.

The 'Chilton Tuning Catalogue' provided early advice. Since the 1970s Malbrad Saab Specialists, owned by Stephen Broadhead, has offered parts with which to tweak your V4. Highgate Saabpart, currently in Tamworth, founded in 1988, was among the early UK suppliers of V4 items, notably the Highgate-type clutch. Some of the upgraded gearboxes made for the 96 by Richard Vigouroux-Henday occasionally turn up on the Internet. British Saab Club member Richard Simpson has created some excellent clutch and gearbox modifications that have stood the test of time in fast road and race/rally use too.[29]

Nils-Gunnar Svensson was development engineer at the Saab Competition Department and he was responsible for the rally and racing engines of 2-stroke and 4-stroke types between 1963 and 1969. Saab's competition manager Bo Swanér was on hand to steer things too.

In late 1966 Saab decided to raise the output of the V4 for Group Two rally classification. Ford in Germany was seemingly less than interested in upgrading the engine and reputedly suggested that 90–100bhp (DIN) was a 'safe' limit for the engine. No tuning instructions were known at Ford for this particular engine, so Saab decided to do their own thing, as always.

Obvious tweaks like changing the compression ratio and altering the camshaft (a camshaft with 7.6mm lift was the first development), together with a larger carburettor or a standard carburettor with larger throttle housing, resulted

SAAB 96 V4: CONTINUOUS IMPROVEMENT

This Rally specification car has the cut-way 'competition' rear wheel arches as well as Saab rally-type fittings.

in improved performance levels, notably with more power and torque that were ideal for rally driving.

Changes to the valve lifters and rocker arms were made to reduce weight in order to allow higher revs. Fitting the largest available Solex carburettor (Mercedes-specification) with a single-port 38mm carburettor (with the throttle housing machined to 40mm with an adapted butterfly) resulted in the sealing surface having a width of only 1.5–2mm. This work was in hand with modification of the ports in both cylinder heads and intake manifold. So were set the revised V4 modification criteria, using a Mercedes-Benz specification carburettor.

The engine was equipped with stronger valve springs, modified air cleaner and a high-capacity ignition coil (Bosch TK12 A10). The exhaust pipes were increased to a larger diameter of 44mm, re-formed in a bow over the driveshafts, with the pipes taken through the rear end of the engine compartment floor and 'siamezed' into a single full-length pipe ending in a silencer. The engine flywheel was reduced in weight and an oil cooler was installed. The engine had been stressed on the dynamometer at just under 90bhp and passed; note that Ford of Germany's warning was not ignored.

These changes were the first 'competition' modifications to the German V4 in its Saab guise.

Saab did what it often did and went testing in a rally, entering the modified V4 in the Bergslagsrundan Rally, held in the region around Kristinehamn on 3 December 1966. Åke

■ SAAB 96 V4: CONTINUOUS IMPROVEMENT

Andersson drove the car to its first victory, with his boss Bo Swanér as co-driver.

By the start of the 1967 season Saab had added a larger carburettor and bigger throttle housing, and the 65bhp engine now produced close to 100bhp. The next step in the development was the introduction of the twin-throat carburettor. Saab used a Ford Transit van specification Weber carburettor and intake manifold on the V4.

Various settings and specifications allowed Saab to set the V4's changes according to which class of rally a car was being entered: Sweden (and Europe) had varying rally 'Classes' or groups with differing regulations and requirements for differing types of stages, these being either the high-speed stages or the slower, but tougher, forest-type twisting sections.

TON-UP, TUNE-UP

With rallying such a huge part of the 92 to 96 V4 story, it became obvious that many modifications had become accepted practice yet never really formalized as the basis for an opportunity to create accessory sales for Saab. In the 1960s a number of tuning upgrades stemming from 2-stroke rally cars became available. For the V4, however, Saab put together and properly marketed a new range of performance accessories.

Fitted with the right engine, breathing, combustion, exhaust and drivetrain parts, the 96 could get to well over 100bhp, with a top speed above 100mph.

Two V4 tuning kits were available from Saab. Kit 1 took the 1500cc engine from 65bhp (DIN) to 80bhp (DIN). Kit 2

You can never have too many lights on a Saab 96, even on a retro-conversion car.

took the 1700cc engine from 65bhp (DIN) to 90bhp (DIN).

Competition modification of the V4 included official Group 2 standard specifications and varied across the period from 1968 to 1972 with 'blue', 'black' and 'red' engine type nomenclature and specifications.

Taking the 1.5-litre V4 engine above 105bhp and perhaps as far as 130bhp (DIN) was now feasible, provided you got the head type and head fitment correct, of course.

Getting the 1.7-litre V4 to between 125 and 145bhp (DIN) was easily possible, though at some cost, and getting beyond 150bhp would soon be achieved.

Modifying your 96 V4 allowed you to consider the following changes as key components of modification:

Cylinders: Bored to 91.03mm (3.584in) for new pistons from 91mm (3.58in)/91mm. (Rebore must not exceed taper out-of-round or limit of 0.14mm/0.0056in.)

Pistons: Forged to replace cast-type for competition only purposes: different dimension pistons also on offer. Forged competition pistons had domed heads that also benefited tuning.

Compression: Increase by milling: if standard cast pistons are used in the engine, then limits apply to reboring the head in order to avoid inducing weakness. The standard block engine must not be milled, but revised heads can be milled to increase compression ratio without changes to combustion chamber.

On the 1.7-litre engine with revised pistons and connecting rods, or a modified-head 1.5-litre engine, there are differing piston diameters and two options for more compression, one being milling the engine block by 1.0mm (0.04in) to make the piston stop at top dead-centre, and milling the head block surface against the intake manifold to create improved flow. A simple method is to mill the cylinder heads alone, dependent on other modifications.

Crankshaft: Saab did not approve modifying the 1.5-litre engine's crankshaft connecting rod, and also recommended that the 1.7-litre engine used a special crankshaft.

Intake ports: These could be re-profiled and special measurements for optimum performance were cited by Saab for such changes.

Valves: According to advice from Saab, these could be chrome plated with differing hardnesses, and separate valve guides improved performance. Relevant changes to the combustion chamber were also recommended by Saab. Torque increased with larger porting areas at intake and exhaust points. The limitation was the 4mm wall thickness and the gasket between the heads and manifolds. Competition valve lifters were also offered.

Rocker arm: This could be ground at the valve end to a diameter of 8mm. A competition-type rocker arm shaft support was another Saab tweak.

Head gasket: A copper ring kit fitment requires grooving to be carried out by hand.

Carburettor: Twin type modifications were an obvious improvement. 2-strokes, of course, could eventually have a triple-carb set-up.

Oil pump: This could be modified with a stiffer spring: Saab suggested polishing the internal plunger to reduce spring wear.

Fuel pump: The standard fuel pump supplied enough pressure up to 115bhp; beyond this figure Saab recommended a stronger flow pump rated up to 160bhp. A fibre gasket could be installed to reduce heat-soak vapour locks.

Oil cooler: This was recommended for the competition engine at high bhp rating. Any tune-up above 110bhp required better cooling flow and a larger radiator and overflow tank were also deemed advisable, especially for competition engines in areas outside Sweden.

Clutch: The Fichtel and Sachs-type clutch (factory or upgraded specification) or the 'Highgate' diaphragm type are recommended. You should beware, however, of drive plate tolerances and thickness issues with alternative non-standard clutch brands as such issues might affect clutch mechanism and function. A key reliability modification is to make sure there is no wear in the thrust arm pivots and that the engine mounts are working as designed and not denuded.

In the early 2000s Richard and Les Simpson made some special Highgate-type derivative clutches with their own modifications to the bearing, together with improvements to the flywheel and cover. Further changes were made to the flywheel face, with better lining material and improve-

■ SAAB 96 V4: CONTINUOUS IMPROVEMENT

ABOVE: **Last of the line 96, fitted with side stripes and black-painted trim for the end of the 1970s.**

Green was always a Saab hue, and this 1970s Opal Green was a thick paint that resisted rot well. Just bung a couple of big lamps on the front and it is a Saab that shouts its name.

ments to the release bearing clips. These may be of interest to racers and rally drivers, or to road-going enthusiasts.

Saab also offered a lightened flywheel effect achieved by reducing the outer diameter behind the starter gear by turning (to 240mm/19.45in) or by milling/turning the flywheel so that only a small amount of coating material remains around the retaining bolts. The surface is then polished and the flywheel balanced and tightened to 7.9kg m (50ft lb). In this way the flywheel clutch mechanism can be lightened from a standard 7.25kg (16lb) to 5.67kg (12.5lb) or 5.22kg (11.5lb), respectively, saving a considerable weight. A competition clutch kit increased the clutch pressure plate and disc effort.

SAAB 96 V4: CONTINUOUS IMPROVEMENT

Non-standard and non-factory, but this remains an enthusiast's delight and somehow its unorthodox appearance makes it very Saab. This Targa 96 V4 features a roll-over bar.

Gearbox: Changes to gear ratios were expected for tuned and competition engines. Saab suggested a lower ratio of below 7:36 for ring and pinion gear: the competition setting was 6:35. Changes to intermediate shafts, cog ratios and shaft diameters were all part of the early 96 V4 tuning specifications.

Modifying the gearbox for high engine power was to be a particular concern for Saab. The gearbox oil viscosity rating was changed from EP80 to EP75 grade to assist in very cold conditions. According to Chris Partington, it is still important not to overfill the V4's gearbox to avoid damage to the nylon worm drive for the speedometer, although you could add a breather modification to increase oil capacity to protect the lubrication on the top shafts.

FURTHER MODIFICATIONS

A limited-slip differential was a rather exotic extra for a front-wheel drive, Ford-engined V4 Saab at factory 'competition' specification. A modified rear axle was used by Saab on all its rally cars. Competition brake pads were an obvious option.

Given that the 1970s Ford 'Cologne' V6 engine was effectively an enlarged version of the Cardinal Project's German V4 (not to be confused with the 'Essex'), as fitted to the Saab 96, it is surprisingly easy to fit the German Ford V6 into a 96. However, the extra engine mass badly affects the Saab's handling and there remains the old Saab issue of gearbox strength, so perhaps a madly understeering 96 V6 with approaching 70 per cent of its weight over or ahead of the front axle is not such a sensible idea. When it comes to re-engining Saab 96s, caution is wiser than imbecility. Saab knew that and stuck with a 'hot' V4 1.7-litre for 'fast road' specification.

Owners also undertook V4 upgrades for road use as well as for races and rallying. These included fitting an electric fan, a Jetex sports exhaust, or adding a Group 2 rally sump guard. Throw in roll cages, steering wheels, special seats, add-on headrests, leather-covered steering wheels, a tachometer and fire extinguisher, topped off with a Saab rally jacket and the 96, and the owner's every need was covered.

Richard Vigouroux-Henday, who has been mentioned above regarding his rebuilt gearboxes, also investigated the effect of tyre sizes and castor/camber angles on the handling of the 96 V4, and how its different weight and centre of gravity compared to the 96 2-stroke. Tyres below 165-section (155-size) seem fine for the 96 V4, but in his discussions with British Saab Club members he found that most agree 165-size provides better grip. Going for a tyre size bigger than 165 can lead to issues, however, as Saab's factory suspension/steering angle settings were apparently less about 'turn-in' sharpness and response, and more about ride and dynamic/directional reaction in the steering's dynamics.

An 'ultimate' Saab enthusiast's modification to the 96 V4 was to fit the 'Mexico' engine support brackets, which were developed in response to earlier rally experiences and rough road running. Designed to reduce engine 'shunt' and overall engine movement on standard engine mountings, this engine support system was Saab part number 101818 and consisted of rubber 'cushion' mounts added to the engine mountings as an extra layer. This stopped the fan and carburettor fittings moving too far out of alignment and upsetting the running of the engine. Two reinforced engine mounts and a third, extra transmission hub mount were fitted. The third, triple-depth rear cushion required a hole to be drilled in the engine floor area centred on the transmission drain, and had to be very accurately mounted, fitted and tightened. But the effects were very beneficial.

In 1972–73 Saab enhanced their enthusiast buyer base by making a further range of 'Sport' tuning kits available in Great Britain. Accessory kit brochures branded as 'Saab Sport & Rally' were produced through to 1979.

Rally spec kits inspired by Carlsson and the Saab works rally department included the option of a new crankshaft,

TYRES

Fitting Koni shock absorbers and Pirelli Cinturato CN36 tyres added the final elements of road holding and suspension/tyre rebound finesse to the car's set-up. The special compound 'grippy' Pirellis, with their new tread pattern and side-wall design that offered enhanced characteristics of hysteresis, really did add to the handling and grip, but wore out rather quickly if subject to hard driving.

Michelin, Avon or Goodyear tyres seemed to go quite well on old Saabs too. Michelin rubber lasted well but could be hard and noisy. A vast array of tyres of different makes have been fitted to the cars with varying results. Dunlops seem to either love or hate an old Saab, depending on its type and set-up. Again, rubber hysteresis, sidewall construction, tread pattern, aspect ratio and, notably in the Saab, castor and camber angle remain vital when it comes to getting the Saab to steer, grip and handle appropriately for the intended use and the tyres fitted.

which increased capacity to 1700cc, a Weber 40 DFI progressive twin-choke carburettor kit, and revised manifold and air cleaner specifications. Stronger valve springs were also brought back. Buyers could choose a new freer-flowing exhaust system, a sports steering wheel, 'golf ball' type alloy wheel design and even new decals.

Chris Partington, who was to rise to be technical director at Saab GB, was then the expert-in-chief and his modified cars, including a 95 V4 estate that was used as a rally support car, really flew. Specifying the full modification kit for a Saab 94 V4 would cost £299.93, a not insignificant sum, but performance, response and handling were taken to new levels.

The mechanical modifications introduced by the factory added nearly 15mph to the car's top speed and reduced the 0–60mph time to 11.5 seconds. A top speed in excess of 90mph, perhaps even 100mph in still-air conditions, was achieved. The car's 0–80mph time was halved to 23 seconds. For £300 British and other Saab 96 V4 owners could transform their cars into something that was faster and very capable. Mellde's genius was proven yet again.

Further enhancements came from the 'Chilton Tuning Catalogue', which contained a series of improvements for

SAAB 96 V4: CONTINUOUS IMPROVEMENT

WGU 561M appeared earlier in this book. With its retro-front panels, allied to chromed grille, it really looks fantastic. R. GUNN

private Saab owners. A milled cylinder head, stronger valves, machined camshaft and compression changes would all boost power. Chilton also reminded its clients that lowered ride height from shorter springs, wider tyres and sports dampers would lower the roll centres and centre of gravity, provide a wider tyre footprint and improve the car's handling and ultimate breakaway point prior to a skid.

Sydney Hurrell, who had raced a Saab at Le Mans, founded an accessory company called SAH Tuning, from which some Saab accessories could be obtained.

LATER 96 V4: TRIMMED UP

Saab did not rest on its laurels. From 1968 the 96 V4 was given a laminated windscreen that was 7cm taller, a bigger rear windscreen that was 11cm deeper, a new safety steering wheel, revised instrument trims and a proper textile carpet that complemented the standard nylon or woollen weave trim options. The 95 was also given the taller windscreen aperture, which made looking up at traffic lights a lot easier for Saab drivers who had developed a technique of bending their neck to see upwards out of the old, narrow windscreen. The improvements kept on coming in the form of a 'De Luxe' variant that had side rubbing strips, opening rear side windows, and rather overworked, fussy, chrome wheel rim embellisher rings. The 96 'Super V4' perhaps promised more than it delivered.

Saab's inveterate fettlers or tinkerers kept on fiddling with or perhaps rather improving the 96 V4's specifications. From 1969 through to 1974 there were constant programmes of upgrades and modernizations. Year on year, there were changes. One notable change brought in by Björn Envall, when he returned from a period working in the design studio of Opel in Germany, was to echo the styling of the new 99 and give the 96 rectangular headlamps (due to legislative requirements the US versions had to have round lamps). A more curved bumper design and a new grille were also fitted. This was the first year that Saab fitted a collapsible steering column across all its cars. Between 1970 and 1974 changes were made to dashboard colours and trims. This period also saw the introduction of car production at Saab's new factory at Uuskiaupunki, Finland, as a collaboration between Saab-Scania AB and Oy Valmet.

The 96 was getting bolder: brighter, stronger colours in blue, orange, yellow and brown echoed the fashion of the decade and bigger indicator lenses made a bolder statement too. The amount of stainless steel brightwork 'chrome' trim on the car was reduced: notably the air vent trim on the scuttle was deleted. Constant revisions in 1971–3 saw new side protection strips, bigger rear lamps, the innovation of an electrically heated driver's seat, halogen headlamps and some rich new paint colours, such as Amber Yellow and a shade of blue that Saab fans called 'unmentionable'.

For 1974 the Saab 96 V4 was given a more extensive makeover. This featured a new black plastic radiator grille with a Saab 99-style bright crossbar trim, revised badging, inertia-reel seat belts, better rustproofing and more (Olofsson-inspired) 'abstract' colours: Sunset Orange with a Manilla Brown interior trim was rather challenging to the

■ SAAB 96 V4: CONTINUOUS IMPROVEMENT

Another reverse-engineered 96, this time in blue and with all the makings of a cult car for a film appearance. You cannot knock Saab enthusiasts' sheer belief.

eyes. There were also bright blue and vivid green interiors to complement new exterior colours. Saab decided that these improvements warranted a trim motif and so was born the 96 De Luxe and 96 'L'. In 1976 Saab fitted the 96 with the smart, black rubber, self-repairing cell-construction bumpers that had appeared on the 99. For 1977 the high-backed seats from the 99 were also fitted to the 96, and a clever full-width rear boot spoiler also improved the management of airflow off the car's tail.

It was in 1975 that Saab also had the idea of creating an updated 95 estate. Something with cleaner lines and a more contemporary style was envisaged. Envall got busy and the result was Project X14 or the Saab 98, a three-door cross between an estate and a hatchback with a sloped rear end. The building of the one-off protoype was assisted by Carrozzeria Cogglia in Italy. Today it would be called a 'sportback': then it was sadly discarded.

Great Britain in 1975 also saw the Saab 96 V4 Silver Jubilee edition. Three hundred specially trimmed cars were fitted out to mark the anniversary of Saab GB. These cars were finished in Crystal Silver metallic with black-painted rear 'C' pillar vents and fitted with a special design of side body moulding. The interiors were a melange of orange and brown trim materials that was best described as distinctive.

96 V4 1.7S RALLY EDITION

In this period the Saab engineering department had to clean up the V4's exhaust emissions to meet new Swedish legislation, as well as US regulations. The 1.7-litre (low-compression in the USA) engine had become known for use in the 96 V4 in America, and had been taken up elsewhere by private owners with fast road or rallying ambitions. Saab claimed that the 90bhp 1.7S would be made available, including in Europe, while the 1975 Saab brochure said that Saab was 'producing on a limited scale' a special model: a 1.7-litre V4 with alloy wheels, extra instruments and a leather-trimmed steering wheel rim, twin headrests, special side stripes and a Simons-type rally exhaust. This was the 96S Rally Edition.

Saab intended to build ninety-six of these cars, but production figures up to 150 have been claimed. Most were in Indian Yellow, but there are reports of cars in Sunset Orange or green. The special edition had a production run from early 1975 to 1976, with the cars going from the factory to the Trollhättan Competition Department for fettling. Was the 1.7S Rally Edition a marketing trick? Maybe, but it was still hugely desirable and went well. Initally on sale in Sweden at the end of 1974, a right-hand-drive version was offered via Saab Great Britain for 1975 and left-hand-drive cars were on sale in Europe as well for more than twelve months.

For 1978 the V4 became the 'V4 Super' and more enhancements were made to create a 'GL' badged status. These included a power hike to 68bhp, more Saab 99 trim items, larger indicator lamps all round, and a range of metallic colours: one of these, Cardinal Red, became one of the few Saab paints to suffer from quality and corrosion problems across both the 96 and 99 ranges.

The Saab 95 estate was withdrawn from production when the last 95 body was welded up on 28 February 1978.

By 1978 all the 96s were being built in Finland to a very high build-quality standard. The cars of the 1979 and 1980 model years were given de-chroming and black painted window frames. This was a small design detail yet it made a surprisingly large visual difference to the car. Minilite-type alloy wheels and 'golf ball' 99 EMS style wheels were fitted and these also created visual changes to the design. The famous Acacia Green was also introduced.

A limited edition run of 150 special edition 96 V4s was seen on the British market in 1976, each with its own numbered dashboard plaque. These were the 'Souvenir' editions

The Sonett and Sonett V4 were developed from the 93 and 96. Parking a rally-specification 96 V4 next to a Sonett V4 highlights the free thinking that went into Saab design.

SAAB 96 V4 PRODUCTION FIGURES, 1967–8 JANUARY 1980

Year	Production	Year	Production
1967	37,622 (includes very low numbers of 96/95 2-stroke remaining, including in USA)	1974	22,762
		1975	21,468
1968	36,037 (28 Saab 96 2-strokes sold in Sweden)	1976	19,744
1969	32,384	1977	14,014
1970	34,120	1978	8,951
1971	28,369	1979	8,837 (final car driven off production line 8 January 1980 after Christmas break)
1972	28,795		
1973	27,431		

designed to mark the end of the right-hand-drive Saab 96 in Britain. They were little different from the standard 96L. A lot of the European run-out special edition very late-model 96 V4s sold very well in the Netherlands, where today they command high price premiums.

In 1980, the 96's 'run-out' year, there was a special Swedish/European market edition of 300 cars produced in Aquamarine silver blue metallic, with colour-coded wheels and interior trim. Less than a thousand examples of the venerable thirty-year-old base design that had been behind the story of the 92 to the 96 were sold in Sweden in 1980. In total, Saab sold 547,221 examples of the 96, and the 95 estate sold 110,527. Sales for the early cars saw 52,731 Saab 93s and 20,128 Saab 92s built and sold (not including prototype and pre-production examples).[30]

The last car rolled off the Finnish factory line on 8 January 1980, bringing to an end the story of the first Saab. With manufacturing ceased, the last cars eased themselves out of dealers' showrooms and quietly a great car died. Saab sold just 967 96 V4s to dedicated Swedish enthusiasts in the first months of 1980 before the final end. The Dutch, always Saab fanatics, snapped up 150 of the very last 96 V4 Anniversary cars.

Erik Carlsson ('Mr Saab') drove the last 96 out of the factory and into the Saab Museum. It was less the end of a love affair and more the end of a generation. It brought a close to the story of the original Saab, calling a halt to a motoring epoch marked by mechanical analogue excellence before digital authoritarianism ruled. Above all, the Saab was fun, a true car and faithful companion. That these cars continue to do so is testament to the original design and the men who created and built it.

On the road again. An orange 96 V4 makes a maximum impact as part of the 'Save Saab' convoy.

BELOW: **An interesting letter, dated 14 February 1980, from Bob Lutz at Ford to Marcus Wallenberg at Saab. Who knew how portentous the sentiments expressed could be.**

Ford of Europe Incorporated
Chairman of the Board

Brentwood Essex CM13 3BW
England

February 14, 1980

Dr. Marcus Wallenberg
Chairman, SAAB-SCANIA AB
S-58188 Linköping
Sweden

Dear Dr. Wallenberg,

Now that the contract between Ford-Werke/Ford Sweden and SAAB-SCANIA for the supply of Cologne manufactured V4 engines for your Saab 96 production line has run out after 14 years, I -- as Chairman of Ford of Europe Incorporated -- want to tell you how much we appreciate the excellent relationships and the fine cooperation that developed during this long and close association of our companies.

And may I add, that we here all hope it will be possible to find some way, possibly in some other areas of our mutual business, to continue in the same spirit in the future.

Sincerely,

Robert A Lutz

SAAB 96/95 V4 MODEL DEVELOPMENT

1967 Launch of Ford-sourced V4 1.5-litre 73bhp (SAE rating at 5,000rpm), 65bhp (DIN rating at 4,500rpm) engine in 'new' 96 V4 model. Much improved performance. Very early V4s reputedly as engine and trim variant builds of partially complete 2-stroke cars. First 96 V4 chassis number 420001

1968 Sales increase of 41.5 per cent with new V4 model by 1968. New safety steering wheel and anti-reflective dashboard finish. Nylon-type seat covers. Export-specification V4 De Luxe model introduced. Twin side-rail brightwork reinstated. 1968 model 96 V4 from chassis number 4700001. Saab 95 V4 De Luxe described in export documents as 95 V4/C with 1968 chassis numbers starting 520001.
NB The 96 2-stroke was still available in limited colour and trim range in 1968, but fewer than 30 units were sold in Sweden that year. 2-stroke deleted from model range at end of 1968 model year

1969 New frontal styling with rectangular headlamps (round lamps in US market due local legislation). Higher bumpers, revised lighting clusters, trims, hubcaps, colours. Telescopic safety steering column introduced. Launch of Finnish-built cars for 1970. 1969 96 V4 chassis numbers from 96520001

1970 Further specification revisions with new dashboard and 'two-dial' instrument designs. De Luxe model phased out during 1970 model year. 96 from chassis number 96560001. Finnish built from 60600001.
500,000th Saab manufactured

1971 Minor trim and specification changes. Headlamp wiper wash system fitted. Single-strip side brightwork rails now standard. Revised cabin heating ducts. Electro-dip paint-primer process introduced. 96 from chassis number 96600001. Finnish built from 61600001.
NB Late 1970 saw the introduction of the 1.7-litre V4 engine revision primarily for US market

1972 First fitment of electrically heated driving seat as Saab innovation (with auto-temperature sensor trigger). Revised wheel trims and new black rubber bumper overrider horns. 96 from chassis number 96722000001. Finnish-built from 96726000001.
Saab-Scania divides into Saab Car Division and Scania Division

1973 Revised trim and specifications. New instruments and revised badging. 96 chassis numbers from 96732000001: Finnish-built from 9673.
Finnish-built Saab 96 production expands.
Saab-Scania completely absorbs the old AB Svenska Järnvägsverkstäderna (ASJ), which had been part of the 1930s Saab amalgamation

1974 New black-painted, plastic-moulded front grille finish and revised grille styling to create new 'face' of Saab 96/95. Revised seat and cabin trim colours. Revised engine specifications include large cooling capacity and electrical upgrades. 96 chassis numbers from 96742000001. Finnish-built from 96746000001

1975 Minor changes to trim include start of black trim to wipers. Strengthening to gearbox casing. 'Jubilee' cars launched in spring 1975 to celebrate Saab anniversary: special colours for Jubilee cars start with Silver Crystal. 96 V4 was offered as 1.7S Rally Edition into 1976 with 96 built. 96 chassis numbers from 96752000001. Finnish-built from 96756000001.
NB 95B model Finnish-built chassis numbers from 96752060001

1976 L Model created: the 5mph-type 'Impact' bumper type added to the 96 and 95 on revised bumper mounting beams. New carburation. Revised rear floorpan gave more rear seat legroom. Revisions to trims, badges, addition of new steering wheel, more equipment and 'day' driving light setting, creates 95L and 95L specification types. 96 chassis numbers from 96762000001. Finnish-built from 96766000001

1977 The year of the 96L and L/B. Reduced export market availability, but 96 and 95 retained for Northern European markets. 96 fitted with high-backed front seats (from Saab 99). New external mirror. Twin-strip bright trim to bumpers. Late 1977 cars for 1978 model year had two-stage carburettors raising engine to nearly 70bhp and also improving fuel consumption (cited as 1977 model B). 96 chassis numbers from 96772000001. Finnish-built from 996776000001. 96B model chassis numbers from 96773006001. Finnish-built from 96776006001

1978 The year of V4 'Super' GL type. Revised lighting clusters, notably on rear of 96 as well as front of 96 and 95. Aerodynamic spoiler in black rubber fitted to boot lid on 96. Larger 1.7-litre engine of 68bhp available. Top spec 96 now defined by 'Super V4' badging in all markets. High-backed seats now fitted to the 95 as well. 'GL' emblems fitted. Final year of 95 estate with total of 110,527 units across model life from 1959 to 1978. 96 chassis numbers from 96783000001. Finnish-built from 96786000001

1979 All 96s now Finnish-built. Further black-trim specification finish and addition of black side-stripe decals on lower panels. Black rocker panel on rear lamp valance. Black hubcaps on domestic market cars. Acacia Green metallic paint offered on 96 from 99 and 900 ranges. 96 chassis numbers 96796000001

1980 The end of 'original Saab' production. Final sales ex-showroom across Europe into mid-1980 with 967 units sold in Sweden in early 1980. Low numbers remaining on sale in other markets. Last-of-the-line cars with 'Minilite' type wheels, Saab 'plush' seat fabric and Aquamarine Blue Metallic paintwork as part of final '300' model run

CHAPTER EIGHT

SUPER SPORT: MR SAAB AND MOTOR SPORT MOMENTS

The Saab was great because the brakes were weak. I liked the drum brakes because they did not do much and I rarely used them because you could not slow the thing down anyway – this is one reason why the Saab was so fast. Don't use the brakes! Just coordinate use of power, gears and available left-foot braking. You have to constantly rev the ... thing.

Erik Hilding Carlsson in conversation with the author

For more than three decades the 92, 93, 96 and 96 V4 stormed the world rally scene. The famous names of Saab rally driving are beyond legend. Erik Carlsson deserved every plaudit he received, but other less well-known names deserve a mention, as Erik always agreed. He sometimes became frustrated with his Saab steeds, and the occasional stubborn shout of 'Blooody Sorbs' might not have been as fictitious as some have suggested. But wear a tie, speak properly and show your enthusiasm, and Erik was pure kindness, pure gold and a wonderful chap. The love for the man was palpable at his memorial service. Many thought of him as almost beyond an icon, but he would hate to be stuck with this label. His wife Pat was treated with a similar level of affection and respect.

In recent years the wonderful Saabs have continued to thrill on the classic rally stages of the world's historic rally movement and in privateer hands at national and regional motor sport and club level.

The speeding Saabs were the rally icons of their era and in many cases remain highlights of the Saab clubman/woman movement and of historic rallying. 'Historic' rallies, the Swedish national classes, the Roger Albert Clark 'RAC', the Per Eklund Trophy rally and events in North and South America all add to the continuing historic Saab scene.

In 2006, for example, Team Pearl consisted of Nicolina Hübert of Gothenburg and co-driver/navigator Anna Sörensson of Stockholm in a 1960 Saab 96 2-stroke. Backed up by a male support crew, they competed in various Swedish historic rally classes before heading to Mexico to take part in that year's La Carrera Panamerica road race in the true spirit of Saab and inspired by the events of 1969 and 1970.

BAJA 1000, 1969 AND 1970

The 1969 Baja 1000 race in Mexico had been the location of an epic early part of the Saab story. Thanks to Len Lonnegren, who worked in the Saab USA public relations team from 1963 to 1989 and eventually became the PR chief, a record of the event was published in the Saab Club newletter *Nines* in 1992, and this is the basis of the following account.

The Saab 96 V4 had competed in the 1969 Baja 1000 rally with full Saab USA support thanks to Ralph T. Millet and Erik's ability to raise works support from Saab. This would be his first time at the wheel in a major competitive outing since his retirement nearly three years before. At one stage Erik and his co-driver Torsten Aman led the race. Erik put up a good show, but he was maybe a little out of practice and suffering with his back on the tough Baja dirt tracks. His Saab suffered too and his race lead was taken from him by driveshaft issues. The mechanic on the outing was Leif Melin (sometimes called Burt) and at one stage he hung onto the back of Erik's car using specially attached handles, in order to travel with the car to fetch a spare alternator from a service store some miles away.[31]

It was fellow 96 V4 driver Ingvar Lindqvist, the Southern Californian Saab dealer, however, who drove a second 96 entry (with co-driver Sven Sundqvist) and won the main

SUPER SPORT: MR SAAB AND MOTOR SPORT MOMENTS

Erik Carlsson's Saab 96 V4 at Baja 1000 in 1969–70. Not everything went according to plan.

The three Saabs that headed the Carlsson memorial service convoy.

■ SUPER SPORT: MR SAAB AND MOTOR SPORT MOMENTS

The Saab ladies team arrive in Monte Carlo.

saloon car classification race. A brand new model Saab 99 was sixteenth in the event.

Many famous names in V8-powered American cars, including the actors Steve McQueen, who was about to shoot the film *Le Mans*, and James Garner, were impressed by the V4 that had beaten them all. Len Lonnegren stated that Erik let Steve McQueen drive the 96 V4 rally car after the event.

Another Californian Saab dealer, Olle Andersson, entered a Baja 1000 rally after the 1969 event, joining Saab and Lindqvist, who went back for more in 1970. So did Erik, but this time he got stuck in sand while attempting a short-cut.

Lindqvist had previously built a series of Lin-Saab 'Specials'. The first used a Saab 93 GT750 (748cc) engine and a range of parts, some of which were by Saab, in a curious open-bodied racer that stormed the race tracks of California in 1958. He even modified the car into a Saab GT750-powered Mk2 Special, fitted with a Porsche gearbox. It was Lindqvist who built a Lotus-chassised but Saab 2-stroke, rear-engined one-off that was later raced in South America. A Lotus 11 chassis and body and a screaming Saab 2-stroke that revved to 8,000rpm was Lindqvist's achievement.

If you are passing through Solvang in southern California, drop into the local garage and try to spot the Saab memorabilia: one of the mechanics on that 1969 race used to run the garage and old Saabs and Saab parts are still found in and around Solvang.

1956 AND 1957

Back in 1956, the Saab rally story in America began with Bob Wehman and Louis Braun's victory and placings at the Great American Mountain Rally and this provided Saab with massive launch publicity. In 1957 at what the Americans called 'Little Le Mans' at the Lime Rock Park circuit in Connecticut, and in Rolf Mellde's presence, Saab 93s stormed to class victory, even if they did have to 'borrow' some extra tyres from road-going, privately owned Saabs in the car park.

From 1958 to 1962 Saab and Volvo battled it out at Lime Rock Park. Among the early American drivers racing Saabs were Hal Mayforth with Dick Thompson, and Bill Rutan with Gaston Andrey.

Saab went to Le Mans as early as 1959 and the fact that historic Saabs returned to Le Mans in classic context fifty years later only adds to the legend.

In 1957 Harald Kronegård, who mainly drove for Porsche, Lotus, Alfa-Romeo and Abarth, competed in a new Saab 93 with navigator Léonce Beysson in the Atlas-Oasis Rally in Morocco. Together with Charlie Lohmander he also won their class in the Mille Miglia: their original 93A was recently restored and driven in a 2011 Mille Miglia re-enactment by Saab's then managing Director Jan-Åke Jonsson and his son. One of this car's restorers was the long-retired Saab Competition Department's Rolf Ebefors.

SUPER SPORT: MR SAAB AND MOTOR SPORT MOMENTS

Erik and Pat at Monte Carlo. Wonderful people and great memories of an age that will never be seen again.

Saab had also taken second and third spots in the Tulip Rally in 1956, second place in the Acropolis Rally in 1957, and won the 1959 Canadian Rally.

Erik Carlsson and Gunnar Palm came second in both the 1963 Liège–Sofia–Liège (first in class) and 1964 Spa–Sofia–Liège rallies. Carlsson won the RAC Rally three years in a row (1960–62) and the Monte Carlo Rally in both 1962 and 1963. His third place in the 1964 Monte Carlo Rally seemed somehow inevitable, especially after his unexpected fourth in a 95 estate in 1961.

But it was not just the tough little Saabs that were rallied. Early Sonett outings included a 1969 Monte Carlo Rally third in class placing, which was deflated by a scrutineering row and the organizers' alleged dysfunction – to the Saab's cost. Its driver, Simo Lampinen, was not happy to be demoted for what he thought was the race officials' actions.

RALLYING AND THE SAAB LEGENDS

Erik Carlsson drove a Saab, as history will always recall, but alongside his amazing record others have also created vignettes of Saab magic. One of these came in 1974 at a Finnish rally when Juan Manuel Fangio, then closely involved with Mercedes-Benz, drove a Saab 96 V4 rally car and was entranced by its feel and response. As has recently been revealed by Larsson and Johansson in their new book, Rudolf Caracciola had discussions with Saab about a potential drive in the earliest days of the marque.

Erik Carlsson is forever associated with Saab rallying. He became its star and his wife, Pat Moss Carlsson (sister of Stirling Moss), also became a successful proponent of Saab rally driving. Carlsson made the legend and quite rightly is

■ SUPER SPORT: MR SAAB AND MOTOR SPORT MOMENTS

Erik at speed in '283'.

Erik nears his destination at Monaco.

the most revered name in the story. He is our hero as 'Mr Saab'. Yet Saab's interest in rallying on a global stage did not begin with Carlsson, but with 'car-crazy', DKW rally-driving motorcyclist Rolf Mellde, who had joined Saab in late 1946: it was Mellde who went on to create the branding and iconography of Saab rallying and its competitions department (later run under 'Bo' Hellborg). Mellde, Carlsson and a small group of men and women took Saab to the world through their rallying exploits.

Mellde was rather busy at Saab in the 1950s with matters like engines and their design, new cars, the Sonett (MkI) and rally development. Before it went upmarket in the late 1970s, Saab's success was rooted in its rally-ing pedigree. Landbü, Mellde and Carlsson contributed to that legend in their respective ways, as so did all the other Saab rally drivers.

As early as December 1949, a Rolf Mellde-prepared Saab 92, driven by K. G. Svedberg, took the Östergötland road race. Within weeks Mellde and Svedberg, alongside Greta Molander and Margareta von Essen, were entered in their two Saab 92s in the 1950 Monte Carlo Rally: Molander and von Esen finished 55th overall, 8th in class and 2nd in the Ladies class. Svedberg and Mellde were 69th overall.

The female drivers who took early Saab 92s and 93s to 1950s rally successes included Greta Molander, Helga Lundberg, Margareta von Essen, Ewy Rosqvist (Ewy von

SUPER SPORT: MR SAAB AND MOTOR SPORT MOMENTS

Erik en route in 1962 on the Monte Carlo Rally.

Erik on the 'Monte' in 1964.

Korff-Rosqvist), Monica Kjerstadius and later Ursula Wirth. Elisabeth Nyström rallied a Saab with Pat Moss-Carlsson.

As the 1950s and Saab evolved, however, one name would come to the fore: the giant talent and plain-speaking brilliance of Erik Carlsson, a 'Viking' legend who had grown up crossing the Swedish countryside on both two wheels and four.

Erik Carlsson and Pat Moss-Carlsson

Erik Hilding Carlsson had been born close to the Saab factory in Trollhättan and began developing his feel for handling by riding Norton motorcyles on slippery rural Swedish roads. Here he learned his craft of handling and anticipation. Carlsson was immersed in speed and Saabs from his formative years. He became a legend, driven by genius, talent and a strong, competitive personality. Rolling the Saab on its roof earned him the sobriquet of 'Carlsson-on-the-roof', but it was perhaps a touch unfair – the rally and road stages were rough, the Saab fast and he was not the only driver to have roll-overs. So strong was the little Saab that sometimes the roof was undented after a roll and no one suspected or ever knew the car had been rolled over. Ford tried to emulate the Carlsson technique of 'roll over and carry on regardless' with a MkI Cortina in the 1960s, but the results were not pretty.

In the early years after World War II Carlsson worked for the motorcycle dealer Per 'Pelle' Nyström, from whom he learned the craft of rally car navigation, somewhat ironically from the spare seat of Nyström's Volvo. Nyström's daughter Elisabeth would later pair up with the Saab ladies team and Pat Moss in the 96.

Carlsson came to the attention of Saab after he bought a secondhand Saab 92 and competed as a privateer. Mellde offered him help preparing his private entry car in the early 1950s and by 1954 Carlsson had won a series of local and national events. Saab lent Carlsson a newer car to drive and from that developed the relationship that led to the 'works' drive and the unique legend of Erik Carlsson. That story entered a second chapter with the 93 2-stroke cars and Carlsson's co-driver/navigators, Gunnar Palm and Torsten Åman. Erik also drove the 96 2-stroke and finally the 96 V4 in competition. But we might suggest that his heart lay in the 2-stroke, in a little red 93 rally special with many personal modifications.

Despite leading the East African Safari Rally on several occasions, the gentle giant never won this prestigious rally. The honour of being the first European to do so went to the brilliant 'flying Finn' Hannu Mikkola.

Irrespective of that missing trophy, Erik Carlsson was probably the most gifted, fastest thinking and most astute blend of mind and technique that rallying had ever seen. In Britain, where Carlsson lived for decades, he won the RAC Rally three times in a row in 1960, 1961 and 1962, the first of these with his renowned British co-driver Stuart Turner.

After Erik's death in 2015 the tributes to Carlsson matched his stature: the *Daily Telegraph*'s obituary, written by the author, covered more than half a page; the BBC ran archive footage of Erik's greatest drives; and even the American mass media bothered to mention him.

Carlsson was an inspiration to thousands of young people, but his wife Pat had the distinction of being a huge inspiration to women on horses and in cars. Pat Moss was the younger sister of Stirling Moss. She learned to drive in Land-Rovers on the family farm, and acquired advanced hand, eye and leg co-ordination skills on horseback. Aged fifteen, Pat Moss had a class victory at the 1950 Horse of the Year Show and in 1953 won the Queen Elizabeth Cup at White City.

Switching from four legs to four wheels, her early drives were in a Triumph TR2 and she won first time out in a

'The Boss': Erik in retirement at the wheel of the Philpotts' 96 V4. M. PHILPOTT

SUPER SPORT: MR SAAB AND MOTOR SPORT MOMENTS

Erik at full charge – best get out of the way.

Erik and co-driver Stuart Turner.
SAAB/MAGEE

SUPER SPORT: MR SAAB AND MOTOR SPORT MOMENTS

Erik during the RAC Rally, 1965.

Erik on the RAC Rally again, this time in 1966.

regional rally. A Triumph factory drive did not happen, but MG snapped up the young Pat and she drove an MG TF to a top three Ladies Class place in 1955. Her first drive in the Monte Carlo Rally was in 1956 as a crew member in an Austin – all on board survived a crash over the barrier on a mountainside hairpin bend.

Various drives in a range of car makes came and went, but it was winning the 1960 Liège–Rome–Liège rally outright in a big Healey 300 that marked Pat Moss out as something special. Pat might have won the 1961 RAC Rally if she had not stopped to assist Erik Carlsson, who needed a spare tyre. The following year she won the Tulip Rally in a Mini Cooper. Pat married Erik Carlsson in 1963 during her time with Ford. Not surprisingly, it was not long before Pat found herself driving for Saab: she finished fifth in 1964's Monte Carlo Rally and third the following year, with Ursula Wirth and Elisabeth Nyström, respectively.

Pat switched to driving for Lancia – with that easy familiarity that the Swedes and English have with the Italians. Drives in the fast but fragile Renault Alpine followed and then a brief spell driving for Toyota. 'Mrs Carlsson' retired in 1974 and died in 2008. Pat and Erik's daughter Susie continued the love of horses and Saabs. The sight of a line-up of roaring red 'original' Saabs at Erik's 2015 memorial service, headed by

SUPER SPORT: MR SAAB AND MOTOR SPORT MOMENTS

'Old faithful': Carlsson's little red rally Saab.

Susie at the wheel of Erik's replica car, was not just moving, it was beyond a tribute: it was typical of Saab and its people.

Ewy Rosqvist, Ursula Wirth and Cecilia Koskull

Ewy Rosqvist (née Jonsson) was one of Sweden's most successful rally drivers. In 1957 she drove for Saab and took the 93 to victory in the Ladies Class of the Viking Rally of Norway with her sister-in-law Anita Rosqvist-Borg as her co-driver.

Together with Ursula Wirth, another early Saab driver, Ewy later took a lumbering Mercedes-Benz 220 SE saloon to a major rally victory in Argentina's Gran Premio Internacional Standard Supermovil YPF in 1962. Ewy remarried in 1965, this time to Baron Alexander von Korff, a senior Mercedes-Benz competition manager, and extended her name to Ewy Baroness von Korff-Rosqvist.[32]

Another name from Saab's early rally era about 1950 to 1953 was Cecilia Koskull, who achieved fame in a Porsche 356 with a Swedish Midnight Sun Rally victory in 1950 and partnered Greta Molander in a Saab 92B for the 1951 Monte Carlo Rally. Saab's commitment to equality was obvious in the 1950s and a lot of women rallied Saabs.

By the later 1950s Carl-Magnus Skogh and Ewy Rosqvist had joined the Saab 92 and 93 rally car operation at the now

■ SUPER SPORT: MR SAAB AND MOTOR SPORT MOMENTS

fully formed Saab Competition Department. Rosqvist would move on to Volvo in 1960, and then to Mercedes-Benz.

Carl-Magnus Skogh

Skogh became a well-known Saab rally driver even if he also drove Volvos! He joined the emerging Saab Competition Department early on with Erik Carlsson in the 1950s. Skogh won the Midnight Sun Rally in 1960 and 1961 as a driver (having won it as Erik Carlsson's co-driver in 1956) and piloted the Saab Formula Junior car. Skogh took more than fifty wins for Saab across various rally classes. Skogh joined Volvo in 1963 and again had several world-class rally victories and podium finishes. His co-driver on several Saab outings was his brother, Rolf Skogh. Carl-Magnus's other Saab co-drivers included Karl Erik Svensson, Fergus Sager, Håkon Fløysvik and Åke Kristiansen.

Skogh was not just a brilliant 2-stroke rally driver, competing in twenty major rallies for Saab, he was also a Saab Competition Department test driver and highly regarded within the company. At the time of writing he was in his mid-nineties and still driving.

WORKS TEAM AND PRIVATEERS

Before long the standard 38bhp engine was being tweaked by Mellde's people to churn out an ear-shattering 50bhp or more. Ultimately a Saab 2-stroke would get to 86.5bhp, but it worked best under rally conditions as it was a touch recalcitrent on occasion.

These rally events were using very early production Saab 92s and it would not be long before Mellde sought official management sanction and funding for Saab's growing rally preparation needs. The Saab 'works' team was born and the staff rose from two to six, with David Persson as the first service manager. Always short of funds, the Saab rally team drove to most of its European events, often taking long ferry crossings to get to their destinations.

Other top rally names associated with the Saab 92, 93 and 96 include Carl-Otto Bremer, Bengt Carlqvist and Simo Lampinen.

Ove Andersson was a Saab rally regular and another of those who came to cars through motorcycles. He first drove for Saab in 1962, then won a team place in 1964 and was fifth in the Swedish rally championship. He then moved to Lancia, followed by time at Renault and then at Toyota in the 1970s.

The single-seat Saab 2-stroke assembled from Saab mechanical parts.

MAJOR SAAB RALLY SUCCESSES, 1949–64[33]

1949	K.G. Svedberg wins the Tour of Östergötland in the new Saab 92's first event
1950	Rolf Mellde/K.G. Svedberg and Greta Molander/Margareta von Essen enter the Monte Carlo Rally and then Swedish Rikspokalen Rally. Mellde also drives with Bengt Carlqvist
1952	Greta Molander/Helga Lundberg win the Ladies Cup in the Monte Carlo Rally, starting from Oslo
1953	Rolf Mellde with Pelle Nyström races Saab 92 'P9101'. Mellde wins that year's Swedish national rally championship
1955	Erik Carlsson wins the Rikspokalen Rally, with Sten Helm as his co-driver on this and other events
1956	Bob Wehman/Louis Braun win the Great American Mountain Rally. Rolf Mellde finishes 6th and another Saab is placed, securing massive US launch publicity for Saab.
	Carlo-Otto Bremer finishes 6th in the 1957 '1000 Lakes' Rally in a Saab 93. He wins the same rally in 1960 and is Finnish Rally Champion in 1957 in a Saab 93
1957	Ewy Rosqvist takes the 93 to victory in the 1957 Viking Rally in Norway with her sister-in-law Anita Rosqvist-Borg as her co-driver.
	Erik Carlsson/Carl-Magnus Skogh win the Midnight Sun Rally.
	Erik Carlsson/Mario Pavoni win the Finnish '1000 Lakes' Rally
1959	Sture Nottorp/Gunnar Bengtsson finish the Le Mans 24 Hours in 12th place and 2nd in class.
	Erik Carlsson wins the Midnight Sun Rally with Pavoni, scores 2nd in the Adriatic Rally and 5th on the Tulip Rally, both with Karl Erik Svensson. E Carlsson also wins Swedish and German national rallies and is 2nd in the rally championship rankings
1960	Erik Carlsson wins the British RAC Rally with Stuart Turner
1961	Erik Carlsson, with Svensson, enters Saab 95 estate with four-speed gearbox in Monte Carlo Rally and finishes 4th
1962	Erik Carlsson/Gunnar Häggbom win the Monte Carlo rally overall
1963	Erik Carlsson/Gunnar Palm win the Monte Carlo Rally for the second time (a rare consecutive winner). Further Saab placings in the Monte Carlo event included: 1963 with Arne Ingier/Finn R. Jacobsen (29th), 1964 with Pat Moss-Carlsson/Ursula Wirth (5th) and 1965 with Pat Moss-Carlsson/Elisabeth Nyström (3rd) and Ove Andersson/Torsten Åhman (13th)
1964	Erik Carlsson/Gunnar Palm place second in the Spa–Sofia–Liège road rally and win the Rallye dei Fiori in Italy (followed in second place by Pat Moss-Carlsson/Valerie Domleo-Morley). They are also second in the East African Safari and third in both the Monte Carlo and Geneva rallies

■ SUPER SPORT: MR SAAB AND MOTOR SPORT MOMENTS

Saab 92 and 96 rally cars remembered.

John Sprinzel and Walter Karlsson were also on the team. Erik Carlsson's British rally event navigators/co-drivers were Stuart Turner, John Brown and David Stone. Saab GB encouraged British Club privateers and supporters, but its main official support during the RAC Rally campaigns was to Carlsson.

There was a notable list of entries on the 1965 Monte Carlo Rally driving Saab 96s, including:

- Pat Moss-Carlsson/Elisabeth Nyström (3rd)
- Hans Lund/Björn Wahlgren (18th)
- Erik Carlsson/Gunnar Palm (20th)
- Per Ekholdt/John Haraldsen (21st)
- Arne Ingier/Finn R. Jacobsen (30th)
- Ingemar Wollert/Isbeth Ljunkvist
- Christoffer Norlin
- Reidar Buran/Svein Nordvang
- Paul Macchi/Aldo Macchi
- Jan Nielsen/Lars Usterud Svendsen
- Laila Schou-Nilsen/Nancy Pettersen

For the XXV Polish Rally of 1965, Saab entered Erik Carlsson/Torsten Åhman (3rd) and Pat Moss-Carlsson/Elisabeth Nyström (5th), and sent three Saabs, including a 95, as service/backup cars. Rallying Saabs remains a notable theme of Polish motor sport: visiting Swedes in Saab 96s included Bo 'Ploppen' Pettersson/Ulf Ottosson in 1976 and more recently Peter Svensson. Krzysztof Rozenblat has been responsible for supporting the Saab classic rally and support network in Poland.[34]

The Saab 'historic' team inside the Saab Club Italia cannot go unmentioned for their continued rallying of old Saabs.

The Swiss drivers Paul and Aldo Macchi should not be forgotten in the record of Saab rallying. They first entered a Saab 96 in a major rally in 1961 and were regulars in the Monte Carlo and Geneva rallies until 1967. They took third place in the 1965 Rallye Stuttgart-Lyon-Charbonnnières and drove a Sonett in the 1966 Geneva Rally.

SAAB AT LE MANS

The tale of the Saab 93B at Le Mans is a perfect example of just how seriously Rolf Mellde took competition. Erik Carlsson was then the test driver for the Saab works team and he tested the Le Mans car before the race.

SUPER SPORT: MR SAAB AND MOTOR SPORT MOMENTS

The Saab historic outfit took this 93 to the Le Mans Classic.

As so often, the entry of a Saab into a race was 'supported' by Saab but not entirely officially sanctioned. In 1959 Sture Nottorp decided he would race a Saab at Le Mans. The obvious candidate to ask for help was Mellde and this was soon forthcoming. Nottorp's co-driver in car no. 44 was to be Gunnar Bengtsson, an experienced Swedish race and rally man. This was not to be the only Saab racing at Le Mans that June. There was also a privately entered British Saab 93 750 GT, car no. 43, driven by Sydney Hurrell and Roy North. Although it suffered a seized piston and had to withdraw, it did provide the brief sight of two Saab 93s racing at Le Mans.

Nottorp's car was stripped down to the bare essentials. Next the engine was internally blueprinted: polished and honed to the closest degree possible. It would run at a 4 per cent fuel/oil ratio. A large 21.5 gallon fuel tank was fitted, with its own quick-access refuelling valve. Triple Solex carburettors were fitted and a Saab four-speed gearbox included in the spec sheet. This little 750cc car managed 65bhp at dynometer measurement. Top speed was 105mph from a 2-stroke 3-cylinder engine.

The Nottorp/Bengtsson Saab raced all day and all night, finishing the Le Mans 24 Hours in twelfth place overall and second in its class, amid fifty-five total entrants. Apart from greasing, servicing and some attention to the alternator, the Saab performed as intended, covering 232 laps of Le Mans at an average speed of 81mph. Amid the Le Mans exotica, the slippery Saab had scored some major profile for Saab and its fledgling competitions department.

In the 1960s and 1970s the hard-charging Saab 93, 96, 96 V4 and 99, all revved up and simply flying along against heavier and more powerful cars, scored victory after victory. With their deft handling and easy revving, and Carlsson's development of a constant power-on technique for the 2-strokes, Saabs simply were invincible. The low power of the Saab meant it had to be kept on-song and revved up, with a light touch on the brakes, steering and gears. The car had to be kept at speed because it took a long time to accelerate back up to pace.

In 2008 Bo Lindman entered a Saab 2-stroke with a tuned engine built by Niklas Enander as a 'replica' of the original Saab 93B at Le Mans. The drivers were Lindman, Fredrik Tornerhielm and Göran Dahlen.

The Le Mans Classic of 2010 saw the green Saab 93 of Chris Partington, Chris Nutt and Chris Parkes return the model to the La Sarthe circuit and show the world a low-flying dark green Saab flying along like a meteor in a snarl

SUPER SPORT: MR SAAB AND MOTOR SPORT MOMENTS

of tuned-up 'strokerism'. The Saab 'bumble-bee' LDH 781D revved to a sound that echoed across northern France. This had been a dream for Chris Partington for many years. He also had the ex-Saab racer Ferdinand Gustafson on the team. The dedicated Saab owner and journalist John Simister played a supporting role and drove his 96, YSL 941, all the way to Le Mans and back.

V4 RALLY CAR

The V4 and the upgrades Saab created for it transformed the 96. As early as 1967 the tweaked V4 driven by Åke Andersson won the Rikspokalen Rally and Simo Lampinen was the most successful Saab entrant in the Swedish KAK Rally. Lampinen secured many results with the Saab and also ran the Saab rally team in his native Finland. In Poland in 1962, Lampinen had driven the 96 with Jyrki Ahava. Lampinen matched Erik Carlsson in the 1968 RAC Rally by winning it in a Saab 96 V4 with John Davenport. This was the marque's fourth RAC win.

One of the most successful members of the Saab team was Carl Orrenius, who had many results in a Saab 96 V4 between 1967 and 1972. The pairing of Per Eklund and Björn Cederberg also had a notable spell in a Saab 96 V4 from 1973

STIG BLOMQVIST, THE ORIGINAL 'STIG'

Stig Blomqvist's original name was Lennart, but 'Stig' was a great PR tool that was picked up decades later by the BBC's *Top Gear* programme. For many years Blomqvist was based in Essex, but more recently he enjoys the roads of New Zealand.

Blomqvist first rallied a Saab 96 in 1964, but his name was perhaps best associated with the 99 EMS and 99 Turbo from 1975. The long list of his major international victories include the Swedish Rally, 1000 Lakes, RAC Rally, Cyprus Rally and the 1976 Boucles de Spa. On snow or ice Blomqvist was a speed sensation, often with Arne Hertz, Hans Sylvan or Björn Cederberg during his Saab days, driving the 96 V4 with amazing style and then working around the 99 Turbo's 'lag' and lack of low-speed urge: just as the old 2-strokes had had to be kept 'on-song', so too did the turbocharger in the 99. Such was his success that Saab was the major rallying name in the 1970s, long before Audi and Lancia stormed to prominence.

Erik and Pat's daughter Susie about to depart in the memorial convoy in the red Saab.

Erik Carlsson in Charly Walmsley's red 96 in Buenos Aires. Walmsley also owns a very early 92 and is active on the Saab scene in Argentina and Uruguay.

to 1976 before moving on to the Saab 99 EMS and Turbo.

Håkan Lindberg, another works-supported driver, won the 1967 Swedish Rally Championship in the Group 1 standard-tune class in a Saab 96 V4.

Erik Carlsson, so long associated with the 2-stroke Saabs, briefly took to the 96 V4 in July 1967, taking outright victory (with his co-driver Torsten Åhman) in the Rally Vltava in Czechoslovakia. This was Erik's last major victory in an international class rally, but he would go on to drive the V4 in the 1969 and 1970 Baja 1000 rallies in a post-retirement bout of enthusiasm.

The lesser-known name of Tom Trana joined the Saab rally team from Volvo in 1967 and won first time out in a Norwegian rally, driving a 96 V4 with Knut Moberg. The V4 would go on to major success in the rallying world and the name of Stig Blomqvist rose to the fore via the 96 V4 prior to the switch to 99EMS and the stunning 99 Turbo.

Saab had a curiously bad year in the 1970 RAC Rally. Even though Stig Blomqvist led at one stage in a 96 V4, not one of the four team cars finished, forced out by gearbox problems and crash damage. The only Saabs to make it around were two privately entered 96 V4s driven by Lasse Jönsson/Alf Qvist (9th) and Jack Tordoff/Brian Marchant (13th). The unfortunate Saab teams were Stig Blomqvist/Bo Reinicke, Håkan Lindberg/Brian Coyle, Tom Trana/Sölve Andreasson and Carl Orrenius/Arne Hertz.

SAAB MOTOR SPORT IN URUGUAY

As early as 1962 Marco Baca, Saab's representative in Ecuador, rallied a GT750 in an Ecuadorian speed trial and won. Baca's brother also entered the event in a standard specification Saab and finished fourth.

There would be more Saab sporting activity further south when José Arijón Rama, who supplied Saabs in Uruguay, raced a 96 Sport in Uruguay and Argentina.

Héctor Marcial Fojo was the leading name in South America Saabs, rallying a 96 Sport with co-driver Nestor Uccellini. His fame was secured when he came second in the 1965 Rally Grand Prix of Argentina. First place was taken by Carlos 'Yuyo' Lepro in an Alfa Romeo GTA and third place went to a young Carlos Reutemann, who was driving a Fiat 1500 in his first year of racing. Between them was Marcial Fojo in his Saab 96 Sport.

In 1964 the strength of the Saab 96 had been well and truly proven when a driver who had entered a local Uruguayan rally under the name 'Torres de Oza' (actually José Arijón, who had picked a name in honour of his home town) managed to flip over his 96 Sport, which did not have a roll bar or roll cage fitted, and it carried on rolling over many times at high speed. Jacques Bourgeois was the co-founder of the Saab supplier Automotora Boreal and other key names of the early era of Saabs in South American competi-

■ SUPER SPORT: MR SAAB AND MOTOR SPORT MOMENTS

tion included Carlos Montagna, Ramiro Balcarcel, Enrique Duhart, Angel Longo and Rogelio Belloso.

In 1965 Ramiro Balcarcel, Oscar De Barros and Rafael Fernández Someca entered their Saab into the six-hour race at the El Pinar circuit near Montevideo. In the Punta del Este 1968 Rallye there was an interesting match between two Saab 96s, those of Balcarcel in car no. 13 and Arnaldo 'Pipo' Casto in car no. 15. Balcarcel also entered a 93 with his co-driver Carlos 'Pelado' Montequín in the 19 Capitales Rally of 1971. This rally was held for the first time in 1968, when a white Saab 96 had been part of the sweep team. From then until 1981 Saabs entered the rally regularly, but victory remained elusive, although placings were achieved. Balcarcel came as close as anyone in 1971: he had a big lead near the end when his car took off and landed very heavily, cracking the gearbox casing.

In 2004 the rally was revived as a historical re-enactment: in the first two years of the event, the Argentinian-Uruguayan pair of Carlos Quarta and Ricardo Durhart won in a 1964 Sport and a long-nose Sport, respectively.

A team of three Saabs competed in the 2008 event. Angel Longo, who had driven in the original rally, also took part in 2008 with his co-driver Gustavo Soberal in a 1965 Monte Carlo Sport. Ricardo Joubanoba and Adolfo Chelle drove a 1967 V4, and well-known Saab 92B owner Charly Walmsley drove in from Argentina with Linda Walmsley in the family's red 96. Starting from Montevideo with 150 other entrants, the Saabs (registered as K102005, SAQ 1007 and BAH 306, respectively) careered across the Uruguyan countryside and along sections of main road, and raced around the El Pinar race track. The teams were introduced to Ramiro Balcarcel who told them the story of his drive back in 1971.

The three Saabs survived the 2008 event with minimal on-the-road repairs throughout 2,000km of rally stages. The story of the 2008 re-enactment was told by Ricardo Joubanoba in *Saab Driver* magazine in September 2008, translated by Charly Walmsley.

In 1994 P. Ponce de Leon, Ricardo Duhart and Angel Longo raced their Saab to a placing in the 1000 Millas Uruguay event.

At the centre of Club Saab Uruguay, which was founded in 2008, are Alberto Domingo, who has had a decades-long passion for Saabs, and Carlos and Juan Abeiro, who have rallyed a Saab 96 in Uruguay in recent years.[35]

VINTAGE SAAB RACING GROUP (USA)

The following accounts are just a selection from the many that could be told about members of the US Vintage Saab Racing Group. First up is a particularly long-lived 1960 93F, which was originally raced in the 1960s by Rex Harison of Salt Lake City with an '850' Sport engine. It was eventually acquired by the Christ family of Orwigsburg, Pennsylvania, and restored by Chuck Christ in a vivid orange to replicate the 1964 Saab race season car raced by his father, Joseph Christ. This car has been raced at Elkhart Lake, Watkins Glen, Sebring, the Virginia International raceway and many other tracks, and is one of the best-known vintage Saabs in North America. As recently as August 2021 it has also been hill climbed by both Mary Anne Fieux and Chuck Christ.

Another 1960 Saab 93F was raced in hill climbs by Dennis Snyder in the 1960s. The car stopped competition in 1974 and passed through several hands until it was restored from 1989 by Wendell Francis into a vintage racer. It competed at Road Atlanta, but in the same year the car was rolled at the Summit Point 'Blue-Gray Challenge' event and once more rebuilt. In recent years it was driven competitively by Randy Cook for its owner Thomas K. Cox.

The late Bertil Sollenskog owned a 1966 96 Monte Carlo and it held the Bonneville Salt Flats record and the Ohio Mile title. Bertil broke the then existing class record at Bonneville in 2011 with a two-way average of 110.187mph. In late 2014 he got to 112.642mph. Tom Donney set further records with the car including three new records at the Ohio Mile in 2013 and a speed of 107.6040mph in the J/Pro classification. This car had fuel injection.

The orange 96 V4 named the 'Pumpkin', recently owned by Bill Jacobsen, was a 1970 V4 that had been updated to the Ford 1700cc specification. This car raced at major circuits including Bridgehampton and reached 152mph whilst nudging 8,500rpm!

For information about other US Saab owners who have been active racing and rallying their Saab 96s, including Willie Lewis, Reinertsen Motors Racing, George and Stefan Vapaa, Tom Donney and, of course, Bruce Turk, please *see* Chapter 6.[36]

THE BRITISH SAAB 'HISTORIC' RALLY TEAM

This team of rally-prepped Saabs, headed by Jim Valentine's red 96 Sport, AJM 101A, brought together a dedicated group of Saab believers who put time and money into achieving something that would be more than re-enactment. Of interest, the team's support truck was resprayed in the superb shade of Saab Hussar Blue. For clarity, we should note that there has been a Netherlands-based Saab 'historic' team of differing context, and neither is the British team to be confused with the Saabs United Historic Rally team. AJM 101A has also been more recently driven by Maxime Castelein on Belgian plates.

The 'regulars' who took rally car Saab to new heights in the British historic scene were Jim Valentine, Julian Stocks, Andy Harris and Chris Nutt. Their first project was to bring together a team of five Saabs prepared to relive some classic moments in the historic 2010 Roger Albert Clark Rally '50' anniversary event, with five Saabs. As it happened, the 2010 event saw ideal Saab conditions: 17 degrees of chill and a foot of snow on some stages.

The Roger Albert Clark is an 'RAC' rally by name but not by lineage from the Royal Automobile Club (which of course Roger Clark and Erik Carlsson dominated in their respective days). From 2017 the 'Roger Albert Clark' RAC has been a biennial event and the Historic Rally Team has kept up its entries.

In the event four Saabs competed in the 2010 event. Nick Pinkett and Mark Casey earned a win in Class B1 and a seond place in the historic class, even without a limited slip differential device on the Saab. Jim Valentine and Andy Harris took a third in the historic section and second in the B1 class. Colin Hope and Nick Patrick were fourth in class C3 and gained many places over their start position. Richard Simpson and Debby Myers retired after challenging for the lead.

Both Jonathan and Caroline Lodge are regular Saab competitors. Sometimes they are in a Saab together, but in 2011 Jonathan was crewing with Jim Valentine, which he often does. Caroline had planned on sitting it out in a chase car, but was persuaded to crew a 96 for Stephen Higgins, a driver she had never met. That 2011 RAC Historic was marked by plenty of mud and snow.

The 2012 RAC saw even worse conditions and many retirements, but the Saab spirit has endured throughout these events. Four of the six Saab Historic Team cars retired, but the remaining two won two classes and took third and fourth places in the Historic Class. Jim Valentine steered 'AJM' through the brutal conditions, this time with Caroline Lodge.

Other Saab 96 V4s that have taken part include those of Peter Lumsden/Paul Darlington and Ceiriog Hughes/Emyr Hall.

Despite the RAC being cancelled one year, Saabs of the Historic Team have been seen on the event more recently.

Björn Cederberg at speed in the Saab 96 V4.

SUPER SPORT: MR SAAB AND MOTOR SPORT MOMENTS

Rally and race specification included window stays, air vents, extended arches, full roll cage and the 'Saab Sport & Rally' department's decals.

The full works applied to the 96 rally and race car interior specification. Note the turbo boost gauge!

Stephen Higgins's ride with Caroline Lodge in the 2011 Roger Albert Clark Rally seems to have whetted his appetite and he became a Saab regular as part of the historic rally set-up.

Key names in more recent Saab Historic team entries in the 'RAC', notably in 2017, have included:

Nick Pinkett	96 2-stroke
Colin Hope/Nick Patrick	96 V4
Jim Valentine/Jonathan Lodge	93 2-stroke and 99
Stephen Higgins	96 2-stroke and 96 V4
Gavin Chisholm	96 V4
Maxime Castelein	96 Sport (ex-AJM 101A)

Later V4s in rally competition include those of Hugh Myers/Debby Myers and John Tatlow/Julie Westwood. Gavin Chisholm/Shannon Turnbull rally a 96 and a 99 EMS, which they used in the 2017 and 2019 Roger Albert Clark rallies.

Stephen Broadhead's Malbrad Saab Specialists has provided much support to the historic Saab rally team and to Saab owners and drivers. Malbrad's own team has included David Ledgard, Jonathan Taylor-Smith and David Brook.

Richard Simpson became famous for his forays in his Saabs and sterling efforts to keep them on the road, both when driving with Leslie Simpson, Craig Wallace or Debby Myers, and in the sense of maintainence and repairs.

The beige 96 V4 VWM 553L, driven by John Wood and Ian Whittley, was the only Saab entry in the 2008 Viking Classic Rally.

In 2014 Stephen Higgins and Don Bramfoot competed in six stages of the RAC Rally Championship in a Malbrad-prepared white 96 2-stroke, KMN 171Y. They started in February and March in the 'Red Kite' Historic Stages rally. They then tackled the mid-Wales stages a month or so later. With places and points from class wins in the bag, it was off to the North East for a Tour of Hamsterley rally in April and then on to the Severn Valley and DMACK Carlisle stages, finishing with the Trackrod Historic Cup.

Hugh and Debby Myers showed similar commitment to the historic rally scene in their green 96 V4, OYX 966L, from 2012 to 2014, and Debby chronicled their exploits in *Saab Driver* magazine.

The Welsh team of Ceiriog Hughes and Emyr Hall from Bala Motor Club flew around many rally stages in their 96 V4, JCG 130L, and also featured in the pages of *Saab Driver*.

Competitors from all the nations of the United Kingdom have campaigned Saabs across what is often known by Saab enthusiasts as 'Mud Island'. Johan Denekamp ran the bright 'Bugatti' blue 96 that he briefly owned for the first time at the Silverstone Classic in 2013, and came second in class with Jonny Pinhorn in the 2015 Tour of Wessex.

SUPER SPORT: MR SAAB AND MOTOR SPORT MOMENTS

LUK 3K: FROM TUTHILL TO MATHER

The famous Porsche name of Tuthill has graced an original Trollhättan-built 96 V4 rally car in competition and this car is today being restored by well-known competition driver Justin Mather, who won the 2019 hill climb speed overall championship in a modified Porsche 924/944. The Mather 96 V4 has a rare provenance: it was driven in the 1972 British rally season by garage business owner John Bloxham in five rallies including the Scottish Rally and the Fram Castrol International Welsh Rally, where it came fourth. (Bloxham's connection with Saab went back to driving a Saab GB 96/60-2-stroke in the 1962 autocross season.) Francis Tuthill shipped this Saab to Kenya and rallied it there on the Safari and Malindi rallies in the 1970s, before it was eventually sold to Mather.

After its current renovation the Mather 96 V4, LUK 3K, will be one of the most interesting and valuable V4's still extant.

Tuthill has also restored an ex-works rally Saab and entered it in the 2017 Roger Albert Clark Rally with Peter Lythell. He remains a devotee of the car.

The ex-Francis Tuthill 96V4, registered LUK 3K, seen in action in Kenya. The black-painted bonnet/hood reduced glare.

Sheer Saab sporting style – doing what a 96 rally car should do. This is LUK 3K in East Africa with its owner (then and now) Justin Mather doing the Saab rally thing in real style.

(continued overleaf...)

199

■ SUPER SPORT: MR SAAB AND MOTOR SPORT MOMENTS

(continued from previous page...)

LUK 3K at the start of the Safari Rally. The vehicle has real provenance as a Saab rally car.

Originally orange, then resprayed, LUK 3K seen on an East African rally stage point. Today the car is under full restoration by owner Justin Mather (who is also a Porsche Club national hill climb championship title holder) and of course the Saab has prior Tuthill ownership provenance.

SUPER SPORT: MR SAAB AND MOTOR SPORT MOMENTS

Erik in the snow. The author's tribute painting to a Saab hero.

The Saab Historic Rally 'Team Yke' was founded in 2009 by Roger van Keulen and runs Saabs of 1964 96 2-stroke and V4 types. Besides van Keulen, who acts as both driver and navigator, there are co-pilot/navigator Sytze de Bok and chief mechanic and fixer Gert van Keulen. Roger's white 96 2-stroke is an ex-UK car that participated in the 1988 Pirelli Classic Marathon.

The Dutch 'historic' Saab scene also supports the K&K Saab Historic Rallyteam and the Saab Historic Rally Team, which runs about fifteen Saabs, including a Sonett 3 and a 96 TT Monte Carlo.

Sweden's Saab movement is still packed with historic rallyists, and that enthusiasm extends to Norway, Denmark, Germany and Poland, where Saab fanatics fettle old Saabs for fun.

Key names of Saab 93 and 96 rallying in Sweden in the first two decades of the century, notably on the Midnight Sun Rally Historic and as part of many Swedish Saab group meetings and trials include: Fredrik Ekendahl, Peter Svensson, Pekka Stenhagen, Helge E. Roald, Sibylla Gustafsson, Niklas Enander, Christer Esberg, Carl-Gustaf and Axel Engbert, Sten and Janne Säfström, Gunnar Fredriksson, Lars-Ove Runesson, Lennart Forsberg, Lennart Westerberg, Jonny Andersson, Göran Huggare, Bertil Trued, Mikael Jordström and Anders Wallin (in a 92).

These are just some of the names associated in motor sport with the Saab 92, 93, 96 and 96 V4, stretching beyond the much-loved 'stars'. They and their cars are legends and a vital part of the spirit of Saab.

CHAPTER NINE

BUYING AND RESTORING A CLASSIC SAAB

Values for the Saab 92 and 93 have risen steeply in 2020 and an asking price of 50,000 Euros for an old Saab is now a reality. Until recently prices for the 96 V4 were static, but they too have started to rise and excellent examples, especially perfect original or well-renovated cars and the later special editions, have now reached a price range in the vicinity of 10,000 Euros or pounds. Rarer 96 V4s, such as the Rally editions and the late special editions, now easily exceed this figure or double it. Any car (including a 96 V4) with a special build history or proven competitive provenance, and with rally and competition specification, can easily be valued at 20,000–35,000 Euros/pounds. The 95 estate in 2-stroke guise can now fetch about 10,000 Euros or pounds without trouble.

The truth is that the values of original or well-renovated Saabs with a history from a known Saab expert are rising fast and have made strong gains since 2019.

Values of 2-stroke Saabs have always reflected issues of type, specification and provenance. The 92 in good original condition or expertly restored can be worth 20,000–50,000 Euros/pounds.

In a similar condition, 93s can be purchased for 15,000–35,000 Euros/pounds. Values of 96 2-strokes are rising as well, and a good, interesting car cannot be undervalued.

Any 2-stroke car with special build history, notably one with a Trollhättan Works Department rally-build specification, has a strong value. If such a car has an interesting rally history and ownership trail, at the time of writing values in excess of 35,000 Euros/pounds are known and the US market has no problem with the arrival of the $50,000 2-stroke 'Stroker'. Saab Sonett values are also rising.

KEY AREAS FOR INSPECTION

Legend has it that Saabs resist rust better than most cars. This may have been true, but the fact is that, despite all the quality assurance in the world, Saabs still rust, even if it is at a slower rate than the normal consumer-disposable motor car.

The tough conditions of hard Swedish, Northern European and East Coast/Mountain region American winters inevitably took their toll under floorpans, sills, wheel arches and underbody crevices. These are key parts of the car's structure rather than easily replaceable outer panels, and expensive replacement and welding may be required at great expense.

Body

Wings, doors, boot lid, rear valance. Note inner wing joints. Floorpan and bulkhead can have serious structural implications, as can any corrosion in the windscreen frame and A-pillars.

Key 92, 93 and 96 areas to inspect include: the underfloor area to the rear, under and behind rear footwells, seat pan and sills/sill ends. Inner rear wheel arches. Check suspension mounts front and rear.

Front scuttle, windscreen frame and pillar inserts. Rear windscreen aperture and frame corrosion can be serious.

Cabin to front bulkhead floor panels and join.

Air intake box.

Doors.

Cars that have been rallied or driven off-road may show similar body damage to that seen in impact damage. Check the rear/boot floor for giveaway signs of rippling in the paint finish.

BUYING AND RESTORING A CLASSIC SAAB ■

RESOURCES

For those wanting to purchase, renovate, restore or modify an *old* Saab of 92-93-96 type, the following individuals and outlets in Great Britain and beyond, represent a wealth of wealth of Saab knowledge. This list is not definitive and any omissions are accidental, space-related, or by circumstance: no warranty or liability is implied or given:

Macdonald Classic Cars, Herefordshire	www.macdonaldclassiccars.co.uk
The Saab Sanctuary, Kent	
Carnetix, Leicestershire	www.carnetix.co.uk
Malcolm Miles Motor Engineers, Leicester	https://malcolm-miles.co.uk
Malbrad Saab Specialists, Huddersfield	https://malbrad.co.uk
Jam Saab, Bristol	www.jamsaab.co.uk
SAABits, Devon	www.saabits.com
Two Stroke to Turbo, Hertfordshire	https://twostroketoturboparts.co.uk
Stevelewissaab, Caithness	https://stevelewissaab.com
The Saab V4 web pages (Alec Dearden)	www.saab-v4.co.uk
Saab Enthusiasts Club UK	http://thesaabenthusiasts.co.uk
Saab Owners Club of Great Britain	www.saabclub.co.uk
Saab Car Club of Australia	www.saabclub.org.au
Saab Club Nederland	www.saabclub.nl
Club Saab Uruguay	www.facebook.com/clubsaaburuguay
Saab Club of Canada	https://saabclub.ca
Saab Club of North America (publishes *NINES* magazine)	https://saabclub.com
Vintage Saab Club of North America	www.vintagesaabclub.org
Saab Heritage Museum, Sturgis, SD	www.saabmuseumusa.com
Tom Donney	www.tomdonneymotors.com
Bruce Turk	
Albany Saab Shop, Voorheesville, NY	
Stefan Vapaa	www.at-speed.com
Grieco Brothers Automotive, Boonton, NJ	
West of Sweden, Richmond, VA	
Planet Saab, San Francisco, CA	
Saabplanet.com	www.saabplanet.com
Swedecar, Torrance, CA	https://swedecar.com
2 Guys from Sweden, Los Angeles, CA	www.2guysfromswedenlosangeles.com
Swedish Motors Inc., Marietta, PA	www.swedishmotors.com
Rocky Mountain Saab Club	www.rockymountainsaab.club
Imparts BV, Ede, Netherlands	www.imparts.nl
Saab Veterans Archive, Trollhättan	https://wiki.saabveteranernatrollhattan.com
Saab Car Museum, Trollhättan	https://saabcarmuseum.se

Engine

The obvious differences between 2-stroke and 4-stroke engines need no further narrative. The 2-stroke models have few major moving parts, no valves, no tappets and no 'sump'. Yet the V4 engine should not be underestimated, despite its more complex mechanism and repair requirements. Certain key issues apply to both 2-strokes and V4s, and require similar checks:

Head: Gaskets, valves, valve seats. Compression issues across cylinders: check for expected values. Check for correct/incorrect skimming or modifications.
Balancer shaft: Check pulleys for variation/play. Replace V4 fibre timing gear with metal or expensive alloy type.
Cylinders and pistons: Check for wear, corrosion, scoring and so on.
Oil system: The V4 is notably sensitive to the type of filter used. Timing is by gears, not belt or chain type.
Driveshafts and engine mountings: These need careful assessment.
Exhaust: Check manifold and pipes. Consider replacing with a Jetex Sports exhaust.
Radiator: Assess for cooling issues/blockages. Consider fitting a Kenlowe electric cooling fan to a 96 V4.
Gearbox: Check casing and wheel strength, cogs, crown wheel and whine when engaging the column shift. Freewheel function and positioning. Clutch judder is common but can indicate serious wear. Note whether ribbed-type gearbox casing or earlier (pre-1969) type is fitted.
Tuning: For tuning details and specifications to check and cross-reference any car under consideration, see Chapter 7.

Suspension and Steering

Brakes: Check front brake calipers. Check rear brakes for corrosion and cylinder leaks.
Front suspension: Check ball joints and arms, and note the type of springs and dampers fitted.
Wheels and tyres: Assess for correct specifications and any modifications. Note if wheel reinforcement kits have been welded in for rallying. Assess wheel bearings. Be wary of cheap, low-grip tyres for fast-road running.

REFERENCES

1 Luciak, I., 'The Life of Axel Wenner-Gren', in *Reality and Myth: a Symposium on Axel Wenner-Gren*, ed. I. Luciak and B. Daneholt (Wenner-Gren Stiftelserna, 2012); Luciak, I. A., 'With Vision and Reality: Axel Wenner-Gren, Paul Fejo, and the Origins of the Wenner-Gren Foundation for Anthropological Research', *Current Anthropology*, 57, no. 514 (October 2016), pp. 302–32.
2 Saab Editorial Board with B. Olson, *The Saab-Scania Story* (Streiffert, 1986), pp. 20–31.
3 Möller, H., 'Så borjade vi tillverka bilar' [1973], SAAB-veteranerna Trollhättan, https://wiki.saabveteranernatrollhattan.com.
4 Ljungström, G., 'Från flygplan till bilar', *Saab-minnen* [Veteranklubben Saab], 1 (1988); see also Larsson, G., and G. Johansson, *Saab, We did it!* Gunnar Ljungström and his Pioneers (Saab Car Museum Support Organization, 2018).
5 Sköld, B.-Å., 'Sixten Sason', in *Svensk industridesign: en 1900-talshistoria*, ed. L. Brunnström (Prisma, 1997).
6 Cole, L., *Saab Cars: The Complete Story* (The Crowood Press, 2012); see also the exhibition 'Sason föregängare inom Svenska industridesign', Västergötlands Museum, Skara, 6 June–7 September 2008, and personal communications at the museum.
7 Personal communications with Björn Envall, 1998.
8 Scibor-Rylski, A.J., *Road Vehicle Aerodynamics* (Pentech Press, 1975).
9 Möller, 'Så borjade vi tillverka bilar'.
10 Ibid.
11 *Motor*, 12 April 1950.
12 Crawford Moore, B., 'The Airmen's Stories: Sgt A.R. Moore', *The Battle of Britain London Monument*, www.bbm.org.uk.
13 Lonnegren, Len, 'Baja, humbug', *Nines: The Saab Club Newsletter*, no. 214 (June 1992), pp. 12–13.
14 Personal communications with Charles Walmsley, Buenos Aires, April 2021, and with Erik Hilding Carlsson, Buckinghamshire, 2011.
15 Elg, P.-B., *50 Years of Saabs: All the Cars, 1947–1997* (Motorhistoriska Sallskapet Sverige, 1997).
16 Granlund, O., 'Till minne av Josef Eklund', SAAB-veteranerna Trollhättan, https://wiki.saabveteranernatrollhattan.com.
17 Elg, *50 Years of Saabs*.
18 Personal communications with Bruce Turk, USA, 2020.
19 Eklund, J., 'Minnen från tillkomsten av "Monstret"', 11 August 2010, https://wiki.saabveteranernatrollhattan.com.
20 Cole, L., *Saab Cars: The Complete Story* (The Crowood Press, 2012).
21 Elg, *50 Years of Saabs*.
22 Möller, 'Så borjade vi tillverka bilar'.
23 Archives of Club Saab Uruguay and Club Saab Argentina, and Saab Veteranerna Arkiv.
24 Cedrup, L., 'Saab in Siam', *Vips: Vi på Saab*, 3 (1961–2), p. 14; trans. R. Beaufoy.
25 Cedrup, L., 'Saab in Hong Kong: Rally success has led to increased sales', *Vips: Vi på Saab*, 6 (1962), Eng. trans. available at www.supportsaabmuseum.com.
26 Personal communications with Joy Rainey, with further information from Drew Bedelph and Steven Wade/Trollhättan Saab/Saabs United, Tasmania, 2008.
27 Granlund, Olle, 'Minnesanteckningar från införandet av fytaktsmotorn i Saab 95/96 1966', *Veteranfordonsklubben i Tjust*, 17 October 2010, https://tjustbil.se.
28 Cole, *Saab Cars: The Complete Story*.
29 Saab Owners Club of Great Britain archives.
30 Elg, *50 Years of Saabs*.
31 Pucket, J., 'Lindqvist Saab Double-ender', *Vintage Motorsport* (March–April 1993), p. 28. Additional information from Len Lonnegren.
32 A comprehensive survey of the life and racing career of Ewy Baroness von Korff-Rosqvist (Ewy Rosqvist) has been compiled by Mats Brunberg at www.ewyrosqvist.com. Further communications from the late P. Carlsson.
33 Cole, *Saab Cars: The Complete Story*.
34 Personal communications with Krzysztof Rozenblat and the Rozenblat Family Foundation, 2015.
35 Archives of Club Saab Uruguay and Club Saab Argentina, courtesy of Charles Walmsley.
36 Vintage Saab Racing group archive, courtesy of communications with Bruce Turk.

BIBLIOGRAPHY

Autocar (1950–75) [road tests and archives]
Bakrutan [magazine of Svenska Saabklubben]
Cole, L.F., *Saab 99 & 900: The Complete Story* (The Crowood Press, 2000)
——, *Secrets of the Spitfire* (Pen and Sword, 2012)
——, 'Sixten Sason, Sweden's Secret Genius', *Classic Cars* (1997)
——, 'Saab's Secret Fighter', *Aeroplane Monthly*, 26/8 (August 1988)
——, 'The Death of Saab', *Daily Telegraph*, 7 January 2012
——, 'Erik Carlsson: Obituary', *Daily Telegraph*, 4 June 2015
Cumberford, R., 'Competitive Tuning', *Sports Car Graphic*, 1/6 (October 1961)
Dymock, E., *Saab: Half a Century of Achievement* (Dove Publishing, 1997)
Elg, P.-B., *50 Years of Saabs: All the Cars, 1947–1997* (Motorhistoriska Sallskapet Sverige, 1997)
Hansson, S.A., *Hur jag för ut mest av min Saab* (Forum, 1956)
Luciak, I. A., 'With Vision and Reality: Axel Wenner-Gren, Paul Fejo, and the Origins of the Wenner-Gren Foundation for Anthropological Research', *Current Anthropology*, 57, no. 514 (October 2016), pp. 302–32.
Maddock, P., *Swedish Memories, 1955–2007: a Life in Product Design* (2007)
Saab Driver (1960s–2020) [magazine of the Saab Owners Club of Great Britain]
Saab Editorial Board with B. Olson, *The Saab-Scania Story* (Streiffert, 1986)
Schilperood, Paul, *The Extraordinary Life of Josef Ganz* (Rvp Publishers, 2012)
Scibor-Rylski, A.J., *Road Vehicle Aerodynamics* (Pentech Press, 1975)
Sjörgen, G.A., *The Saab Way: The First 35 Years of Saab Cars, 1949–1984* (Österbergs, 1984)
Sköld, B.-Å., 'Sixten Sason', in *Svensk industridesign: en 1900-talshistoria*, ed. L. Brunnström (Prisma, 1997)
——, 'Sixten Sason', *Svenskt biografiskt lexicon*, 31 (2000–2002), p. 441, available at https://sok.riksarkivet.se
Vips: *Vi på Saab* (1960–66).
Wennlo, S., *Mitt liv med Saab* (Streiffert, 1989)

Translations of the following articles were kindly provided by the Saab Veteranerna Arkiv, Trollhättan:

Eklund, J., 'Minnen från tillkomsten av "Monstret"', 11 August 2010, https://wiki.saabveteranernatrollhattan.com
——, 'Vi Minns Rolf Mellde', SAAB-veteranerna Trollhätten, 24 March 2009, https://wiki.saabveteranernatrollhattan.com
Frick, A., 'Vad hände på "Hemligheta"', Sonettväldern, 3 (2002), available at https://wiki.saabveteranernatrollhattan.com
Göthberg, S.-O., and P.-B. Elg, 'När Saab blev bil eller om ett fynd i arkivet pa Saab Bilmuseum'
Granlund, O., 'Minnesanteckningar från införandet av fytaktsmotorn i Saab 95/96 1966', Veteranfordonsklubben i Tjust, 17 October 2010, https://tjustbil.se
Gustavsson, H.O., 'Grattis Saab 60 Ar!', Corren, 8 June 2007
Gustavsson, H.O., and S. Lenngren, 'En katt bland hermelinerna eller Hurledes grunden lades till SAABs bilproduktion vid flygmaskinfabriken', Bakrutan, 14/4 (October 2006), pp. 24–33
——, 'Huruledes grunden lades till Saabs bilproduktion vid flugmaskinsfabriken', Saab-minnen, 15 (2005)
Lenngren, S., 'Några personliga minnen från tillverkningen av första bilen', Bakrutan, 14/4 (October 2006), pp. 21–3
Ljungström, G., 'Från flygplan till bilar', Saab-minnen, 1 (1988)

INDEX

Abeiro, Carlos 196
Abeiro, Juan 196
AETA Aero Enoch Thulin Aeroplanfabrik 20
AFF Förenade Flygverkstäder 20–21
Åkerlind, Bengt 127
Albin 93
Albinmotor 57
Aman, Torsten 180
ANA Nyköpings Autofabrik 20, 103, 127
Andersson, A. J. 34
Andersson, Ake 169
Andersson, Alvar 93
Andersson, Hans 127
Andersson, Ingvar 93, 154
Andersson, Ove 190
Andersson, Sixten see Sixten Sason
Andreasson, Sölve 162
Andrey, Gaston 182
Argentina 130–132
ASJA Svenska Järnvägsverkstädernas Aeroplanavdelning 20, 21, 32
Automotora Boreal 131, 195

Baca, Marco 132, 195
Balcarcel, Ramiro 196
Baerendz, Bertil 32
Barmen, Oddmund 132
Baxter, Raymond 71
Bedelph, Drew 13
Bedson, Gordon 139
Belloso, Rogelio 196
Berglöf, Björn 163
Bernadotte, Sigvard 38
Bertil, Prince of Sweden 95
Bengtsson, Gunnar 191
Berqvist, Gosta 65
Bertoni, Flaminio 38
Beysson, Léonce 182
Binstead, Geoffrey 132
Blomqvist, Stig 16, 194
Bloxham, John 199
Bock, Hugo 102
Bofors 19
Boheman, Erik 95
Bourgeois, Jacques 195
Bråsjö, Arthur 54
Bratt, Erik 39
Bremer, Carl-Otto 190
Brising, Lars 54
Bristol Company 22, 35, 45
Broadhead, Stephen 168
Braun, Louis 182

Carlsson, Erik Hilding 8, 14 22, 237, 64, 67, 71, 75, 78, 80, 92, 102, 105, 113, 128, 134, 142, 146, 162, 166, 180–201
Carlsson, Pat Moss 183, 185–186, 188
Carlqvist, Bengt 65, 190

Casey, Mark 197
Cederberg, Björn 194
Cedrup, Lennart 132
Chilton Tuning 168, 173
Christ Charles 123
Christ, Joseph 123
Chrysler, 20, 23, 99
Civill, Arthur 120, 128
Clark, Budd 123
Claesson, Anne Marie 41
Clark, Roger Albert (Rally) 197
Clements, Roy 71
Crawford, John 162
Crawford, Robert 123
Cook, Randy 122
Coleman, Simon 111
Cox, Tom 123

Davenport, John 194
Day, Chris 12
Day, Lucienne 40
Day, Robin 40
Dean, Alex 161
Dean, Sheila 161
De Barros, Oscar 196
De Leon, P 196
Dellner, Gunnar 33
Denekamp, Johan 198
DKW 22, 24, 27, 31, 39, 59, 67, 83, 104, 152, 184
Domingo, Alberto 127, 132, 196
Donney, Tom 12, 122, 144–147
Dover, Ken 74
Drafft, Waller 162
Duhart, Enrique 196
Duhart, Ricardo 79, 196

Ebefors, Rolf 102
Ekkers, Erik 32, 56
Eklund Josef 10, 11, 37, 88, 93, 102, 121, 158, 160
Eklund, Per 180
Envall, Björn 38
Envall, Sune 38
Engström, John 127
Ericson, Gustaf 18
Ericsson, Lars Magnus 65
Essen, Margareta von 67

Fangio, Juan Manuel 183
Fend, Fritz 38
Fieux, Mary Anne 196
Fladån, Tage 31
Francis, Wendell 196
Frederiksson, Rune 121
Fojo, Héctor Marcial 195
Ford (V4) 156–162
Frick, Arne 32

Garbing, Borje 53

Ganz, Joseph 29
Gillbrand, Per 137
GM General Motors 11, 19, 40, 77, 157
Granlund, Erik 63
Granlund, Olle 127, 154, 156
Grestock, Tony 9, 73, 135
Grieco, Mike 12
Gullstrand, Tore 155
Gustafson, Ferdinand 194
Gustafsson, Sigvard 102
Gustafsson, Sibylla 201
Gustavsson, Arne 93
Gustavsson, Hans Ingevar 32, 50

Häggbom, Gunnar 191
Hagstrom, Göran 131
Hall, Emyr 197, 198
Hansson, Per Albin 20
Heinkel 88, 89, 132, 152, 141
Heinz Manufacturing Inc 54–55
Hellborg, Bo 184
Hertz, Arne 194
Higgins, Stephen 197
Highgate 168
Historic Rally Team (GB) 197–198
Hjorden, Leif 41
Holm, Svante 28, 32, 84, 127
Holm, Tryggve 8, 32, 50, 72, 86, 103, 120–121, 153, 158
Holmqvist, Brynolf 131
Hope, Colin 197
Hughes, Ceiriog 197
Hull, Chris 85, 100
Hurrell, Sydney 175, 193
Husqvarna 38, 40

Ilhage, Bertil 17
Irion, René 131
Issigonis, A 28

Jacobson, Bill 196
Jaray, Paul 10, 21, 28, 29 46–47
Järkvik, Åke 93
Johansson, August 65
Johansson, Olle 93, 102
Jonsson, Åke 131
Jonsson, Jan-Åke 182
Jonsson, Tore 93
Jorgensen, Leon 75

Karlsson, Walter 192
Kazumoto, Yabe 12
Kern, Walter 12, 123
Kjerstadius, Monica 186
Knutsson, Kjell 102, 154
Koskull, Cecillia 189
Kronegård, Harald 182

INDEX

Lampinen, Simo 183
Landbü, Olof 10, 33, 53, 59, 65, 67, 184
Larsson, Gunnar 33
Ledwinka, Hans 10, 21, 28, 29
Lidmalm, Tord 54
Lidro, Nils 32
Lightburn, Harold 139
Liljevall, Kurt 59
Lindgren, Olle 56
Linköping 7, 18, 21, 27, 43, 49, 50, 64, 72, 81, 111, 113, 151
Lindqvist, Ingvar 75, 180
Lindqvist, Olle 154
Ljungström Birger 35
Ljungström, Fredrik 10, 34–36
Ljungström, Gunnar 6, 10 19, 26, 28–32, 33, 34, 37, 41–48, 53, 63, 68, 70, 71, 83, 88, 89, 93, 120, 146, 143, 203
Lodge, Caroline 197
Longo, Angel 196
Lonnegren, Len 180, 182
Lowe, David 133
Lund, Hans Erik 136
Lundberg, Helga 67
Lutz, Robert 11, 178

Macchi Aldo 192
Macchi, Paul 192
Maddock, Peter 40
Malbrad 168
Mannerstedt, Folke 65
Marchant, Brian 195
Mather, Justin 199–200
Mayforth, Hal 182
Macdonald, Graham 11
McQueen, Steve 182
Meakin, Ian 105
Melin, Leif 180
Mellde, Rolf 6, 10, 11, 27, 32, 33, 53, 58, 64–66, 78, 83, 93, 121, 127, 153–160, 174, 182, 184, 190, 192
Michelotti, Giovanni 114–115
Millet, Ralph T 72, 75, 84, 96, 122, 180
Mills, Chris 123
Moberg, Chris 12, 122
Molander, Greta 63, 67
Möller, Hugo 32, 33, 41, 50, 120
Monö, Rune 40–41
Morecombe, Eric 13
Moore, Robert 14, 71
Moore, Georgie 71
Mortimer, Vernon 12
Moss, Stirling 162, 184, 186
Montagna, Carlos 196
Müller, Hans 88, 93, 141
Muller, Victor 11, 12
Myers, Debbie 197

New England Saab Association 123
Nilestam, Erik 32
Nilsson, Nils Gustaf 38
Nohab 19
Nohab Flygmotor Company 34
Nordic Diesel Auto AS 75
Norlin, Stig 121
North, Roy 193
Nottorp, Sture 191
Nutt, Chris 193
Nyberg, Karl 53, 59
Nymans Plåtslageri 49
Nyström, Elizabeth 186, 188
Nyström, Pelle 186

Ohlsson, Dick 93
Olofsson, Pierre Sager 38
Olsson, Bo 32
Olsson, Lars Olov 154
Olsson, Sven 102
Orrenius, Carl 194
Orr, James 123
Otterbeck, Sven 49, 51
Ottosson, Ulf 192

Palm, Gunnar 183
Pallo, Jackie 13
Parkes, Chris 193
Pärsson, Ove 121
Partington, Chris 95, 133, 173, 174, 193
Patrick, Nick 197
Payne, Ken 122
Perdersen, Bertil 154
Percy, Tony 12
Pernby, Åke V 38
Pettersson, Bo 192
Philipson, Gunnar 7, 22, 25–31, 53, 57, 63, 65, 70, 81
Philpott, Alistair 153
Philpott, Mike 166–167
Pinkett, Nick 197
Porsche, Ferdinand 29
Pye, Ray 12

Quarta, Carlos 196

Rama, José Arijón 131, 195
Rankin, Alex 114, 115
Redmond, Chris 134–135
Reinertsen Motors Racing 196
Roland, Magnus 120
Rosen, Lennart 154
Rosqvist, Ewy 67
Rozenblat, Krzysztof 192
Rutan, Bill 182
Rydberg, Arne 137
Rydberg, Erik 33
Ryder, Neil 122–126

Saab-Scania 131
Saab (cars by model):
    UrSaab 18–41
    92 model 42–61
    93 model 62–83
    95 model 84–103
    96 model 104–119
    96 V4 model 120–151
Saab Club of Australia 12
Saab Competition Department 67, 92, 102, 131, 141, 168, 176, 182, 190
Saab Great Britain 9, 71, 146, 151, 176
Saab Motors USA Inc. 122
Saab Museum 17, 34, 102, 111, 177
Saab Owners Club of Great Britain 12, 13, 135, 152
Saab Owners Club of New York 123
Saab-Scania 131
Sason, Karl Erik Sixten (Andersson) 6, 7, 10, 19, 21, 223, 25, 26, 29, 37–41, 42–51, 54, 61, 62, 64, 77–83, 86, 92, 103, 114, 130, 121, 146, 154, 204
Sax o Mat 92–93, 128
Sayer, Malcolm 34
Scania (Scania-Vabis) 7, 12, 18, 18, 20
Scibor-Rylski, A J 46
Simister, John 184
Simonsson, Svante 33, 93
Simpson, Richard 168, 197
Sjögren, Bertil 33

Sjögren 'GAS' 77
Sjögren, Monica 79
Sjögren Kurt 25, 36
Sinclair, Robert 12, 72, 122
Skogh, Carl Magnus 92, 102
Sköld, B A 38
Soberal, Gustavo 196
Sollenskog, Bertil 147, 196
Someca, Rafael Fernández 196
Sörgardt, Hakon 156
Sparre, Claes 33
Sprinzel, John 192
Ståhlgren, Karl Erik 120
Stone, David 192
Sundqvist, Sven 180
Svanström, Gunnar 32
Svedberg, K. G. 63, 184
Svenska Järnvägsverkstäderna 38
Svensson, Gösta 120
Svensson, Nils Gunnar 154, 168
Svensson, Peter 192
Swaner, Bo 170
Sylvan, Hans 194

Tatra 10, 28, 29, 39, 46
Thompson, Dick 182
Thulin 19
Tjaarda van Starkenborgh, Johan 47
Tjaarda, Tom 47
Trana, Tom 195
Trollhättan 7, 9, 18, 20–27, 31, 43, 50, 54, 59, 62, 78, 83, 103, 11, 113, 139, 144, 176, 199
Tordoff, Jack 195
Törnqvist, Bengt 93
Turk, Bruce 12, 15, 77, 90, 98, 122
Turner, Stuart 14, 186, 187, 191
Tuthill, Francis 199

Uccellini, Nestor 13
Ullstrom, Bengt 93
Uruguay 130–132
Uuskiaupunki, Finland 175

VABIS Vagnfabriks-Aktiebolaget i Södertelge Company 12, 18, 19
Valentine, Jim 196–197
van Keulen, Roger 201
Vapaa, George 196
Vapaa, Stefan 196
Västergötlands Museum 40, 41
Vickers 68, 121, 162
Vigouroux-Henday, Richard 168
Vintage Saab Club of North America 122
Vintage Saab Racing Group 122
Volvo 12, 18, 22–23

Wade, Steven 13
Wahrgren, Ragnar 25, 32
Wallenberg, Marcus 7, 20, 62, 67, 178
Wallenberg, Marc 158
Walmsley, Charly, 14, 195
Walmsley, Linda 196
Wänström, Frid 22
Wehman, Bob 182
Wenner-Gren, Axel 40, 41
Westlund, Gunnar 33
Wickham Company 34
Wirth, Ursula 67, 188, 189
Wise, Ernie 13